THE WAR ON WOMEN

THE
WAR ON
WOMEN

Elly Armour, Jane Hurshman, and
Criminal Violence in Canadian Homes

BRIAN VALLÉE

With a Foreword by STEPHEN LEWIS

KEY PORTER BOOKS

Library and Archives Canada Cataloguing in Publication

Vallée, Brian
    The war on women: Elly Armour, Jane Hurshman, and criminal violence in
Canadian homes/ Brian Vallée.

ISBN 978-1-55263-828-6

    1. Armour, Elly. 2. Abused wives—Nova Scotia—Biography. 3. Trials
(Murder)—Nova Scotia. I. Title.

HV6626.V343 2006   362.82'92092   C2006-901810-3

ONTARIO ARTS COUNCIL
CONSEIL DES ARTS DE L'ONTARIO

The publisher gratefully acknowledges the support of the Canada Council for the Arts
and the Ontario Arts Council for its publishing program. We acknowledge the support of
the Government of Ontario through the Ontario Media Development Corporation's
Ontario Book Initiative.

We acknowledge the financial support of the Government of Canada through the Book
Publishing Industry Development Program (BPIDP) for our publishing activities.

Key Porter Books Limited
Six Adelaide Street East, Tenth Floor
Toronto, Ontario
Canada M5C 1H6

www.keyporter.com

Text design: Marijke Friesen
Electronic formatting: Jean Lightfoot Peters

Printed and bound in Canada

07 08 09 10 11 5 4 3 2 1

To Miss Elly

Violence and injury enclose in their net
all that do such things,
and generally return upon him who began.
TITUS LUCRETIUS CARUS

I've kept silent for more than fifty years, but I ache in my heart
and soul when I see so many women and children being abused
and killed in their homes. By telling other women what I lived
through, I hope they will realize there is help out there and that
they will find a way out without doing what I had to do.
ELLY ARMOUR

Battering isn't the taboo—talking about it is.
And it can only continue if we keep silent.
JANE HURSHMAN

CONTENTS

Acknowledgements

I WOULD LIKE TO THANK ELLA ARMOUR'S FRIENDS AND FAMILY —in particular, daughter Karen Gardiner; son John Melanson; constant companion for the last sixteen years of her life Bill Lyons; cousin Dorothy and her husband Allister "Tin" Watters; cousin Harry Muir and his wife Jean, and former Calgary police detective Jim Fisher. I would like also to thank Douglas Ince for his hospitality and the generous gift of his time and insights during my visit to Stellarton, Nova Scotia, and for his helpful responses to many questions during numerous telephone conversations. Also, a special thanks to Julian Austin and the dozens of musicians—in Calgary, Nashville, and elsewhere—who knew Ella as "Miss Elly," the tireless promoter of country music who helped many new artists get their start in the business.

At Key Porter, I would like to thank Jordan Fenn for recognizing the importance of the issue of criminal domestic violence against women and supporting this book; and my superb editor, Clare McKeon, for her patience and encouragement from the inception of this project to its completion.

Foreword

Stephen Lewis

EARLY IN 2006, THEN SECRETARY-GENERAL KOFI ANNAN appointed a panel on UN reform. The High-level Panel on United Nations System-wide Coherence in the Areas of Development, Humanitarian Assistance and the Environment consisted of fifteen people, twelve of whom were men.[1] He then appointed a secretariat of three, all of whom were men. With troubling irony, all of the appointments were made right at the moment when the UN was trumpeting the principle of gender equality in all decision-making bodies. It was a travesty.

In a speech in March 2006 at Harvard Law School, I confronted the situation directly and said, as any responsible person would, that it was completely unacceptable. I called on the Secretary-General to use the vehicle of the reform panel to advance the need for a new international agency for women, in order to break the pattern of gender inequality that was causing such damage to women around the world—damage that covered the gamut from economic servitude to sexual violence to maternal mortality.

The women of the world went to work. Activist women's organizations the world over, many of which had been fighting for equality for decades, picked up the same themes and joined their

13

voices to the demands for a new agency. My close colleague, Paula Donovan, a strong feminist with years of experience at the UN, wrote a hard-hitting brief on the need for a new agency and orchestrated intense lobbying activity, including the vital involvement of the International Council of Nurses, based in Geneva.

The upshot, much to everyone's amazement, was the panel's recommendation, issued at the end of 2006, to create a powerful new international agency for women. It was a first in the sixty-two-year history of the United Nations.

To be sure, there have been small women's units in the UN, but they've never been allowed to amount to very much, have always been kept subordinate to the overarching powers that be. UNIFEM (the United Nations Development Fund for Women), for example, has been a department of the United Nations Development Programme and has had no real clout of its own.

Many activist groups have insisted that there be an Under-Secretary-General to head the new agency and a budget of a billion dollars or more a year to start. Most important of all, the new agency must have the capacity to do targeted programming for women on the ground: that is, in every country, a sufficient cadre of people who are expert in the field and could effectively influence their governments and other UN agencies.

Within the panel, there was initially a struggle—to put it mildly—around funding, but Gordon Brown[2] of the United Kingdom made it clear that it was useless to create such an agency without sufficient resources. His view prevailed, and the momentum for a billion dollars a year is building. Many formidable African women leaders have made it clear that anything less is self-defeating.

So the recommendation is now in the hands of the new Secretary-General, Ban Ki-moon, who will take it to the General Assembly of the UN for approval. This will be the crucial opening test of his tenure.

If passed, and fully funded, the new agency would provide for the women of every country a tremendous force for advocacy and intervention. The women activists on the ground would have a vehicle, a voice, and some resources and could make impassioned and persuasive submissions to governments. It would, I think, provide a liberating sense of hope at the country level.

As I told the panel on UN reform in Geneva, it matters not the issue—levels of sexual violence, or HIV/AIDS, or maternal mortality, or armed conflict, or economic empowerment, or parliamentary representation—women are in terrible trouble. And things are getting no better.

Many governments, especially Western governments, have invested huge amounts of money and time in "gender mainstreaming" as an easy solution to gender inequality. They want to see it make a dramatic difference, want to see that the needs and rights of women are woven into the body of every aspect of institutional life.

Well, the sad truth is that these governments must learn to face defeat. Gender mainstreaming is not easy. When it's sloughed off to non experts and made to stand on its own, rather than alongside targeted programs to promote women's empowerment and human rights, it doesn't work. The original intention was to use gender mainstreaming as a *transformative* strategy—that is, there would be a radical transformation in gender relationships. That has not happened, least of all within the United Nations itself. I have not read a single assessment—and there have been many—of gender mainstreaming that is fundamentally positive. Every single one of them falls into a range from the negative to an unabashed indictment.

Time and time again over the last two years, Kofi Annan has called for a "deep social revolution to transform relationships between men and women at all levels of society." By that he means women's empowerment and gender equality. Gender equality is not achieved in hesitant, tentative, disingenuous increments. It's achieved by bold and dramatic reform of the architecture of the United Nations.

Witnessing the AIDS pandemic has sharpened everything I've ever known about gender inequality. And I can say without fear of contradiction that where the women of Africa are concerned, the UN has been a colossal failure. Confirmation of that can be seen in the work of the UN Theme Groups on HIV/AIDS at the country level. I've watched them now for five years, and try as they might, they can never get their act fully together to reduce the impact of the virus on women. For the young women in particular, there is a palpable sense of betrayal.

I want to change that view. I want the world to understand that if we had an international organization for women, with real power and dollars and staff, we could save, liberate, and enhance hundreds of millions of lives. I make that argument because this agency can be built on the foundation constructed over the years by the kaleidoscope of women's groups that have operated outside the UN, partly because there's been so little to affiliate with on the inside.

That's why a billion dollars is such a paltry sum. And let no one sow confusion: by an international organization for women, I don't mean a specialized agency like the WHO or ILO.[3] I mean one of the powerful funds or programs like UNICEF or the World Food Programme.

There is a long road ahead. I remain determined that we will drive through. It must happen. It *has* to happen. Women's groups around the world are rallying. It's a pleasure to watch, and incredibly encouraging.

The new agency would be a dramatic shift toward multilateralism for the UN generally. If we get the funding it needs, and the right woman heading it up—and all kinds of people are interested—it would have an inevitable impact in the West as well as in the developing world. I think that the agency would start with sexual and intimate-partner violence in the developing world because the numbers there are so stunning and so horrific—particularly rape as a war crime. But it will inevitably move toward the recognition that domestic violence is its own holocaust.

This is the moment when the women's movement, and all who support it, should confront every member of the international community and lobby with indefatigable tenacity. We must find a regional champion in each of the major areas of the world and have that country carry the banner of women's rights, calling on an ignited civil society for support.

We're not just fighting for women's human rights; we're fighting for women's lives. Over and over again, we're guilty of the same folly. I remember Lord Acton's dictum: "There is another world for the expiation of guilt, but the wages of folly are payable here, below." Women, worldwide, are paying here, below, for that folly with their lives.

March 2007

About This Book

ONE OF THE MOST EMOTIONALLY TROUBLING PROJECTS I undertook during my ten years with the CBC's *fifth estate* was the documentary *Life With Billy*.

This film told the story of Jane Hurshman,[1] the Nova Scotia woman who, after five years of severe abuse by her common-law husband, Billy Stafford, shot him to death while he was passed out drunk in the front seat of his half-ton truck.

The Royal Canadian Mounted Police considered Billy Stafford a well-armed, dangerous bully who would one day end up in a shootout with them. One senior officer who knew Billy well said Jane deserved a medal for killing him. She offered to plead guilty to manslaughter, but the Crown insisted on a charge of first-degree murder. She was then forced to testify publicly and in graphic detail about the degrading sexual torture she had endured and the unremitting mental and physical abuse Billy had inflicted on her and their five-year-old son.

The jury acquitted Jane, but the Crown appealed and won a new trial, though this time it accepted Jane's manslaughter plea. The judge said Billy Stafford was "on the outer fringe of a definition of humanity" and sentenced Jane to six months. But she was allowed to attend nursing school during the day and was released after two months. Her case led to the acceptance of "battered wife syndrome" as a legal defence in Canadian courts, and Jane became an indefatigable warrior on behalf of abused women and children. With her cooperation, I wrote the book *Life With Billy*. The TV movie of the same name aired on the CBC in 1995 and went on to win three Gemini awards. Jane often said that if the telling of her story led to even one woman leaving an abusive relationship, it would be worthwhile. And women's organizations and shelter workers have confirmed that her story inspired hundreds of battered women to flee their abusers.

Ten years after Billy died, Jane took her own life with a bullet to the chest in the front seat of her car in a deserted parking lot on the Halifax waterfront. In a follow-up book, *Life After Billy*, I explained as best I could why Jane killed herself.

The most shocking revelation in my research for the documentary and books was not the savagery of criminal domestic violence, but how commonplace it was. Several battered women subsequently contacted me through the CBC and my publisher, asking me to tell their stories. I said I couldn't. The subject was too bleak and painful. And although the *level* of violence varied—from verbal to near-lethal—the *patterns* of abuse in all their stories were consistent with Jane's experience. So I was convinced that there was no need for another book. Change the geographic locations and the names of the people involved, and the stories would be remarkably similar.

But by 2002, as I witnessed the endless media reports of the ongoing slaughter and abuse of women and children by the men in their lives, I had come to realize my logic was seriously flawed. I began clipping newspaper accounts of these cases until the file was several inches thick.

In Toronto, the city where I live and work, seven women and two children were killed by male intimates in the first six months of researching and writing this book. Three of the women were stabbed, two were strangled, one was thrown from her tenth-floor apartment window, and one was hacked to death along with her three-year-old and five-month-old children. The number of "domestic" deaths in the city in that half-year equalled the usual average for an entire year. And there were similar stories across the country.

I didn't get it. Members of Parliament were no longer laughing when discussions of spousal abuse arose;[2] public awareness of criminal violence against women was increasing; judges, lawyers, and the police were taking the problem more seriously; and more and more shelters to protect abused women and their children were being opened. Yet the slaughter continued. Why?

This book seeks to answer that question and to personalize the terror far too many women go through in their homes. But understanding the *why* involves more than reciting shocking statistics and case histories. It also means recognizing and exposing that elephant in the living room—gross gender inequality, the root cause of the criminal violence against women.

Enlightenment came through extensive research and interviews with knowledgeable, dedicated women who, against overwhelming odds, have slogged in the trenches for years to put an end to the violence. They have suffered funding cuts and a prolonged conservative backlash that has led to disillusionment and burnout. "Our office is a complete disaster," says Eileen Morrow, coordinator of the Ontario Association of Interval and Transition Houses. "I'm the only staff for a seventy-five-member provincial association. It's ridiculous. The Ontario Rape Crisis Coalition has no office and no staff. The Disabled Women's Network has a website and that's it."

Morrow says governments "seem bent on looking narrowly at violence against women, providing poorly funded emergency services and post-violence responses that are still often inadequate. The first step is to realize that violence against women is a gender equality issue, but the government says, 'We can't work with that—it's too vague.' But equality *is* the issue, and violence against women is a part of it. Violence is the most terroristic of the tactics that men use to keep women in their place, but it's not the only one."

Women like Eileen Morrow and other advocates around the world have a powerful ally in their quest for gender equality and an end to violence against women—Stephen Lewis, the incisive and eloquent orator whose two decades of work at the United Nations included four years[3] as Canadian ambassador and five and a half years[4] of tireless advocacy on behalf of African women as the UN Special Envoy for HIV/AIDS in Africa.

"Yeah, he's a hero, that one," says Morrow.

Always a steadfast champion of women's empowerment and equality, Lewis's resolve stiffened when he witnessed first-hand the suffering and death on the ground in Africa. "The AIDS pandemic in Africa is exacting a carnage amongst women that knows no parallel in modern history. What is more, in the presence of AIDS, it's virtually impossible to talk plausibly of women's human rights—every right a woman might have had can be held to the ransom of the virus... The proof is in the dying."[5]

As for the United Nations, Lewis says it has completely botched its goal of "gender mainstreaming," and it even "flunks the test of gender parity, failing to reach its own target of 50:50 in staffing percentages in the vast majority of departments and agencies." He says an agency like UNIFEM (United Nations Development Fund for Women) "does its best, but its best is shackled by a lethal combination of parsimony and misogyny within the international system...

"At some point in time, history will demand an explanation for the torpor that transfixed the international community while women were being decimated, and are still being decimated, in numbers that would numb the mind of Einstein."[6]

Lewis believes an end to gender inequality and violence against women requires worldwide action that must start at the UN with a fully funded, separate new agency for women, as he indicates in the foreword he graciously agreed to write for this book.

ONCE I DECIDED TO WRITE THIS BOOK—with my ever-expanding newspaper file of dead women and children beside me—Jane Hurshman was never far away. I knew I needed a compelling personal story like hers to engage the reader.

I couldn't speak to those who had experienced the ultimate violence—they were dead. I could piece their stories together from interviews with family, friends, and neighbours and from police reports and court transcripts, but that would miss the most important part: the intimate thoughts and emotions of the women themselves. The challenge, I realized, was to find a survivor of severe abuse willing to share her story with a male stranger.

Then, early in 2005, I received a telephone call from a woman in Calgary. "I want you to write my story," she said. And what a story she had to tell.

Her name was Ella Goodchild. She was in the process of reverting to her birth name, Ella Armour, but, "Everybody just calls me Miss Elly," she said. She was seventy-two years old, likeable, incorrigible, with a bawdy sense of humour. We talked for an hour in that first conversation, and by the end of it, I had agreed to write her story. "I guess this was meant to be," I told her. "I've been wanting to write a new book, and you call me out of the blue."

But Elly had not called out of the blue. She had been looking for someone to write her story for some time. She was angry because, "Every time I pick up the newspaper or turn on the TV, it seems like there's another woman being killed or children being abused." Then she heard about *Life With Billy* and decided to contact me. I told her about my thick file of clippings on domestic killings and said I shared her anger and concern.

For more than half a century, Elly had carried around a secret that only a handful of people in her wide circle of friends had an inkling of. Through the years, with limited resources, she had done her best to help by taking into her home several abused or needy children for periods varying from weeks to years. But her health was failing and she was worried about the future of her mentally challenged daughter, Cynthia. She wanted to ensure that if she died first, Cynthia would never be institutionalized. Now, she decided, it was time to go public, and she hoped her story, like Jane's, might inspire battered women to flee their abusers to protect themselves and their children.

After several lengthy telephone conversations ranging from painful to entertaining to frustrating, I told Elly that she reminded me of two polar opposites rolled into one—Mother Theresa and Mae West. She had a good laugh at that. A few weeks later, I flew to Calgary to meet her in person.

JANE HURSHMAN OFTEN SAID THAT A DAY didn't go by without her wondering how many women and children "right this minute" were living in fear or being abused or killed, "all behind closed doors." That got me to thinking that I could be writing in just about any city in the world and the abuse and killing would be going on around me. I decided that it might be useful to share a bit of the stories behind the headlines I was reading as I wrote this book, and I have inserted one at the beginning of each chapter.

IN THEIR OWN HOMES

1

Domestic Terrorists

Rosalinda Concepcion, 32. Mother of three. Welland, Ontario. Rosalinda was found strangled to death in her home after she failed to pick up her children from school. Police and child welfare authorities arrived at the home and discovered her and her common-law partner in the house. Leonard James Kelly was taken to hospital with a "medical condition" and later charged with first-degree murder. (January 2006)

WE LIVE ON A PLANET BESET BY WAR. IN NORTH AMERICA alone, the most familiar wars—those spotlighted by the media—include the War on Drugs, the War on Terror, the War on Crime, the Gulf War, the war in Afghanistan, and the war in Iraq.

Once the politicians decide that war will be waged—in a foreign country or on the home streets—the lives of the women and men in the military and in law enforcement are at risk.

In the seven years from 2000 to 2006, 2,697 American soldiers were killed by hostile forces, mostly in Iraq and Afghanistan. Another 726 died there accidentally in "non-hostile" incidents. At home, 611 American law enforcement officers were

27

"feloniously killed" in the line of duty (including 72 in the terrorist attacks of September 11, 2001).[1] Another 554 officers died on the job from traffic accidents, heart attacks, accidental shootings, suicide, and other "non-hostile" incidents. So in those seven years, the total number of front-line military and law enforcement deaths was 4,588.

In that same period, forty-four Canadian soldiers were killed in Afghanistan, including four who died in accidents and six killed by "friendly fire." At home, sixteen law enforcement officers were killed in the line of duty, while another forty-one died from "non-hostile" causes (including sixteen in car accidents, seven in aircraft accidents, and three in motorcycle accidents). The combined total of all Canadian military and law enforcement deaths for that seven-year period was 101.

We pay tribute to these fallen men and women, often with national television, newspaper, and magazine coverage. Whenever a police officer is shot or otherwise feloniously killed in the line of duty, hundreds of police officers from all over North America gather for the funeral services. In June 2006, all of Canada mourned the death in Afghanistan of Captain Nicola Goddard, the first Canadian female combat soldier ever to be killed in battle, and watched live national media coverage of her funeral and subsequent burial with full military honours at Ottawa's National Military Cemetery. In the United States, the Public Broadcasting Service has run a silent roll call of those killed overseas and other networks periodically air similar tributes. And at the federal level in both countries, public ceremonies honour both war and law enforcement dead.

There is another war—largely overlooked but even more deadly—with far more victims killed by "hostiles." But these dead are not labelled heroes, nor are they honoured in the national media or in formal ceremonies. From time to time they may attract a spate of publicity as the result of a high-profile trial, or an inquest that will likely conclude that society let them down once again and recommend changes to prevent future deaths, though these recommendations will be mostly ignored. This war is the War on Women.

Compare the raw numbers. In the same seven-year period when 4,588 U.S. soldiers and policemen were killed by hostiles or by accident, more than 8,000 women—nearly *twice* as many—were shot, stabbed, strangled, or beaten to death by the intimate males in their lives.[2] In Canada, compared to the 101 Canadian soldiers and police officers killed, more than 500 women—nearly *five times* as many—met the same fate.

Here is another revealing comparison. Fighting fires is a dangerous occupation. In the ten years before the September 11, 2001, terrorist attacks, an average of 97 on-duty firefighters lost their lives in the United States annually,[3] while on that one day, more than 340, from 61 New York City firehouses, died—many of them in stairwells of the Twin Towers as they raced up to rescue victims. The civilian death toll that day was more than 2,300.[4] From 2000 to 2006, including those killed on September 11, 2001, a total of 1,037 on-duty firefighters died in the United States, many from job-related heart attacks and vehicle accidents.[5] Add that number to the number of military and law enforcement deaths cited above, include the 2,300 civilians killed on 9/11, and the total is *still less* than the number of women who were murdered by the men in their lives in those seven years. In Canada, sixty-six firefighters died in that period. Add that number to the 101 military and law enforcement deaths, and the total is still *just one-third* of the more than 500 women who were killed in so-called "domestics."

Those are the deaths. Then there are the wounded. In the same period, about 24,000 U.S. military were wounded in Iraq and Afghanistan,[6] while about 80 Canadians were wounded in Afghanistan.

In the United States, it's conservatively estimated that in addition to the 1,200 to 1,300 women killed each year by intimate partners, *another 5.3 million*, age 18 and older, are victims of non-lethal domestic abuse. Based on those numbers, the violence costs the country more than $5.8 billion annually—nearly $4.1 billion in direct medical and mental health care, and $1.8 billion in lost productivity and lost earnings due to homicide. These numbers are believed to underestimate the problem for several reasons,[7] and additional efforts are needed to determine more accurately the full cost of intimate-partner victimization of women in the United States.[8]

In Canada, the federal government estimates the annual cost of violence against women at $1.1 billion in direct medical costs alone.[9] That figure rises to more than $4 billion a year when social services, lost productivity, lost earnings, and police, court, and prison costs are factored in.[10]

Wars usually produce large numbers of refugees: witness the United Nations camps scattered around the world. And the War on Women has its own refugee camps, in the form of the 2,500 or so shelters for battered women and their children across North America. In the United States, more than 300,000 women and children seek safety in shelters each year.[11] In Canada, the number is between 90,000 and 100,000.[12]

These comparisons are meant solely to draw attention to the ongoing scourge that continues to take the lives and to damage the bodies and minds of thousands upon thousands of women and children living in fear of the domestic terrorists in their own homes. If our governments became aware of terrorist cells that planned to kill and maim thousands of their citizens, would they not muster the full resources of the state to go after and stop them? It is an outrage that this slaughter of women should continue in so-called progressive Western democracies, or anywhere else in the world.

2

Shelters and Fear

Rose Boroja, 54. Mother of three. Markham, Ontario. Rose was found strangled to death in her home, with "obvious signs of trauma" to her body, after a relative made an emergency call to police. Her husband, Pero Boroja, later surrendered to police and was charged with second-degree murder. (January 2006)

WHEN *LIFE WITH BILLY* WAS PUBLISHED IN 1986, THERE WERE about 235 women's shelters across Canada. Two decades later, that number had more than doubled to more than 550.[1] Sadly, most of them are usually full and have long waiting lists. The same problem plagues the United States, where the number of shelters has grown to about two thousand since the first one opened in the early 1970s.[2]

A surprising—and unintended—consequence of the burgeoning number of shelters in the U.S. was a 70 per cent drop in the number of *men* killed by their (usually abused) spouses, ex-spouses, or girlfriends since 1976.[3] "We have given women alternatives, including hotlines, shelters, counseling, and restraining orders," says James Alan Fox, a professor of criminal justice at Northeastern University in Boston. "Because more battered women have escape routes, fewer wife batterers are being killed."[4]

So shelters were saving men's lives. But the drop in the rate of women killed by their male intimates was not nearly as dramatic—less than 25 per cent. Less even than "the overall decline in the rate for non-domestic homicides," said Andrew Klein, senior research analyst specializing in domestic violence at Massachusetts-based Advocates for Human Potential, in a 2005 report to the U.S. Congress.[5]

The startling decline in male deaths was about the same in Canada, but the rate at which women continue to be killed by intimates "is holding stable," according to Leslie Tutty, a professor in the faculty of social work at the University of Calgary. She says that shelters in Canada have become "indispensable" and are regarded by many as "the major institutional response to violence against women." But the fact that abuse against women is still endemic can be perceived as "a massive failure of Canadian society (and societies worldwide) to prevent the violence that forces women to seek the safety offered in shelters."[6]

Dr. Tutty headed a study, released in June 2006, revealing that 77 per cent of 368 women surveyed in ten shelters across the country were at "extreme" or "severe" risk of being slain by spouses, ex-spouses, or boyfriends.

Of these women, 65 per cent had been stalked, 55 per cent had been threatened with death, 50 per cent had suffered choking incidents, 49 per cent had been forced to have sex, 39 per cent had been threatened with a weapon or had a weapon used against them, and 25 per cent had been beaten while pregnant. The study concludes that these "violent behaviours" can result in serious injury and sharply increase the risk of homicide.[7]

"It hadn't occurred to me that so many women that go into shelters were at risk of being murdered by partners," says Tutty. "I think this issue is falling off the radar, despite the fact that women are dying."[8] Tutty's work validates other studies that show that women are in the most danger when they flee, or attempt to flee, their abusive male intimates. "Leaving an abusive relationship is typically more dangerous than remaining, as is clear in the extent to which abused women are stalked, threatened and murdered after separation," she says.[9]

In Canada, between 1974 and 1992, the rate at which women were killed by husbands from whom they were separated was *six times higher* than the rate at which women were killed by husbands with whom they were living.[10] And those numbers don't include women killed by their boyfriends and ex-boyfriends. Ex-boyfriends killed two of the seven Toronto "domestic" victims in the first half of 2006. And both men were under court orders to stay away from the women they were later charged with killing.

In his report to the U.S. House of Representatives in 2005, Andrew Klein said, "the majority of domestic homicides, including the murder of the abused women's children, occur when women attempt to leave their abusers. Leaving abusive relationships is almost always tremendously difficult. It takes incredible courage and fortitude. It can be extremely risky, even lethal."[11] University of Toronto sociologist Dr. Aysan Sev'er concurs: "Whether in divorce statistics, general surveys, victimization studies or intimate femicide statistics, the elevated risk women face during or after separation...is irrefutable."[12]

Even when an abused woman makes it to the safety of a shelter, "realistic fears about her own safety and that of her children are likely to resurface once she must re-establish herself in the community," says Tutty. Carolyn Goard, a director at the Calgary YWCA, explains that when an abused woman attempts to take back control of her life, it's "a very scary time for the partner who has been controlling the relationship. Escalating levels of abuse are a response to try to keep his partner and the relationship under control—to keep her from leaving."[13]

And what happens if a woman decides to stay home and is killed there? Invariably, it's later revealed that there was a long history of abuse before the murder, and invariably the refrain is, "Why didn't she just leave him?"

Why indeed? The answer to that question has been much pondered in the explosion of research and writing about violence against women over the past thirty years. Several theories, often competing, have been constructed and tested, and even leading experts in the field agree it's "an overwhelming and constantly ongoing task" just to keep up with the rapidly growing body of social science knowledge.[14]

Tutty says that most women are abused in multiple ways, all of which contribute to a cumulative effect, leaving them feeling trapped and ineffective in either addressing the abuse or fleeing the abusive relationship. She points out that a number of researchers have identified in abused women "a cluster of symptoms" similar to those experienced by other victims of violence such as rape, robbery, and physical assault. Those symptoms include anxiety, recurrent nightmares, sleep and eating disorders, flashbacks, hypervigilance, and increased startle responses. Women who experience these symptoms may be diagnosed as having post-traumatic stress disorder (PTSD). And it's not uncommon for women exposed to prolonged and severe abuse to suffer from depression, which can lead to panic attacks, thoughts of suicide, or substance abuse.

Although such reactions could imply the abused woman is mentally unbalanced and in need of psychiatric help, they also, by definition, are normal responses to abnormal events in her life. So abused women should not be blamed for creating the symptoms or "cluster of symptoms" affecting them. "This also supports the argument that women who have been assaulted by their partners are not necessarily in need of therapy, since anyone in such a situation would respond with similar reactions," says Tutty.[15] "Their responses are seen as reactions to larger events over which they have no control—the abusive behaviours of their partners."

A similar sentiment is expressed on the website of the Domestic Abuse Women's Network (DAWN) in Washington State: "People often wonder why a woman stays with an abusive partner. By asking why she stays, we hold her responsible for the problem, when responsibility for violence always rests squarely with the abuser. A more appropriate question is 'Why does this person abuse his partner?'"[16]

Madame Justice Bertha Wilson of Canada's Supreme Court, in a unanimous 1990 judgment restoring the murder acquittal of battered wife Angelique LaVallée, said: "A woman who comes before a judge or jury with the claim that she has been battered...still faces the prospect of being condemned by popular mythology about domestic violence. Either she was not as badly beaten as she claims or she would have left the man long ago. Or, if she was battered that severely, she must have stayed out of some masochistic enjoyment of it...Each of these stereotypes may adversely affect consideration of a battered woman's claim to have acted in self-defence in killing her mate."[17]

A lower court had acquitted LaVallée, who shot her husband in the back of the head as he was walking away from her. The Manitoba Court of Appeal overturned that decision, but the Supreme Court overruled the appeal court and restored the acquittal. This case was the first in Canada to recognize the "battered wife syndrome" as a defence for murder.

I AM NOT A SOCIOLOGIST OR PSYCHOLOGIST or an expert on domestic violence. However, I have extensively researched the subject, interviewed several severely abused women, seen accounts of the abuse suffered by many others, and read countless books and numerous reports and studies. I could be considered anecdotally informed. I am familiar with the concepts of battered wife syndrome, learned helplessness, PTSD, cyclical violence, traumatic bonding, and victimization. All of those may be relevant to why a woman stays in an abusive relationship. But I'm convinced there is one word that trumps all the others—*fear*.

Fear is no doubt a component of just about every theory and label out there, but it's also the word I heard over and over again in my interviews and encountered in nearly all the accounts, studies, books, or reports.

In my many conversations with Jane Hurshman, she often talked about "the fear," but I didn't really appreciate what she was telling me until I saw it manifested during our on-camera interview for *the fifth estate*. The husband she killed had been in the ground for more than two years when we spoke in the house in rural Nova Scotia where she had endured five years of terror under Billy Stafford's rule. As she described to host Hana Gartner the horrific incidents that had occurred three, four, or five years before, her eyes bulged unnaturally and soundman Gerry King thought there was a problem with his equipment until he realized he was picking up the frantic pounding of Jane's heart as she recalled Billy's brutality.[18] He was long buried and no longer able to hurt her, yet the fear she felt was still as palpable as if he were right there in the room. That was the first time I understood "the fear"—and why Jane had stayed with Billy.

Unless you have personally experienced that fear, it can be almost impossible to comprehend. But anyone who does understand it would never proclaim, "I don't know why she stayed. I wouldn't put up with that for a minute."

Understanding necessitates a knowledge of the dynamics of the abuse and an appreciation of the vicious, criminal web that abusers weave to win over and entrap their prey.

Several victims of battering used the term "knight in shining armour" to describe the man they thought they were getting at the start of a relationship, only to end up in an unimaginable hell. Andrew Klein says we haven't been successful in reducing homicides of women by their male intimate partners "because we have failed to appreciate the true danger and intransigence of abusers. Domestic violence is not about relationships, good or bad. . . . It is about abusers and their use of violence. Domestic violence is not accidental. Abusers do not strike their partners because they are out of control. They strike their partners to maintain control over them; humiliate and debase them; isolate them; or punish them for asserting their independence."[19]

Eileen Morrow, coordinator of the Ontario Association of Interval and Transition Houses, agrees: "It's not rage—it's control. You know, as soon as the cops knock on the door, he's perfectly fine; or the phone rings and he answers, has a normal conversation, and when he's finished talking, he hangs up and goes right back to being out of control—it's just another tactic. If you want to end violence against women, you have to address the power and not just the tactics the abuser is using on a woman.

"It's not just about the fist and the knife and the gun. It's about the money. It's about the access to information. It's about representation. It's about kids. It's about who has the power to define and redefine. Power has its own set of elements. In an individual relationship, there is economic power—he takes all the money. And there is redefining. She says, 'I was just dancing with the guy,' and he says, 'You're a slut.' She says, 'I want to go back to school,' and he says 'What, do you think I'm not good enough to support this family?' So he takes everything and turns it into something else. He redefines and defines who everybody is, what they do, when they get punished and how. That's the power. So it's not just about the gun and the knife and the fist. It's about how he's twisted everything. Some women say they feel like they are going crazy. Well, it *is* crazy-making, because they are at the kitchen table in the morning and she's sitting there with a black eye and he's saying, 'You know I would never hurt you or the kids.'"

When abuse is less severe and less pervasive, there can be economic, family, religious, and other reasons for a woman to stay. But at the cruel and horrifying other end of the scale—when lives are at stake—no woman wants to be there. She is often trapped, however, because even if she is capable of overcoming the crushing fear of her abuser, she faces the added fear that the system may be incapable of protecting her and her children if she does leave.

DAWN's website provides a list of reasons a battered woman may stay in a relationship, and the top three are fear-related:

- fear of the perpetrator's violence;
- the risk [implicit fear] of being killed when leaving;
- fear that protection orders and the criminal justice system will not protect her.[20]

In his summation to the jury, Jane Hurshman's trial lawyer, Alan Ferrier, attempted to explain how difficult it is for others to put themselves in the position of a severely abused victim: "This case generally requires you to consider the syndrome of a battered wife. That feeling of putting up with incredible abuse but staying for reasons that make absolutely no sense to a person outside that relationship. It's easy for us to say, 'Well, *we* wouldn't be imprisoned under those circumstances.' First of all, *we* are not Jane Stafford. *She* is Jane Stafford. And we are not Billy Stafford either. And we don't know what it was like to live in that household. We don't know what it was like to be subjected to the kind of violence and abuse and sadomasochistic sexual practices that would drive anybody over the wall."[21]

And in the LaVallée decision, Justice Wilson said, "If it strains credulity to imagine what the 'ordinary man' would do in the position of a battered spouse, it is probably because men do not typically find themselves in that situation. Some women do, however. The definition of what is reasonable must be adapted to circumstances which are, by and large, foreign to the world inhabited by the hypothetical 'reasonable man.'"[22] Psychiatrist Fred Shane, called by the defence in the LaVallée trial, said a woman can be so badly beaten "she loses the motivation to react and becomes helpless and becomes powerless...It's almost like being in a concentration camp...you get paralyzed with fear." He said LaVallée pulled the trigger as "a reflection of her catastrophic fear that she had to defend herself."

One of Jane Hurshman's good friends, Andrea Wamboldt, who fled from Nova Scotia to Toronto to escape her abusive husband, witnessed Billy beat and threaten to kill Jane "many times"—more than once with a rifle in hand. "Jane was *really* afraid of Billy," Andrea said. "She was scared—really frightened. I heard him say it many times: 'Old woman, get it out of your head. Don't think you're leaving me, because I'll kill you. I'll find you and I'll kill you.'"[23]

It was Jane's intimate knowledge and acute memory of Billy's terror that haunted her and compelled her, in the years before her death, to become a tireless advocate for battered women "out there, living that same fear."

A REMARKABLE ESSAY DESCRIBING "the fear" and its devastating consequences appeared in *The Globe and Mail*'s Facts and Arguments page in November 2005. Under the headline "Putting It Back Together after Being Abused," Natalya Brown detailed a three-year common-law relationship in which she suffered severe physical and mental abuse: being isolated from friends and family; kicked in the stomach; dragged down stairs; pushed from a moving car; slapped, punched, and pummelled; thrown against walls, dressers, and mirrors; and called a slut and a whore, and worse. "Most women can hide the physical signs," she wrote. "It's the mental abuse that torments them endlessly. A fist flying in the air is as frightening as being told you're worth nothing, that you don't exist."

Natalya was too afraid to leave: "That kind of fear is more powerful than any emotion I've ever known. It's not the kind of fear that makes you jump during a scary movie...I mean the kind of fear that torments your every thought and penetrates your soul every second of your days and nights. I mean the kind of fear that takes over your mind and haunts you no matter where you are or who you are with. It's the fear of the hell you don't know. Staying with him is better than having to face what he might do if you try to leave. And he reminds you of that every time he throws a heavy object at your head."

Natalya said she owes her freedom to one friend who "listened to my agonizing tales over the phone every day." From most other friends and relatives, all she got were reminders "that I asked for it."

"Reminding an abused woman of her mistakes only adds to her self-deprecation and self-loathing," wrote Natalya. "As easy as it may be to judge a woman who 'chooses' to stay in an abusive relationship, it's a lot more difficult to listen to her story. Listening to her allows her to feel like she doesn't have to hide the evidence any more. Once one person knows your secret, it can be the first step toward finding the courage and support to get out."[24]

Telling "your secret." That was the lesson Jane Hurshman taught over and over: "Do not be silent screamers. Do not keep it behind closed doors. The more we come forward and speak out, the sooner society's attitudes will change and there will be an end to the violence. Publicly tell your story, no matter how shocking or unbelievable it may sound. Be honest and sincere, and help and support will be there for you. Society needs to be educated and made aware that domestic violence is unacceptable criminal behaviour."[25]

ANOTHER, LARGELY IGNORED ASPECT TO domestic brutality is sexual violence. "Sexual violence is not readily admitted to by its victims, by those who bear silent witness to it, nor by those in the helping professions," says Carolyn Goard.[26] "Recent research focusing on battered women and women residing in women's shelters found that between 40 and 50 per cent had experienced sexual assault by an intimate partner."

The truth about sexual violence against women remains as much in the shadows today as did "domestic"—physical—violence in the early 1970s, when it was no more than an often-ridiculed euphemism. That began to change when brave women began to speak out and society came to realize that they were talking about more than just a slap or "a boot to the backside." Sexual violence against women in abusive domestic relationships can go well beyond forced intercourse—rape—which is itself a criminal act.

Jane Hurshman experienced further and unimaginable humiliation when she was forced to detail in court some of Billy Stafford's sexual practices. She told about the pain and embarrassment when he tied her to a chair and plucked out her pubic hairs one by one with a pair of tweezers. She described him returning from ports around the world, when he worked on gypsum boats, loaded down with pornographic magazines, which, she said, incited him to increasingly degrading and painful sexual rituals, usually involving beatings and bondage. When, to stop the pain, she bit down on an artificial penis he was shoving in and out of her mouth, he got angry, grabbed her by the hair, and as punishment forced her to drink a glass of his urine. And when he found forced anal penetration of Jane too painful *for him*, he inserted a four-inch length of plastic plumbing pipe an inch in diameter into Jane's rectum. "This'll fix it so you get used to it," said Billy. She was forced to leave it there whenever he was home, and for several months it could be removed only when she went to work or if Billy wanted sex.

The list of Billy's sexual atrocities against Jane is endless, but perhaps the worst was the day he brought his St. Bernard dog into the house and tried to force her to fellate the animal. Jane vomited. Billy forced her to clean up the mess and then fellate him while she simultaneously copulated with the dog.

"To me, I was violated in the most degrading ways possible," said Jane. "Courage is often learning that you can survive doing things that frighten and hurt you. Do it often enough and the fear gets somewhat tamed, but it's always there gnawing away at you."[27]

Sexual violence is not all that unusual in cases of severe domestic abuse. As the true scope of the problem emerges through new studies and the first-person testimony of victims, we are learning that sexual torture is often a routine adjunct to severe physical violence against women by their intimates.

U.S. psychologist Angela Browne, known for her work with women in prison, compared 42 battered women who had killed their abusers with 205 battered women who had not. She found that nearly 75 per cent of the homicide group were victims of forced intercourse, compared to 59 per cent in the other group. And over 60 per cent of the homicide group and 37 per cent of the comparison group reported being forced into sexual acts they considered unnatural or abusive, including "the insertion of objects into the woman's vagina, forced oral and anal sex, bondage, forced sex with others, and sex with animals." In one case, a battered woman's police officer husband sexually assaulted her with, among other things, a wine bottle, a broom handle, and his gun.[28]

At an April 2006 Calgary YWCA panel discussion on domestic violence against women, a woman named Sara bravely told her story of emotional, physical, and sexual abuse at the hands of her husband. "Early in my marriage, my husband held a rifle to my head and told me that if I ever left him, he would kill me." The fear that he would follow through with his threat left her trapped in the relationship for two decades.

Sara attempted to flee in the early 1980s, but her husband called the police and reported she had stolen his car. He was drunk when the police came to talk to him, and he threatened to commit suicide. The police then went to Sara's parents' house to speak to her. "My parents were so devastated to have the police there, they told me to leave. The police also strongly suggested I go home and take care of my husband."

She stayed, and over the years made many trips to hospital emergency rooms as a result of the physical and sexual abuse. "The sexual abuse I suffered caused a perforated uterus and subsequent major surgery. I also suffered a flipped and twisted bowel that required major surgery and the loss of a major part of my upper colon. At the time the injuries occurred, I lied to hospital personnel to cover for my husband without really knowing why. I just instinctively knew that you didn't tell. In private, my husband referred to them as 'sexual accidents' and was very proud of his sexual prowess."

About a year before Sara finally escaped the relationship, she was having lunch with a friend who described how her fiancé had accidentally hurt her during a playful wrestling match. "She told me he cried. I remember feeling very uncomfortable, and later in the day the memories of sexual abuse caused my body to start twitching." It was then that she decided to seek counselling.

"That was the beginning of my rebirth and years of trauma therapy," said Sara. "Unfortunately [until she left], the more help I sought, the more the abuse escalated...He even tried to convince my sister to have me committed for mental illness and he told me I would not be allowed to keep my children if I continued on the path I was pursuing towards self-knowledge."

The physical and sexual brutality endured by Sara and by Jane Hurshman was extreme but not all that uncommon. Jane shot Billy Stafford to end the abuse and save her children. Sara's terror ended when she was finally able to leave. But are severely abused women ever really free? Jane killed herself ten years after Billy's death, and Sara, in her own words, faced "years of trauma therapy."

Then there was Ella Armour.

ASPHALT CROSSING

3

Ella

*Shao-Sang Liang, 38, her daughter, **Vivian Yuen-Yee Chau**, 3, and her son, **Ian Chau**, 5 months. Toronto. Shao-Sang and her two children were stabbed to death in their basement apartment while neighbours listened to their screams. Neighbours had often heard banging and screaming in the home but had never intervened. They expressed disbelief and surprise at the murders and variously described the family as "anti-social," "not normal," and "nice people, like a happy family." Media reports emphasized the trauma suffered by police when they entered the scene and the difficulty they have dealing with the death of children. Huc Minh Chau, common-law partner of the woman, was arrested at the scene and charged with three counts of first-degree murder. (February 2006)*

ELLA ARMOUR AND JANE HURSHMAN WERE BORN SEVENTEEN years and two hundred miles apart in small towns on opposite sides of Nova Scotia—Ella first, near the northeast shore facing Prince Edward Island, seventy-five minutes by ferry across the Northumberland Strait, and Jane in the small coastal town of

Brooklyn on the province's craggy south shore, which challenges the powerful and erratic North Atlantic.

Ella's love-filled, mostly languid early years were in sharp contrast to Jane's. Jane's father went off to fight in the Korean War six months after her birth in 1949. When he returned in 1952, he decided to make a career in the Canadian army and eventually became a chef.[1] Jane had an older brother, by sixteen months, and two younger sisters.

When she was five, she witnessed her father being dragged off to jail after a fight in a restaurant. That same year, he was transferred to the army base in Truro, Nova Scotia, where he began to drink heavily and beat his wife. He became angry and unpredictable. "I used to sit alone on the stairway, especially when they were fighting," said Jane. "I could see them but they couldn't see me. He would stay up all night drinking, go to work, do his job, and come home and start the vicious cycle again."[2] Her father's drinking exacerbated the family's financial problems, which led to more violence.

While Ella had an abundance of warm childhood memories, Jane had few. Recounting the three years they spent in Truro, she said, "Mom used to take us picking blueberries. We would pick all day and then sell them. We were never given allowances, so the berries provided us with some spending money. And sometimes in the winter we helped make ice cream. Those were the nice times, but they were very scarce."

In 1957, Jane's father was transferred to Camp Gagetown in neighbouring New Brunswick and the family moved into a three-bedroom brick bungalow with hardwood floors. Jane entered a new school and found a next-door girlfriend whose family never fought, drank, or smoked. That house became a sanctuary from the madness around Jane. It seemed that in every family she knew on the base, except for her new friend's, there was some degree of alcohol abuse and physical and emotional violence against women and children. "There were all-night drinking sessions and poker games with Dad and groups of his friends," said Jane. One night, one of them, obviously drunk, left a game to get something to eat and drove his car head-on into a truck. He was killed instantly, leaving behind a wife and six children. "I was sad, yet I was secretly thinking, 'Now maybe Dad can see what drinking can do and maybe he'll stop,' but he never did."

Jane never forgot the night her parents, dressed in their finest, a handsome couple and in a good mood, went off to a dance. But when they returned home a few hours later, her father was cursing and ranting and ripped her mother's dress "almost off" as he pushed her to the floor and began beating her. Her mother was crying and worried the children would awaken. "Fuck the kids!" he shouted, hitting her again. When Jane and her brother came downstairs and implored him to stop hitting their mother, he screamed at them and ordered them back to bed. The younger sisters were awake and crying by then. As she often did, Jane took them to the basement, where she held them and sang to them until the violence stopped.[3] Jane was scarcely eleven years old at the time.

Three years later, her family was posted to a Canadian base in Germany, and Jane found a part-time job "washing heads" in a women's hair salon. One day after school, in lieu of pay, she had her own hair done—backcombed, which was the style then—and a touch of makeup applied. "They transformed me into a new person," said Jane. She went home and admired herself in the bathroom mirror. "Dad was drinking as usual. I could hear music and men talking. Mum was running around waiting on them hand and foot." Jane thought she looked pretty and walked into the living room, hoping for a compliment. Instead, her father glared at her. "You made-up whore," he yelled. "Get in the bathroom and wipe that shit off your face and comb your hair." The fourteen-year-old ran into the bathroom, feeling totally humiliated. In an interview a dozen years later, in 1985, the memory of that incident was still painful for her. She said her mother "never in her life" used anything but a bit of lipstick, and "to this day, I seldom wear makeup. When I do, there's so little, it's barely visible."

Returning home from school in Germany one afternoon, Jane could hear her father shouting. Peering through the mail slot in the front door, she saw he was drunk "and had vomited all over everything." He was screaming at her mother to "clean up this Jesus mess." She sat on the front steps, praying silently. Suddenly her father lurched out the door and sat beside her on the steps. "I hate you!" he said, glaring at her with glazed eyes. "I like to believe he was so drunk he didn't know who he was talking to or what he was saying," said Jane. "But at the time, and for many years to come, it left an awful impact. I thought, if my own father hates me, then who will ever love me?"[4]

IN CONTRAST, ELLA ARMOUR LIVED A fairy-tale childhood. By the time she was old enough to pop up around the neighbourhood on tiny legs that never stopped, friends and relatives were calling her "little Shirley Temple." Her dark hair, flashing eyes, and impish smile could thaw the coldest heart. It was the mid-1930s, however, and her environment was nothing like that of the real Shirley Temple, a famous child star living an apparently magical Hollywood life. Ella's backdrop was the bleak landscape and surface buildings of Nova Scotia's Pictou coalfields. Ella Armour was a true coal miner's daughter.

Her parents were descendants of the Gaelic-speaking Scottish settlers who had begun pouring into Nova Scotia in the late 1700s and early 1800s. The influence of the Scots on Pictou County was succinctly described in a 1916 promotional book: "As a result of this emigration from Scotland, the county became predominantly Scottish in character...as more than 27,000 of its 36,000 inhabitants are the descendants of this thrifty and intellectually forceful race who have played, and play today, a conspicuous role in the business, educational, intellectual and political life of the Province and the Dominion."[5]

Both John Robert Armour and Pearl Hughena Muir came from families with eleven children. Pearl's siblings included a set of twin boys. Twins were not unusual for the Muirs. Pearl's great-grandmother was a twin, as was Pearl's grandmother, who had two sets of her own. Not to be left behind, Pearl would also bear a set of twins.

John was proud of the Armour name and bragged that it could be traced back to Jean Armour, long-suffering wife of Scottish icon and poet Robert Burns, who fathered all nine of Jean's children—four before they married in 1788. (The poet also fathered three or four more children out of wedlock with other women.) Jean Armour certainly matched the Muir family's propensity for bearing twins. Four of Jean's nine children were twins. So impressed was Burns that he decided to marry her, writing to a friend, "I am so enamoured with a certain girl's prolific twin-bearing merit, that I have given her a *legal* title to the best blood in my body; and so farewell to Rakery!"[6] The last of their children was born on the day of Burns' funeral. Jean Armour, who outlived Burns by thirty-eight years, was quoted as saying, "Our Robbie should have had twa [two] wives."

Nicknames, particularly for males, were common in Pictou County. John Armour's was "Recky," but no one alive today has any idea of the origin of this moniker. One local suggested it may have had something to do with racking up balls in a poolroom. "I didn't even know his first name was John," said another. "Everybody knew him as Recky." The name was so unusual that in a newspaper photo taken at Salisbury Plain, England, in January 1915, Armour is listed as "John (Rocky) Armour." The editors, understandably, must have thought Recky was a misspelling. The photo was of a First World War honour guard for Private John George MacDonald, "the first Pictou County soldier to die in the war," and in the caption his nickname, "Buglar," was also included in brackets so friends back home would know he was the one being honoured. Outside of immediate family, most wouldn't have known Private MacDonald by his Christian names, John George.

John Armour, like many eager young men of the day, lied about his age to get into the army. He was born on July 14, 1898, but on Attestation Paper No. 46975 his birth year is listed as 1895, which would imply he was nineteen instead of sixteen, his actual age. He had travelled to Valcartier, Quebec, where on September 26, 1914—about seven weeks after Britain declared war on Germany—he signed on to the Nova Scotia Overseas Battalion of the Canadian Expeditionary Force. On his enlistment papers, he is described as five feet, five and a quarter inches tall, with a fair complexion, blue eyes, brown hair, and chest "when fully expanded" of thirty-six inches. Under "religious denomination," he checked Presbyterian. Armour went overseas with the 13th Battalion Black Watch and served commendably for five years, during which he was twice wounded and spent some time in hospital,[7] then returned to Pictou County and the small coal-mining town of Westville, where he had been born and raised.

Like the nearby towns of Stellarton, New Glasgow, and Thorburn, Westville sat on some of the richest coal deposits in the world. The Pictou Coalfield, also referred to as the Stellarton Basin, covered only about thirty-eight square miles but contained the thickest coal seams in eastern Canada. Besides coal, Stellarton would also become headquarters for the Sobey grocery conglomerate, started almost a century ago when Frank Sobey's father opened a butcher shop from which he peddled meat door-to-door on a horse-drawn wagon.[8]

John Armour's father and namesake had also been born and raised in Westville and, like most of Pictou County's men, spent his working life in the mines. Young John followed his path. After the war, he found work underground in a Westville mine operated by the Acadia Coal Company. His job was to make sure the mine shafts were properly shored up so the miners could safely go about the business of extracting coal hundreds of feet below the surface.

With money in his pocket, Armour soon came a-courting to the door of Pearl Muir. They were married on July 24, 1924, ten days after his twenty-sixth birthday. She was eighteen. With a wife and a solid working future ahead of him, Armour found temporary housing adjacent to the Presbyterian church at the end of Irving Street, kitty-corner to the Church Street School. But he and Pearl had plans to eventually build their own house on the other side of Irving, near South Main Street.

They were very much in love, and when their first child, Robert, was born in 1925, they felt their lives were close to perfect. But in May 1928, their beloved three-year-old died of diphtheria. Fear of contagion was justifiably rampant and the child was buried the next day. Seven months later, John Armour's father died of heart failure at the age of seventy-six. Pearl and John were still privately grieving their losses when in late 1931 they discovered Pearl was pregnant again and rejoiced when Ella was born on July 2, 1932. There was no hospital in Westville, and Ella, like Robert, was delivered at the Aberdeen Hospital in nearby New Glasgow. Three months later, her cousin Dorothy was also born there. Dorothy's father, Daniel Muir, a twin, was Pearl's brother.

Dorothy laughed as she studied a seventy-year-old photo of herself and Ella sitting on the front steps of a house, each holding a doll and looking very serious. "Oh, I remember that. I think we were about five. It was a hot day and we had those crocheted caps with tassels on the back of them. We thought we were great. They were big dolls with porcelain heads and arms and feet. I'm laughing because my shoes are on the wrong feet."

Life got even better for the Armours when, three weeks before Christmas in 1936, Pearl gave birth to twin boys, John Ormiston and Charles Langston. They were baptized in February 1937 at the nearby Presbyterian church. Ella, who was four and a half and had yet to be baptized, went through the ceremony along with the twins.

The family's happiness again proved transitory. Pearl had hired a housekeeper to help her with the twins. One day, when they were just three months old, the housekeeper showed up with a cold and "a touch of the flu." Pearl immediately sent her home, but it was too late. Both boys became ill. Dr. P.D. Bagnall was called on March 18, but John Ormiston died eight days later and Charles Langston three days after that. "My parents came home from one funeral and three days later found the other twin dead in the crib," said Ella. "We had two funerals in the same week. It was very hard on them. I was probably four or five at the time. So I grew up as an only child."

Her cousin Dorothy remembers the death of the twins: "They were just babies when they died and it was not a pleasant time. Ella and I were both very young then, but I remember it was very sad. I remember going into the house and seeing the little white caskets, and I know they were buried at the Auburn cemetery."

Given their loss, the Armours understandably tended to spoil their surviving child, but they did not become overprotective and Ella was allowed to pursue an active, normal life.

There was a pleasant rhythm and routine in Ella's early years that she would remember fondly for the rest of her life. On weekday mornings, she didn't see her father because he was typically up and out to work in the mines by 4:30 a.m. In the summer months,

Pearl was usually up early, baking bread and biscuits before the heat of the day. Often, she slipped into Ella's room to wake her. "Get up, it's daylight in the swamp," she would say cheerfully, yanking off the covers. "She loved to sing and dance and would pull me out of bed and dance me all the way to the kitchen. I don't know where she got her energy."

Ella said that if her father was home on a Saturday or Sunday, relaxing on a chair in the kitchen, Pearl would straddle his thighs, facing him, "and start singing, 'Oh Johnny, oh Johnny...how are you doin?' Then she would begin tickling him and he would laugh and say, 'Stop it! Get out of here!' I can still picture it."

Ella usually had assigned chores, but they never seemed like work to her. "Monday was clothes-washing day, and socks had to be scrubbed on the washboard with PC [Procter & Gamble] soap and boiled in a copper boiler until they looked like they just came out of the store," she said. "And the clothes had to be hung on the line just so. On Tuesday we ironed with homemade starch for the shirts and dresses. Wednesday we cleaned the windows and cupboards and wiped the walls, and on Thursday it was cutting the grass, weeding the flowers, and visiting relatives and friends. On Friday we scrubbed and waxed the floors until you could see your face in them. Now it was the weekend, and on Saturday it was baking bread and goodies in the morning and sometimes shopping for clothes in the afternoon."

On Sunday mornings, John Armour was up with Pearl and Ella as they prepared for church and Sunday school, but he never went with them. While mother and daughter were at church, he stayed home and watched that the meal Pearl had left in the oven didn't burn. But that wasn't the sole reason he avoided church. Ella heard his mantra often. "I do my praying at home," he would say. "I don't like looking to see how the other guy is dressed, and all the gossipers passing looks between each other because everybody knows everybody, and some people running around screwing other women's husbands and then going to church on Sunday pretending to be Miss Goody Two Shoes."

Year-round, Sunday was Ella's favourite day. She sang solos and duets in the choir and sometimes at funerals. Then, "Mom always had a big meal ready after church and we came home and ate until we couldn't move. Later in the afternoon, relatives, friends, and neighbours would arrive. One of them played the fiddle, another played the banjo and the mandolin, and Mom played the pump organ. One uncle played the mouth organ and another played the Jew's harp and the spoons. And the Hubbley twins from down the street would tap dance like you wouldn't believe. Then there was always a sing-along—usually country and gospel. It was our own little talent show, and Mom would serve sandwiches and homemade pies and everyone would bring food—homemade bacon, a roast, salads—so it wasn't a big expense to anybody. It was a good time all day and usually no alcohol. It was wonderful.

"The same routine would be followed week after week, but we were always happy and there was always singing and music and lots of love and laughter in our home."

LIVING ON CANADA'S EAST COAST, ELLA CAME to appreciate the four distinct seasons, even the winters, when storms roared ashore with driving snow and lashing winds, creating blinding blizzards. "There could be some pretty awful weather," she said, "but it was a white wonderland too, with the skiing, the skating, and the sleigh rides. I just loved it."

Her uncle John—another of Pearl's brothers—and his family lived behind the Armours across a field. "In the winter, my dad and my uncle cleared off the field, levelled and flooded it, and we had our own great big skating rink," said Ella. "Then they got some empty oil barrels and drilled holes in them and washed them out. They put logs in them and set bonfires, and we used to have marshmallow roasts and hot dog roasts. Sometimes we even had baked beans and brown bread."

Ella also liked to go to the local arena, where she had a reputation as a speed skater. "I used to speed skate at that rink every Thursday night, Saturday night, and Saturday afternoon, because they always had a band playing and I liked to skate to the music."

And during the Christmas holidays, Ella and her friends would go over to John Dan Fraser's livery stable in the centre of town to rent a horse-drawn sleigh. "He had a very friendly light grey horse and we called him Flicker. And we would go for long runs out to what they called the poorhouse, for people who couldn't afford proper food and housing and the town used to feed and clothe them. Every Christmas we used to go there and sing carols, and a lot of people in the town, including my family, would knit and crochet socks and mitts and other things, and everybody got presents. Nobody went without."

There was one Christmas Eve that Ella would never forget. Her uncle Sandy's wife, Margaret, was a Catholic, "and we were all Protestants. But on this particular Christmas Eve, everybody decided to go to the Catholic church for midnight mass so Aunt Margaret wouldn't get upset. They all had a few drinks celebrating Christmas and off they go. My dad had never been in a Catholic church before, and when Aunt Margaret, who was ahead of him, suddenly stopped to genuflect, he tripped over her and then the others fell over both of them and they were sprawled all over the aisle. It's a wonder they didn't get thrown out. They stayed for the mass, but Aunt Margaret said, 'That's the last time you're coming to church with me.'"

When the snow retreated, sometimes as late as April, there was the gradual greening, with wildlife emerging from winter slumber and the sounds of spring sweetening the air. "I used to take a cup of tea and sit on the doorstep and watch the sun slowly peek through the trees and burn the dew from the grass," said Ella. "It was so fresh, and the birds would sing. It was like you had a little piece of heaven all to yourself."

The summers were soothing, with trips to the beach, parties, boy talk, and dancing. "We all used to go to barn dances," said Ella. "Just old-time music—doing polkas. That's why I always loved to dance; I grew up with it." Dorothy sometimes went with her. "They called the dances jam sessions then. Ella was a great dancer. We were just kids having fun."

In those days, there was no alcohol allowed, but there were always a few who found a way around the ban. Ella remembered the time her cousin Harry Muir and his girlfriend, Jean, whom he later married, decided to sneak in a flask of gin. "He was wearing a grey suit. I'll never forget it. So he and Jean are dancing the polka and they're swinging around, and this other couple was swinging too, and they collided and the flask broke and out came the booze right down his suit. God, that was funny." When Harry was reminded of the incident years later, he said, "She got that exactly right."

One memorable summer, Ella's father and Uncle Sandy took her fishing near a dam. "It was high up with fast water, and the fish would jump right over the dam. I never saw anything like that. They had their lines in the water, and all of a sudden Dad yanked his line. I thought he caught a snake. I ran. I hate snakes. It saw me. It was a big eel. I made Uncle Sandy put it in the container he had in his truck to hold fish. I wouldn't get in the cab until he did that. Mum was mad when we got home, because Dad had worn new jeans she bought him. The eel had wrapped itself around his leg and it took out the colour in the jeans."

Autumn was young Ella's favourite time of year, with leaves changing colour and swirling to the ground, rustling in the breeze, or crunching underfoot. "I can still feel and smell the crisp air when I close my eyes," she would say more than sixty years later. "And I see the gold, red, and yellow maples in their glory, and the blue spruce with their different hues of green—just magnificent."

There was a lot of family in the neighbourhood where Ella grew up, and more than a few unforgettable characters. Hugh Allan MacQuarrie, the local undertaker, was a big genial man, known to most as "Allie," who handled most of Westville's burials from the time he took over the business from his father in 1907 until his own death at age sixty-nine in 1942. He and his wife, Millie, lived next door to Pearl and Recky and were there to offer comfort and to provide undertaking services for their twins and Recky's father.

Besides undertaking, MacQuarrie was in the furniture business and was active in civic affairs, serving stints as a town councillor and mayor. He was a Past Master of the Western Star Masonic Lodge and president of the East Pictou Conservative Association. According to his obituary in the *Halifax Herald*, he was "the staunchest of Conservatives but numbered among his friends the most ardent of Liberals, for even in the height of election campaigns he retained his sense of humour and fair play."[9]

Allie and Millie often played cards—bridge and Auction 45 were the popular choices—with Pearl and Recky or various relatives. They never played for money, but they always enjoyed themselves. Behind the MacQuarrie house was a garage-like structure that served as Allie's morgue. "That's where he worked on the remains or whatever he did in there," said Ella. "When someone died in the middle of the night, he would knock on the window and my dad would get up to help him pick up the remains."

One night, she heard MacQuarrie's knock and couldn't get back to sleep. She eventually went outside and saw him and her father lift a body from a hearse to the special basket used to carry remains. Just then, Millie hollered from the house, "There's a phone call—they want to talk to you right away." They set the basket on the ground and MacQuarrie headed for the house.

"You can't leave him on the ground like that," said Ella.

"Why not?" said MacQuarrie. "He's not going anywhere."

Into old age, Ella would chuckle over that incident.

Even more vivid was her memory of the time her grandmother came to visit and a runaway horse galloped along the sidewalk near their first home next to the Presbyterian church. "He could have killed somebody," said Ella. "People were chasing him, trying to catch him. The horse cut through between our house and the church, and in our kitchen there was a shelf with an old-fashioned alarm clock with legs on it. My grandmother was sitting at the table and her chair was just below the shelf. Well, that horse hit the house and the clock fell and hit my grandmother on the head and knocked her out. She was out cold on the floor. Nobody knew what had happened, and when we went out to look, the horse was gone."

DURING THE SECOND WORLD WAR, the sleepy town of Pictou became a busy shipbuilding centre, and many women from there and surrounding towns, including Westville, trained as riveters or worked—often six days a week—at other jobs normally held by men. Those not working in the shipyard contributed to the war effort in other ways. They regularly arranged parties and dances as an antidote to oppressive wartime rationing and were active in fund-raising and salvage drives.

Ella was just eight years old at the start of war, but, spurred by the example of her mother and aunts, she was anxious to do her bit. "My dad's sister, Aunt Peg, and my mother and her friends used to knit socks and mitts for the troops and insert happy notes and messages for them. The notes would say something like, 'See you when you get home,' or 'We all love you,' or 'God bless you.' The Red Cross shipped them overseas. When I got older, they taught me to make homemade quilts on a quilting frame. There was a lot of sewing with the patterns they would design, and I also learned to make homemade rugs and mats."

PICTOU'S NAME IS DERIVED FROM THE Mi'kmaq word *piktook,* meaning "an explosion of gas,"[10] and it seems the Mi'kmaq knew what they were talking about. Pictou's rich coal seams release a lot of gas and are extremely volatile, sometimes resulting in spontaneous fires and explosions. Since 1880, about 650 miners have been killed in accidents in Pictou County—many of them in explosions. The last major explosion, on May 9, 1992, at the Westray mine about a mile from Stellarton, trapped and killed twenty-six miners underground.

John Armour came close to becoming a fatality statistic when Ella was twelve. The earth shifted while he was working underground and the roof of the shaft came down on top of him, pinning him. He was buried for seven and a half hours, and all that time his good friend and fellow miner Jesse Rundle kept digging with his hands, trying to make a hole between the rocks large enough to pull Recky out to safety. "He dug and dug until there was no skin on his hands," said Ella. "He was bleeding, but he didn't care, he was saving his buddy. My dad was never the same physically again after that."

Armour was transported by ambulance to Camp Hill Hospital in Halifax. At first, doctors thought he might not live. "He was there five or six months," said Ella. "His heart was squeezed and his chest was injured. I don't know how he lived, but he did. After months and months of therapy, he could walk around the house and out in the yard. But he couldn't walk half a block on his own."

John Armour's injuries were so severe and his heart so damaged that he would never work again, nor could he undertake anything more strenuous than walking short distances. But he was inventive, and what he could do was pass on knowledge and skills to an eager and receptive daughter. "He taught me all kinds of things. He used to straddle a chair with his arms resting on the top of the back, and he would tell me how to do things. We had already moved into the new house that he and my uncles and a friend had built, and he taught me, with the help of my uncle Ronnie, how to build an addition on to the back. We added another room and I learned to shingle [a roof] and to put up gyproc [drywall] and two-by-fours. Also how to lay a floor. What I hated most was 'mudding' after you put up the four-by-eight sheets of gyproc. They're heavy, and when you get them up you have to fill all the nail holes, and then you had to 'mud' them and then tape them and wait for them to dry."

When Pearl wanted a clothesline set up in the yard, Ella helped dig the posthole, "and then my dad taught me how to mix cement. He couldn't do anything, so he sat there and told me how to make the frame for the cement and how to mix sand, water, and some salt in with the cement and shovel it into the hole. I was about twelve years old then and five-foot-two."

Seeking a better way to support his family, Recky decided to go into the chicken business. "So then we built a henhouse and a long wire fence, and before you know it, he was into raising Rhode Island Reds," said Ella. "And he made money doing that."

Despite all she had been through, losing three children and seeing her once active husband now an invalid, Pearl Armour didn't flinch. Beneath her feminine airs, there was a strength that did not seem to diminish with age. Nor, apparently, did the affection she felt for her husband. He was now infirm. He had packed on the pounds through the years and was no longer the slim young soldier who had returned from the battlefields of Europe. But Pearl—elegant, a couple of inches taller, and svelte by comparison—didn't seem to mind.

Even with her new responsibilities and challenges, young Ella still found time for the things that pleased her. In addition to roller skating and ice skating, she became the only female member of the Westville Pipe Band, and when the lead singer of a local band "took sick," Ella was asked to replace her because everyone knew Ella's abilities from her choir singing. "So I ended up being the lead singer for the band," said Ella. "And they had barn dances and they played at the Oddfellows Hall for Saturday night dances. Jeez, I think I was only about fourteen." And Ella and Dorothy found a way to make $2 each on Tuesday nights. "That's what they would give us for a whole night selling bingo cards," Dorothy recalled. "And that's the place that Ella met Vernon."

4

Vernon

Wendy LaFleche, 41, her daughter, Victoria, 7, and her son, Jesse, 3. Aurora, Ontario. Wendy and her children were beaten to death in their beds. Her estranged husband, John LaFleche, was caught in a police chase near Barrie as he fled and was later charged with three counts of first-degree murder. (March 2006)

DOROTHY WATTERS LAUGHS WHEN SHE REMEMBERS WORKING Tuesday night bingo at the Westville Orange Hall with her teenage cousin, Ella, just after the Second World War. "Besides the two bucks we were paid, we got a free bottle of pop and a hamburger. That was okay in those days, you know. But Ella and I had to cover one long table each. And you'd get these superstitious people who wanted cards with certain numbers on them—like I-66. And you have these armfuls of cards that you'd have to run through, and you only had so long before the next game. After working there, I never went to bingo again."

Back then, she was Dorothy Muir. Today, she lives in Kamloops, British Columbia, with her husband, Allister "Tin" Watters, who was a miner in Stellarton until they moved west in 1952. Now in their seventies, they raised three children, including Timothy "Tim" Watters, who played defence in the National Hockey League for fourteen years with the Winnipeg Jets and Los Angeles Kings.

"Ella and I had fun at the bingos," says Dorothy, "but, unfortunately, that's where she met Vernon Ince."

Vernon sometimes showed up with his mother, Dorothy May Ince, and her boyfriend, Ray MacDonald, who was well over six feet and weighed about 240 pounds. Most people called him "Big Ray." He and Dorothy May had recently moved in together after she separated from her husband, James "Jimmy" Ince, a miner who'd retired due to injury and a long-time alcoholic.

"I didn't know them from Adam," said Ella. "We were each assigned certain long tables to sell the bingo cards, and they always made a point of sitting at the table where I was working. Then they started joking around and said the only reason they came to bingo was me. Because of Big Ray, I thought Vernon's last name was MacDonald."

IN THAT SUMMER OF 1947, VERNON was seventeen and the younger of Dorothy May's two sons. His brother, Douglas, was just over a year older and—one of the few men in the area without a dubious or embarrassing nickname—was known simply as Doug or Dougie.

Vernon wasn't so lucky. He was saddled with the nickname "Dickie." Doug Ince, now in his late seventies and living in Stellarton, recalled, "They had him circumcised when he was six or seven years old, and somebody put that handle on him. To think they put that on him when he was in the hospital and it stuck."

Doug Ince is a congenial, quiet-spoken man enjoying his retirement. He and his wife, Susan, are close to their three adopted

children and two grandchildren. Doug had a heart bypass operation in 1991 and tries to look after his health. His daily routine
includes a morning swim at the YMCA. "After that, I look after any
odd jobs around the house, and then I go down to the post office
and talk with the boys."

Doug's father, Jimmy Ince, was born in England and became
part of the small army of men who came to Canada from the
British Isles to work in the mines. His mother's maiden name was
Field, and her family too had emigrated from England, although
she was born in Stellarton—the only one in her immediate family
not born in "the old country."

"I still write to cousins over in England," says Doug Ince. "I
think they are all from little towns around the Manchester area.
They might be thirty or forty miles from each other. Over there,
they think that's a long way."

When Dorothy May's father, George Field, first arrived in
Stellarton, he took a job at Lee's Dump. "They would dump coal
from the mine with rock and everything in it, and the mine would
give a guy a contract to separate the coal and sell it," explains
Doug. "George worked there picking the coal out." But he didn't
like the work and soon quit and opened a grocery store.

Jimmy Ince had a brother and sister who also came to Canada
from England. The sister went to Toronto, but the brother, William,
was caught in a fall of coal deep underground on April 13, 1938,
when he had been in Canada for nine years and in the Stellarton
mines for seven. He was moving hardwood blocks, or "chucks,"
used as temporary roof support when a large piece of coal or rock
broke loose and fell on him—an accident similar to the one that
almost killed Ella Armour's father. "You've got to know your stuff,"
says Doug Ince. "It's dangerous and tricky work. Recky [Armour]
was a brusher,[1] and if the roof in the mine takes weight and comes
down a bit and there's no room to get a box[2] through, then you

have to use a pick and chip off enough to get it through." William Ince was severely injured, including a "deep puncture wound to his left flank." He was operated on at the Aberdeen Hospital in New Glasgow but died two weeks later at the age of forty.

Dorothy May and Jimmy Ince were the same age as Ella's parents—eighteen and twenty-six—when they were married in a Church of England ceremony in Halifax on July 4, 1928. They returned to Stellarton, to his job in the mine and the home where they would raise their two boys. Doug was born first, followed by Vernon on February 22, 1930.

Doug remembers a fairly typical childhood. "We were like all the other kids growing up around here—playing ball in the old grass fields, skating on the ponds in the winter, playing kick the can. Vernon loved to skate. But I never played hockey. I didn't even play on a ball team—just played in backyard type of games."

Even though Doug was older by thirteen months, he could always depend on Vernon. "He was the baby, but he always stuck up for me. If you got in any school fights, he was right there, boy." When the roles were reversed, Doug confesses, "I just let him fight it out himself. Oh, Vernon had a temper all right. He'd get in fights, but he'd get over it."

Doug had been on an odyssey of sorts since he quit school in seventh grade. "I didn't like school, and my father said, 'If you quit school, you've got to go to work.'" His first job was working with his uncle at the Stellarton grocery store founded by his grandfather, George Field. "And then I went on the 'extra gang' for the CNR railroad in the summertime. They had extra gangs of maybe a hundred guys to dig up all the old railroad ties and stuff. In those days, it was all by hand. Of course, now they have machinery to do the work.

"I had different jobs. I worked in the Trenton car works down here where they made railway cars, and then I was in the shipyards in Pictou for two years when the war was on. I worked in the blacksmith shop, and I loved it. I had a chance to go to Halifax and finish my trade. I often wished I had gone. I've still got tools I made, hammers and stuff. I was only a kid—I could hardly lift the maul.[3] I was a striker, but they put me on the forge. The old fella liked me. He was an old English guy and was like a father to me. I never had to ask for a raise all the time I was there. He would say, 'Look in your pay envelope next week,' and there would be a raise. He was good to me."

The local office of the government's Unemployment Insurance Plan sent a group of Stellarton men, including Doug and some of his friends, to work at a nickel plant in Port Colborne, Ontario. But they had other plans. "We left there and 'hoboed' to Alberta on the railroad. I stayed out there all summer." Doug returned to Stellarton for a few months. "Then one of my buddies said, 'Let's go to Ontario,' and off we went again. We were just young and foolish then, travelling all over the place."

Doug also worked in the mines until, with their long history of fires and explosions and collapses, they were closed because they were too dangerous. "I liked working in the mine and I would have stayed there," he said. But with his job gone, he went to work at age twenty-seven for an uncle who had a concession selling confectionaries.

Doug knew Ella Armour's family, and he liked Pearl and Recky. "She was a nice woman," he said, "and he told a good story and you couldn't help but like him. I bought an old 6.5 [mm] rifle from him for hunting. Jesus Christ, you couldn't hit a barn door with it. It wore out."

There was another connection to Ella's family. For years, her cousin, Harry Muir, cut Doug's hair. Harry's father had been a barber in Westville for fifty-two years and Harry apprenticed with him until he opened his own shop in Stellarton, where he worked until his retirement in 1995. Between them, father and son barbered for a hundred years.

Doug also knows Tin Watters and says, "He most likely got that nickname from kicking tin cans up the alley when we played kick the can. Tin's young fellow turned out to be quite a hockey player, and Tin's father, who was a coal miner, was a pretty good piano player. He played house parties and played in a band at the dances. I liked listening to him."

Tin Watters in turn remembers the Ince boys and says, "Doug was pretty easygoing, but that Vernon—Dickie we called him—was a mean one. I never had any run-ins with him, but I don't think he had a lot of friends and he wasn't well liked. My acquaintance with him was just to say hello and that was about it. His mother was well known as a bootlegger. She was a big woman, and it used to be quite a poker shack she ran behind the store. We had the liquor store, but it used to close at noon on Saturdays. When it was closed, you went to the bootlegger."

Doug Ince doesn't make excuses for his brother. He is acutely aware that Vernon was quick to anger and could be difficult to deal with. Growing up with an alcoholic father and the resulting stresses and squabbling between their parents was rough on both boys. Jimmy Ince was a hard worker, but after years in the mines, he suffered a serious back injury and was in such pain that he was unable to work. Doug says that because his father "wasn't actually hit with anything in the mine," the company refused to pay him a disability pension. The union then decided to send him to Montreal, where he was examined and operated on by renowned neurosurgeon Dr. Wilder Penfield. "He said my dad's injury was just from hard work. And after that the mine started giving him about $30 a month. Then they gave him light work at the Allan Shaft, but his pension was so small, they didn't cut it off. He could work a little as long as they gave him a light job."

Doug says that his father wasn't a constant drinker but was prone to extended binges. "He'd go on a bender for a couple of weeks, and then he'd go without a drink for six months. Neighbours used to say that when they saw my dad dressed up, they knew he was going on a drunk—with a shirt and tie on."

There were no bars in Stellarton to attract him and most of Jimmy Ince's drinking was done in other people's homes. His favourite destination was the cluster of company houses—where the rent was paid to the mining company—in an area called the Red Row and another in Evansville known as the Bull Pen. "He would just drink in people's houses," says Doug. "Some of them were bootleggers and they didn't mind him coming around. Jesus, no, they loved the old man. They knew they were going to get some money out of him. He'd save up and blow it all.

"He had a good sense of humour, and he was funny when he was drinking. He was about six feet and 175 pounds—tall and thin and all bone. If he grabbed a hold of you, you'd have a bruise on you. He didn't play any musical instruments, but he sang hymns when he was drinking."

IN ONE BLACK-AND-WHITE PHOTO of a handsome teenage Vernon Ince, he flashes an engaging, self-assured smile as he stands square-shouldered and cocky, hand on hip. He is wearing work gloves and what appear to be work boots. In an earlier photo, Vernon and a young friend are wearing boxing gloves. A second friend holds Vernon's left arm up in victory while the other pugilist feigns defeat, bent at the waist with both boxing gloves hanging listlessly almost to the ground, but grinning at the camera with a cigarette dangling from his mouth. In a third photo, Vernon smiles proudly beside his mother. He was always close to her, and in this photo he has his arm around her and stands a full head taller. His hair is neatly parted and he wears a white open-necked shirt and a sports coat.

By his late teens, Vernon's five-foot-ten frame had filled out and he weighed close to two hundred pounds. He had trouble finding employment that suited him. "At one time, he was down at the railroad station where he was going to be a telegraph operator, but he didn't get along with the guy and I don't know if they fired him or if he quit," says Doug. "Then he went to the steelworks where they made wheels for the rail cars. He was going to be a machinist, but he wasn't there very long. I don't know what happened. Maybe it was the money, or maybe he didn't like being an apprentice."

LIKE THE MEN, PLACES IN THIS PART of the country often have nicknames. Melford MacLean is a confirmed bachelor who has lived all his life in an area of Stellarton called the Asphalt. "I was born on this property and I'm still on it," Mel says.

Pronounced Ash-felt by locals, that area of Stellarton was one of several enclaves of housing built by the mining companies. "So if somebody said, 'Where do you live?' I wouldn't say Acadia Avenue, I'd say that I live in the Asphalt, and they would know what I'm talking about," says MacLean.

Tin Watters, who also grew up in the Asphalt, doesn't remember the origin of the name, "but it's got something to do with coal. There's a history of coal in that name. The Asphalt is a miner's community—a company town. They were pretty well all miners who lived in those houses. It was an Acadia Coal Company house, and I think my parents paid around $7 a month rent. And coal was around $7 a ton. But we used a lot of firewood in those days too, because we were pretty handy to the bush. There was my mom and dad and my two sisters and four brothers. The mines were my dad's life. A lot of those homes are still there today, but most of them have been renovated.

"There were about four streets in that neighbourhood, with about twelve houses on each street, so about fifty houses in all. We lived on a street at the top end of the Asphalt, and there used to be a ballfield up there and lots of activity."

Doug Ince, who lived across the street from Mel MacLean, says that originally the houses were mostly owned by Acadia Coal and suggests "Asphalt" may have originated from the practice of dumping ashes behind the house. "Years ago, you used to put the ashes out in the garden at the back of the house. That's where I thought they got the name."

Mel MacLean knew the Ince family well but was never close to Vernon. He recalls once seeing Vernon working on his car and he went over to see if he could lend a hand. "I wasn't a mechanic or anything, but he knew I used to fool around with cars. So I was down there just trying to help him get the car going. I think he was having transmission problems and he was underneath doing that, and I was just kind of talking to him. But other than that, I never had that much to do with Vernon. He was a neighbour all his life, you might say, but I would just see him coming and going. With me, he was all right. He never bothered me."

Mel and Doug Ince remain fast friends. But Mel says Vernon "was kind of nasty. I never chummed around with him that much. He's not like Doug—no comparison between the two of them."

HELEN SANGSTER DESCRIBES HERSELF AS "a young seventy-seven." She lives in her own apartment in Stellarton and is often in the company of Mel MacLean. But Helen knew something about Vernon Ince that, until recently, Mel never did.

Helen, whose maiden name was Betts, was the same age as Vernon and as a young teenager often saw him around Stellarton. There was something about him that made her uneasy. "He wasn't like Dougie," she says. "Dougie was a nice fella and friendly, but Vernon had a nasty look about him. I don't know why, but I didn't like him at all. There was something about him. He was a smart aleck or something."

When she was fifteen, at the end of the war, Helen was living with her coal miner father and three younger siblings. Her mother had died in 1944 at the age of forty. "I was just going on fourteen and I had to bring up a three-year-old, and one seven, and another one ten," says Helen. "I looked after them alone until dad got a housekeeper to help. There were two older girls, but they were married and they had their own families. The doctor used to come in, and he couldn't get over me, that age, keeping everything as nice as I did and baking and cooking too."

One summer day, Helen thinks it was in 1945, when she was working in a bakery, she came home quite weary. "It wasn't easy work for my age, but in those days you took anything you could get. I remember I was tired, but I went over to this Charlie Baker's canteen." A canteen was usually a hole in the wall, a mini-version of today's corner store. Charlie's was a one-room operation at the front of a house in the Asphalt, selling cigarettes, soft drinks, hamburgers, and chips. "I knew Charlie and Mary and they lived there in the house. I don't know if I went there for cigarettes or pop. I think I was smoking then. When my mother was alive, I used to sneak them. And when she caught me, boy, did I ever get it. I quit eventually. We were all just kids showing off."

When she arrived at the canteen on that summer day, Vernon Ince was already there. "He was hanging around like kids do in those places, and when I went in, he came over and was trying to get around me." Vernon began touching and stroking Helen's hair. "I had long blonde hair and he was telling me how lovely it was. I just looked at him and said, 'Leave me alone.'"

Vernon walked out and Helen thought that was the end of it, but when she left the canteen a few minutes later, Vernon attacked her. "I thought he went home, but when I opened the door, he came right around the side of the building and kicked me in the stomach. It knocked the wind right out of me and I couldn't breathe. Then he was gone."

Charlie Baker saw what happened and came to her aid. "Helen, I wouldn't take that," he warned her. "That boy will always be bothering you if you don't do something about it."

When she got home, she pondered what Charlie had told her. "It scared me to think he would be bothering me again. I couldn't believe it. I was a stranger to him." She decided she would go to the police. "But then his father [Jimmy] came to our house and was begging me not to press charges. But I did press charges and he got arrested and I had to go to court. It was a small room down in Stellarton in the town hall. Nowadays you'd have to go to Pictou for court."

Helen recalls that Magistrate William Richardson heard the case, but she doesn't remember if Vernon had to pay a fine. "Whatever he paid, I don't know. All I know is he was told to stay away from me and he did."

IN THE WORLD OF MEN WHO ABUSE WOMEN, it's not unusual that they exhibit violent behaviour beyond battering their intimates and have problems with outsiders and police. Among felony assault defendants charged with family violence in state courts in the United States, a major study revealed that 73 per cent of them had previous criminal convictions, though not necessarily for domestic violence.[4] That figure was slightly lower than an earlier Massachusetts government study that found 80 per cent of male abusers had criminal records, including 46 per cent for violent crimes. And 39 per cent had had prior restraining orders issued

against them, of which 15 per cent violated those orders within the
first six months.[5] About half of those with "priors" had abused
multiple victims.

These reports contradict earlier studies that suggested most
batterers usually *do not* have criminal records and are almost never
violent with anyone except their domestic partners.[6]

A penchant for fighting, a nasty temper, and stroking the hair
of a woman you barely know, then kicking her in the stomach for
telling you to stop—these certainly qualified Vernon Ince as a
potential batterer.

VERNON'S CONDUCT IN HIS EARLY years was easily matched by
that of Billy Stafford, the man who later became Jane Hurshman's
common-law husband. Alfie Warrington knew Billy from their
childhood years in Liverpool, Nova Scotia. "We were friends, but
he was always sadistic," Alfie said. "We used to work for his dad
in the junk-collecting business." One day, they were riding in the
rear of Billy's father's truck "with a bunch of strands of guy-wire
ends. Billy started whipping them across my legs. I told him to stop
because it hurt, but he kept doing it. He didn't stop until I struck
him with a piece of metal. After that, he gave me a wide berth."[7]

Billy quickly gained a reputation for violence and intimidation.
And Peter Williamson, who took over as staff sergeant of the
Liverpool detachment of the RCMP, said he and his fellow officers
were wary of him. "He was well known and he was feared," said
Williamson. "He was an intimidating individual. He was a big man
and he...pretty well did what he wanted out there in Queens
County. His neighbours feared him, and they knew that if they
went to the police, they'd have to go to court, and then he might
take some retribution later. He was very obnoxious and resented
the law. He was sort of a bully."

AMONG PEOPLE WHO TREAT ABUSIVE men, there is controversy about trauma or negative experiences these men may have endured in their childhood: How important are these experiences? And how much might they contribute to abusive behaviour when the child becomes an adult? Billy Stafford's father was very strict and Vernon Ince's father was an out-of-control alcoholic. Both boys grew up resenting, perhaps even hating their fathers. Many experts believe the result is internalized rage that stunts normal character development and leads to violence against intimates in adulthood. "They feel helpless, abandoned, manipulated and abused," said Robert Heskett, executive director of Family Nonviolence Inc. in Massachusetts. "So when they get in a position of power, they use it. It's payback time. It's very much an unconscious process. It's automatic. It comes out of their gut."[8] Heskett and others believe this childhood dynamic must be explored and treated in therapy, with the aim of changing and reforming the abuser, thereby ultimately protecting his victims from further battering.

The opposing argument is that protecting the victim is the primary goal. Dealing with an abuser's childhood problems "is not likely to have the immediate effect of stopping a man from acting in controlling and abusive ways," said Gus B. Kaufman Jr., co-founder of Men Stopping Violence, based in Atlanta, Georgia.[9] "The main task...is to challenge men to take responsibility for their abusive actions and choose alternatives. One-to-one therapy is not traditionally focused on that task. Most abusive men will benefit from individual therapy, but not until they have completed meaningful work to stop their emotional and physical assaults."

Beth Gerhardt, director of Respect, an American intervention group, puts it more bluntly: "A lot of these men view their lousy childhood as an excuse. We don't get into their childhood. This is a behavioural education program. If you want to talk about that, go to a therapist. Here we want to discuss why you threw your partner down the stairs."[10]

TWO SUMMERS AFTER THE INCIDENT with Helen Betts, Vernon Ince was wooing Ella Armour. The joking around the bingo tables had progressed to the point where he asked her to go out with him. Ella was flattered by the attention from "an older man [Vernon was two and a half years older]. So the next thing you know, he arrives at my parents' place with his uncle's truck and he says, 'Oh, I just want to take your daughter out to get some ice cream at the dairy in Scotsburn.'"

Ella confirmed that she wanted to go with him and her parents approved. "They thought he was nice, so they said, 'Oh well, he doesn't mean any harm.'"

Vernon brought Ella home promptly after their trip to the dairy, but the outing provided enough time to make his intentions clear. He wanted to see her on a regular basis—to be her steady boyfriend. The fact that she had just turned fifteen didn't seem to bother him, but he knew that Pearl and Recky would probably feel that their daughter was too young for a serious relationship.

Ella was thrilled that a handsome older man was interested in her and agreed to start seeing him. She stressed, however, that their relationship would have to appear low-key so as not to alert her parents.

5

Tarnished Knights

Fallon Mason, 23. Mother of two. Brantford, Ontario. Fallon was found dead in the townhouse she shared with her two preschool children, who were present at the time. Later, police engaged in a lengthy standoff with a man who finally emerged from another home with injuries and blood-soaked clothing. He was said to have had a previous relationship with Fallon and had been charged in February with breaking into her home and harassing her and was released on bail after that incident. Greg Christopher Martins was arrested and taken to hospital. He was later charged with first-degree murder. The children were placed in foster care. (March 2006)

THE KNIGHT IN SHINING ARMOUR IS AN IMAGE THAT appears over and over in domestic violence research and first-person accounts of women who have been battered by their intimates. Therapists and shelter workers often hear the term used by victims describing the charming and considerate men they thought they were getting in the early stages of a relationship. Both Ella Armour and Jane Hurshman used the expression when discussing their early relationships with Vernon Ince and Billy Stafford.

In an article in *Let's WRAP!,* the newsletter of Women's Rural Advocacy Programs in Minnesota, one woman said: "The year before we were married, we spent almost every evening together. When we were dating, he was very good to me. He was attentive and caring. He was my knight in shining armor. He was, literally, too good to be true. After we were married and the abuse had begun, I asked him, 'Why didn't you let me know what you really are?' His reply, 'Fooled ya!' My married years were not a dream come true. In fact, I found myself living a nightmare. The man I loved, the man who vowed to love and honor me, spit, literally, on my face, hit me with a one-ton truck, threatened to murder me, threatened to mutilate me, yelled obscenities in my face, and mentally tortured me. I believe that if I had not broken away when I did, I would probably be dead by this time."[1]

Kristi Sayles, a teacher and freelance writer in Tennessee, was a month away from her second marriage when her husband-to-be was taken away in handcuffs after he pulled the phone out of the wall and attacked her and her thirteen-year-old son. He had knocked them both to the floor after the boy talked back to him. Writing about her experience, Sayles said, "Tommy was my 'knight in shining armor.' He had rescued me from my loneliness after my first husband had fallen in love with another woman." Later, Sayles thought about the signs that should have alerted her to Tommy's true character. He was often overbearing, insisted that he didn't want her working after they married, insisted that they attend the church he liked rather than hers. "And there was that annoying thing he often did—ordering my dinner for me at restaurants without asking me. Those seemed like relatively unimportant facets of our relationship at the time—things I assumed that I could change later. I had wanted him to be 'Mr. Right' so badly that I had been

willing to ignore the warning signs... My knight in shining armor
was an abusive man!"[2]

Jennifer Landhuis, a public educator with the women's crisis
centre in Fremont, Nebraska, and a domestic violence advisor for
the Exploring Womanhood website, said that many women are
deceived by abusive men who often start out "very sweet and kind.
He seems like her knight in shining armor. Then he moves very
quickly, wanting to get married and have children."[3] By the time
she realizes his true nature, she is trapped in a violent and dangerous relationship.

And David Mandel, an expert in child welfare cases involving
batterers for the Non-Violence Alliance, an organization based in
Middletown, Connecticut, says the "ugly private face of chivalry
involves obedience and punishment for failing to appreciate the
generosity and beneficence of the *knight in shining armor*. Whether
it's money, hard work, protection from the dangers of the world,
women are expected to go along with the deal. 'I work hard to earn
the money and you provide sex on demand.' Men who use this
form of entitlement often have difficulty taking full and real
responsibility for their violence. They always want to be seen as the
good guys and may work hard to avoid giving up that image of
themselves. Interventions with these clients depend on teasing out
the *secret deals*, or the unspoken quid pro quos behind his *good
deeds*. For example, 'I'll work hard to support the family but you
must never question my judgment or express unhappiness.' Never
articulated by the abuser, they form the basis of an internal system
of justifications for the abuse when she fails to live up to her half
of a bargain she never agreed to in the first place."[4]

Kathleen Waits, a University of Tulsa law professor and member of the American Bar Association's advisory committee on
domestic violence, wrote a much-heralded 1998 article entitled
"Battered Women and Their Children: Lessons from One Woman's

Story" for the *Houston Law Review.*[5] She called this woman Mary and told her story in the first person, using it as a platform to discuss, with exceptional insight and solid research, the implications for the broad issue of domestic violence.

"Women are brutalized, terrorized, and murdered by intimate partners every day," wrote Waits. "The statistics are horrifying... and yet the statistics cannot tell the whole story. They are too abstract and impersonal. The sheer magnitude of the numbers can desensitize us. Domestic violence is so widespread, we can easily become numb to the human suffering behind the statistics. Telling individual women's stories is one way to address this dilemma."

THERE WERE REMARKABLE SIMILARITIES between Mary's experiences and Jane Hurshman's. "The end of my first marriage was very traumatic for me because I had been raised a strong Catholic," Mary said. "I felt as though I had failed. In retrospect, I think Russ sensed my vulnerability and took advantage of it. He acted the part of a 'knight in shining armour.' He wined me and dined me. I was very impressed. He was never physically violent during our courtship."

As Jane Hurshman was ending her marriage to her non-violent but alcoholic first husband, a then charming and attentive Billy Stafford was there to offer his support. "If you ever need any help, or if there's anything I can ever do for you, just let me know," he said. She moved in with him soon after. "I was full of hope for a new and better life when I went off with Billy," said Jane. "He was my knight in shining armour. He was always telling me he loved me." Billy promised they would have a good life together. "I will protect you always," he said. "You won't be hurt anymore."

Both women experienced their first beatings when they were pregnant. Billy stood just over six feet and weighed more than 250 pounds, while Russ was six-foot-four and 240 pounds. Along with the beatings came the incessant degrading and humiliating verbal taunts and insults. "Your thighs are fat," Russ would tell Mary. "No one else would want you. You're lucky to have me." Mary said she had always felt good about her body, "but the constant stream of criticism tore away at that."[6]

As Jane's pregnancy progressed, Billy called her a "cow," and when she had trouble controlling her bladder because of her condition, he shouted, "Jesus Christ! I can't take you anywhere. It ain't bad enough you're as big as a barrel, now you're like a dog and go around pissing on everything."[7] And there was no let-up after she had the baby. He had been working at sea for two weeks after the birth. On his return, he demanded sex and ordered Jane to strip. "Just look at you," he said. "What a hard-looking mess...stretch marks all over you, legs that look like two broom handles—the only good thing I got out of this is that your tits got bigger."[8]

Both Billy and Russ were capable of controlled violence, as well as explosive rage that resulted from "losing it." The descriptions of how that rage manifested itself are uncannily similar. Jane said Billy's face would flush deeply, "His eyes bulged out, and he started foaming at the sides of his mouth." Of Russ, Mary said, "His face was distorted, inhuman, and filled with rage—his eyes bugged out...he seemed like a rabid dog."

Mary echoed Jane when she said she agreed "to share my story with Professor Waits for the same reason that I speak in the community. If just one person reading this story comes away with a better understanding of abuse, it will be worth it. I am not going to go down quietly...They will not take away my voice."[9] Jane said of Life With Billy, "I want this book to be written, not for myself but for all of those others out there who are living that same hell as I did. If even one person picks up the book and is helped by it—that will be reward enough."[10]

ELLA ARMOUR'S KNIGHT IN SHINING armour didn't arrive on a noble stallion but in his uncle's truck, and although she concealed the true nature of the relationship from her parents, she wasn't shy about sharing her good fortune with her girlfriends at school. Initially, she explained to them, she hadn't really been interested in Vernon, "But he just kept coming around."

"Stay away from him," they warned. "He's way too old for you."

That wasn't something Ella wanted to hear.

"I didn't listen. You know, at that age, when an older guy is interested in you and he's working and everybody seems to like him, you start to feel really grown up. I thought my friends were just jealous. He was a smooth talker, and we went out for about a year and he became my whole world. I began ignoring my girlfriends. I felt that they were wrong and that I knew what I was doing."

No one will ever know the details of how their relationship evolved or the endearments and entreaties Vernon whispered to Ella in their private moments. But the fact that they downplayed the relationship for her parents' benefit and that Ella began avoiding her girlfriends fits a pattern. Early in the relationship, an abuser will often attempt to isolate his victim from her family and friends, proclaiming theirs to be "true love" and the "perfect" relationship and convincing her that he is the only person she needs or can trust.[11] In a list of "Warning Signs That Your Relationship May Become Violent" on the University of Wisconsin–Stout website, the number one sign is "A push for a quick involvement: Comes on very strong. An Abuser pressures a person for an exclusive commitment almost immediately."[12] And at Toronto's Centennial College, a women's safety awareness program warns that an abuser will attempt to isolate a woman "from all personal and social resources. If she has men friends, she is a 'whore'; if she has women friends, she is a lesbian; if she is close to family, she is tied to apron strings. The abuser claims that people who are supportive of her are troublemakers and [he]... may not let her use the car, or try to keep her from working or going to school."[13]

Whatever Vernon was whispering to fifteen-year-old Ella seemed to work. She was smitten. "At nights, I would lie awake and picture beautiful images of my life with him," she said. Soon they were having sex.

For a time, Ella successfully juggled school, family, and her relationship with Vernon. And she still found time to perform with the Westville Pipe Band. "She was the only female," said her cousin Dorothy. "She used to be out front marching and twirling the baton. They were in parades and other events all around the county."

Pearl and Recky were never overly strict with Ella, who was always popular and led an active social life. Sixty years later, her cousin, Bessie Flanders, a retired registered nurse living in Coldbrook, Nova Scotia, remembers Ella as "just a typical young teenager—busy, happy and fun-loving. She came from a good family with lots of laughter and joking and no abuse of any kind that I ever saw." Back then, Bessie was Bessie Smith, the adopted daughter of Pearl's sister Tina and her husband, Alexander "Alex" Smith. Though adopted, Bessie was a Muir blood relative. Her birth mother, Rose, was also one of Tina's and Pearl's sisters. Bessie was nine or ten years old when she and her mother went to Pearl and Recky's place for a family crisis meeting—a meeting that would decide Ella's future.

ELLA AND VERNON WERE BY THEN constant companions, together whenever he could drive out from Stellarton to pick her up after school or on weekends, and they were having regular sex, furtive or otherwise. Ella had never had a birds-and-bees conversation with her mother. As she put it, the topic of sex "was taboo in our house." Predictably, she became pregnant, and was understandably afraid to tell her parents. "But my girlfriends were mad at me," Ella said. They felt jilted because she had been spending all of her time outside school with Vernon and ignoring them. "They said I thought I was too grown up for them, so one of them called my mother and told her I was pregnant, and all hell broke loose. I panicked, because I'd never had a fight with my parents. My mother called Vernon and demanded to see him. He didn't know what she wanted. I was grounded and sent to my room for the night, but I sneaked out and went next door to my aunt's place and I called Vernon to tell him what the trouble was."

"To hell with it, we'll just get married," he said. "I was going to ask you to marry me anyway."

Ella was thrilled that her handsome knight was willing to rescue her from jealous girlfriends and legitimize her pregnancy so they could live happily ever after. But Pearl and Recky didn't see it that way at all—thus the family crisis meeting.

"We were living on River Street in Stellarton," says Bessie Smith. "I think Ella was in Grade 9 or 10 at the Church Street Westville High School when we went out to their house. I was just a kid, but I never forgot it...Ella came home from school and they were all waiting for her in the kitchen. Pearl and Recky didn't want her to get married. Because she was so young, they would do anything—send her anywhere—to keep her from getting married. Aunt Pearl just begged and begged her. I stood there and listened. All of them begged her—my mum too. But she would have none of it."

Bessie's birth mother, Rose, had been dead for six years by then, and four of the six Rankin children were grown and had moved out of the house in Montreal. Stanley Rankin still lived there with two of his daughters. Ella's parents and her aunt Tina urged Ella to go to Montreal to live in Stanley's house until the baby was born. "There were several in the family who would have taken the baby," said Bessie. "But Aunt Pearl wanted her to stay with them and even offered to adopt it. She and Recky really wanted to bring the baby up. They didn't want it to go out to somebody else."

Mostly, though, Pearl and Recky didn't want Ella to marry Vernon Ince. She was just sixteen and they wanted a lot more for their only child. They would look after the baby and she could continue with her education. Offering further alternatives, they tried to convince her to go to a private school in Windsor, Nova Scotia, or to the Home of the Guardian Angel in Halifax, run by the Sisters of Charity. "They were giving her all the options they could think of—just to go somewhere to have the baby," said Bessie. "They wanted more for her than to get married to Vernon. She was too young to get married and raise a child. Up to that point, she'd had a normal upbringing and they had given her everything. She was smart, she had a wonderful personality, and everybody liked her. But I remember Ella just wouldn't agree to anything. She wanted to get married, and that was it."

Ella's parents and her aunt talked and argued with her until they realized it was futile, then they gave reluctant approval to the marriage. "My father said Vernon was a man and I was a kid, but the damage was done," said Ella. Her cousin, Harry Muir, said of her marriage, "She was very young. I don't think Pearl would have let her get married if she wasn't pregnant. Back then, people viewed things differently. Today, nobody would care."

THERE ARE STRIKING SIMILARITIES BETWEEN Ella Armour's marriage in May 1949 and Jane Hurshman's sixteen years later. Both lived in small towns, both were pregnant, both were sixteen, and both married older men.

Jane's father had been posted back to Canada from Germany in 1964. The family arrived at an army base in Winnipeg in the depth of winter with the temperature at forty below. Jane was unhappy at school and with her bleak home life. She eagerly accepted a chance to escape and spend the summer of that year with her grandparents in Liverpool, Nova Scotia. It was there that she met Milford Whynot, nine years her senior.

"He was a nice-looking, quiet-spoken, very talented man," said Jane. "He filled a very lonely spot in my life. I needed him— needed someone. He told me he cared. I'm sure I would have clung to anyone who showed interest and affection. I don't honestly know if I loved him or not. I was still a child myself."

They began dating. Jane was a virgin, and the first time she had intercourse was in Milford's car. Two months after her sixteenth birthday, a doctor confirmed she was pregnant. Lying in his bed in his grandmother's house that night, Jane told Milford the news. He was silent for several minutes. "Well, that's something, ain't it," he said finally. "I guess I have to marry you. When do you want to get married?"

"I don't know. When do you think we should?"

"I dunno either. Go to sleep now and I'll decide tomorrow."[14]

Jane lay awake wondering, "How can I tell Mom and Dad? What will I do with a baby? Will I be a good mother?"

But she was resigned to her fate. "I really didn't know what the future held."

Exactly the same questions and apprehensions had kept Ella Armour awake in her bed sixteen years earlier—two young women, girls really, awed by what was happening inside their bodies and fearing what might lie ahead.

DOUG INCE WAS IN LONDON, ONTARIO, when Vernon told him he was getting married and asked him to be best man. "I was working for John Deere, and I had to come home and stand for him. If I hadn't, I might still be in Ontario."

While Doug was in Ontario, he was on the lookout for a rifle for Vernon, an avid deer hunter. "You couldn't get any down here [in Nova Scotia]," said Doug. Eventually he purchased a .30-30 Winchester carbine. "I got a bargain for him at a time when they were very scarce at Simpson's. They only had two left and I was glad to get one, because Vern loved hunting so much."

Vernon's wedding brought Doug back to Stellarton, where he would meet his future wife and decide to stay in Nova Scotia.

THE WEDDING OF VERNON INCE and Ella Armour on May 18, 1949, was by all accounts a smashing success. The ceremony was held under a homemade arch of roses in the front parlour of her favourite aunt's house in Westville, and the bride was starry-eyed. "I just couldn't believe it. I was getting married and my dream was coming true. We received so many gifts—I couldn't wait to open them all."

Her cousin Dorothy, who was younger by three months and who would marry Tin Watters the following year, drove in from the farm with her grandmother and widowed mother. "If I remember, it was in the afternoon and a very nice day. I think Reverend Buntain married them. I can't remember who stood for her as bridesmaid. She looked beautiful. They both looked nice. If he were as good as he looked, he would have been a fine catch. But some people wondered why she married him, because he was such a jerk. It was a very pleasant wedding, and nobody could have imagined what was to come. Vernon and Ella sort of held hands but it wasn't touchy-touchy, which in those days would have been frowned on by the old aunts. And if there was alcohol served, I didn't know about it, but there were sandwiches, cake, and tea."

The large parlour was beautifully decorated, and, "There were so many friends and family," Ella remembered. "There was no room to dance, but everybody knew everybody. It was like one great big happy family gathering. All of Vernon's family was there, except his father, Jimmy Ince." Big Ray MacDonald was there in Jimmy's place, which suited the groom just fine.

Sixteen years later, Jane Hurshman made her marriage vows at the presiding minister's house at 7 p.m. in the evening. Milford had been raised by his grandparents, but they didn't attend the ceremony. Neither did Jane's parents, nor did they send a gift. A small reception was held in the apartment of one of Milford's friends. Jane didn't know most of the people there. Milford got drunk and they went back to his grandparents' house, where he vomited and went right to sleep.[15] There was no honeymoon.

VERNON AND ELLA PLANNED TO take the ferry across to Prince Edward Island the next day for a short stay at the Charlottetown Hotel for their honeymoon. But for the wedding night, Vernon's mother, Dorothy May, had arranged a place for them to stay. "Out on the old Westville highway, where the mall is now, there used to be tourist cabins, and Mum knew the guy that owned them," said Doug Ince. "I went with her when she booked a cabin for them. It was just ten minutes away."

Vernon had a job when they got married, but he wanted to get hired on at the mines at a higher rate of pay. "He promised my parents he would provide for me well," said Ella. "I thought we would be happy."

6

You Make Your Bed

Yvonne Marsh, 37. Wasaga Beach, Ontario. Yvonne was found dead in her home after a man turned himself in to police, saying he had killed someone. Reports said she had died as the result of an axe attack. Yvonne had rejected a man who was insisting that they have a relationship after she separated from her husband. Adam Newman was charged with first-degree murder. (March 2006)

F OR THE FIRST FEW MONTHS, THE NEWLY WED ELLA AND Vernon lived in a three-room apartment in Ella's grandfather's house on Irving Street in Westville. Widower and retired miner Alexander Muir had died of kidney failure at the age of eighty-one, less than four months before the wedding, but the house remained in the family, and Ella and Vernon were charged minimal rent. With her parents and other relatives close by, nothing much had changed for the young bride—except that she didn't have to go to school and she could sleep openly with Vernon.

Ella was seventeen, but she felt all grown up and with her handsome husband in tow was, in her own mind, the envy of her girlfriends. But it wasn't long before she noticed troubling and erratic behaviour on Vernon's part—behaviour that she'd never witnessed or experienced in her short and sheltered small-town life. And she had no idea whatever how to deal with it.

"Everything was fine for the first few weeks," said Ella. "Then Vernon began going off to his mother and Big Ray's place in Stellarton for poker games that would sometimes go all night. He didn't go out after a high-paying job as he promised. He slept most of the day, and only on rare occasions did he go out to the job he had—if he wasn't too tired. What I didn't know was that what money he made he was losing in poker and borrowing from his mother. He owed her hundreds of dollars.

"Several times, I had to go there with him and wait until he was finished playing poker, and it could be four or five o'clock in the morning. I was tired, and I wasn't used to that, and I would go and lie on his mother's bed. I would be there half asleep, and I would hear people knocking on the door. Dummy me, I didn't figure it out right away. 'Oh, just a minute,' Dorothy May would say, and then she'd come into the bedroom and open the closet door and out would come bottles of liquor. I thought they were having a party in the front because everybody was talking and playing poker. But eventually I realized these guys were buying bootleg liquor from her. I was stupid at first—I thought she was just a housewife."

As her pregnancy progressed, Vernon stayed away more. When he did take Ella out, it usually involved his family and he all but ignored her.

Despite Vernon's aloofness, Ella was still in love and excited about the impending birth of the baby. She thought it would bring them closer and magically transform them into a real family like the one she was raised in. However unrealistic, it was a comforting thought, and her spirits were further lifted when "a very nice couple, Johnny and Jean," moved into an apartment in the house next door on Irving Street. They quickly became friends. Ella began spending time with Jean, and "Johnny and Vern chummed around and went fishing and hunting together."

Soon a pattern developed. The men began drinking together, leaving the women at home. "Now it was alcohol and gambling," said Ella. "So we had absolutely no money for food and he didn't care. He would never give me money for anything. Sometimes I would go to bed crying with hunger pains." She didn't dare complain to her parents after her strident defence of Vernon when they had begged her not to marry him just weeks before. Nor could she seek solace from the high school girlfriends she had belittled and accused of being jealous when they had said Vernon was too old for her. "I was too ashamed to tell my mother or anybody else," said Ella. "I was very confused."

And then her life with Vernon took a frightening and more dangerous turn. "He never gave me money unless it was to go to the store for food," said Ella. "So one day he gave me money to buy bread. And I went to the store. There was no food in the house, except for a can of cat food in the fridge. I loved animals and I had a little cat to keep me company.

"Johnny came over while I was out, and I guess he told Vernon he was hungry. Vernon said he would make him a sandwich. There were two slices left from the old loaf, so he took the cat food and spread it on the bread."

Ella arrived home, put the bread away, and went to the refrigerator to get the food to feed the cat, but the tin was gone.

"Where did the cat food go that was in the fridge?" she asked.

"I made a sandwich for Johnny," said Vernon.

Ella said Johnny jumped to his feet, went into a rage, and charged at Vernon. "He gave Vern a bad beating and stormed out of the house," said Ella. "They never spoke again, and Johnny and

Jean moved away. And then my cat disappeared." She was convinced Vernon killed the animal.

NUMBER NINE ON THE UNIVERSITY OF Wisconsin–Stout's list of warning signs that a woman may be headed into an abusive relationship is "Cruelty to animals and to children: Kills or punishes animals brutally."[1]

In a 1997 U.S. study, workers in the largest shelters for battered women in forty-eight states estimated that abuse of animals takes place in more than 40 per cent of the domestic violence cases reported by victims seeking their help. In an article entitled "Domestic Violence and Animal Abuse: The Deadly Connection," Dr. Murry Cohen and Caroline Kweller say, "The main reason for animal abuse within a domestic relationship is control. Threatening, harming, and killing companion animals can powerfully demonstrate someone's power over a partner or child. Abusers also harm animals to punish their partners for leaving, or trying to."[2]

Similar results were found in an Ontario SPCA (Society for the Prevention of Cruelty to Animals) study in 2000.

And a 2004 Calgary study by Sue C. McIntosh[3] reported that of the interviewed women who owned pets, 47 per cent reported that their abuser had also hurt or killed their pets. About 25 per cent of the victims delayed going to a shelter, fearing for their pets' safety. "This confirms that threatening or hurting a cherished pet is a powerful tool, used effectively by many perpetrators of family violence to manipulate and obtain the silence and obedience of their victims."[4] One participant in the Calgary study said her abuser "killed a cat. He told me it was like an electric charge going through his body and tingly. He would tease them to the point of frustration. I would tell him to stop and he wouldn't until he was satisfied." Another participant simply stated, "He fed my one cat to a dog."[5]

JANE HURSHMAN SAW FIRST-HAND WHAT the women in the animal abuse studies were talking about. She had a dog named Blue and learned to show it affection only when Billy Stafford wasn't around, because he would abuse it if he thought she seriously cared for it. But that didn't stop Billy. Blue had always been a house pet, but one day Billy decided that the dog would be kept outside. "She wasn't used to that," said Jane. "Then he started kicking her around, and he would hold her up by the back of the neck and bite her nose. It broke my heart to see this, but I knew not to say anything, because if I did, he would just do it all the more. If I acted as if I didn't care, he'd usually stop doing it." They also kept a horse and two cows in a small barn at the rear of their property, and when Jane's son once tried to feed the horse, "It went right up on its hind legs. It was right wild from being kicked and whipped by Billy." And one of the two cows died after Billy pushed a shovel handle up its rectum. He trucked the cow deep into the woods and dumped it.

JIMMY INCE WAS NOT WELCOME at his son's wedding, and Ella had never met him before he showed up at their Westville apartment one day when Vernon was out. He was a friendly man, and even though she knew about his drinking problem, Ella instinctively liked him. Jimmy asked her to convince Vernon to move to Stellarton, where they could live rent-free in a house he owned there. "He said all we would have to do is look after the grounds and the garden," said Ella.

With a baby on the way and her husband seldom working—and gambling or drinking away what money they did have—Ella thought a change of scenery and living rent-free might have a positive effect on Vernon. She couldn't wait to tell him about his father's visit, but she didn't get the reaction she expected. "Instead of being happy, he got really angry and pushed me against the wall and started screaming at me," said Ella.

"Why did you do that?" she sobbed.

"That was for talking to him," said Vernon as he turned and left the house.

Ella was shaking when he left. "I began to fear for the baby, and the baby became the most important thing in my life."

About two weeks after Vernon's outburst, Jimmy Ince showed up again, but this time his son was home. "Vernon seemed almost glad to see him and invited him in," said Ella. "His father was drunk. Vernon wasn't drinking that day, but he didn't even get mad. And before you know it, the two of them sat down and agreed that we would move into the house he owned in the Asphalt in Stellarton."

Doug Ince says that the house in question was actually owned by his mother and that his father had signed it over to her when the two separated. The house was on Maple Street at Acadia Avenue, but because it was near the railway tracks, locals describing its location would call it Asphalt Crossing. There was a small store at the front of the house, run by Olive Fleming. At the rear was a three-room apartment with a kitchen and living room on the ground floor and a bedroom upstairs. The apartment was occupied, but the plan was to build a two-room addition along the side of the house for Ella and Vernon. Jimmy stayed sober long enough to help Vernon and some other helpers complete the addition. "I remember my father did all the [electrical] wiring for the two rooms," says Doug Ince. "He could do a lot of things. He knew a little bit about everything."

The young couple moved in early in the fall of 1949. The house was painted black, and when Ella first saw it, she thought that this might be a bad omen. She was also feeling somewhat isolated because her parents didn't have a car and, except for her aunt Tina's family, who lived nearby, she was now surrounded by Vernon's relatives. With no telephone, no money, and her baby due in a matter of weeks, the two-mile distance to her parents' house loomed as large as an ocean.

But with the move, Vernon became more attentive and loving. Maybe, she thought, the move would rekindle the romance they had once enjoyed. That belief was bolstered when Vernon followed through on his promise to her parents and found work in the mines. "He surprised me when he got that job," said Ella. "I thought life would get better, and it did for a while."

Through that autumn, Ella's focus was her baby, with reinforcement from her mother and aunts, who eagerly anticipated the coming birth. "They bought up flannelette by the roll and made diapers, little shirts, undershirts, and nightgowns," said Ella. "And they crocheted beautiful baby outfits and blankets. Then they held a baby shower for me and the baby got everything, including a new English pram."

On November 8, 1949, less than six months after her marriage to Vernon, seventeen-year-old Ella gave birth to a five-pound, two-ounce girl. "She was like a little china doll, very blonde, with long blonde eyelashes," said Ella. She decided to name the baby Estelle, after her high school principal, "Because I thought the world of her and I respected her very much. She said no one had given her an honour like that, and she used to drop in and see the baby."

When mother and infant were released from the Aberdeen Hospital in nearby New Glasgow, they stayed with Ella's delighted parents for the first week. Ella needed all the advice she could get from her mother. "I didn't know how to care for a baby," she said. "I didn't know anything about them."

Back in the Asphalt with Vernon, her joy was soon displaced by anxiety—and fear. "He seemed to kind of straighten out for a while, and I thought everything would be okay," said Ella, "but then he started complaining about the baby crying and everything else he could think of. I couldn't do anything right." He began staying away for longer and longer periods, and when he *was* home, the verbal attacks were now accompanied by escalating physical attacks—from slaps and pushes to kicks and serious hair-pulling.

One night, he came home drunker than usual.

"Who said I wanted a kid in the first place?" he demanded.

"I didn't ask for a child either," said Ella, "but I'm happy to have her."

"Oh, you are. You want another one?" At that, he pushed her to the couch and forced her to have sex. "I had stitches from the birth, but he didn't care. He tore those stitches and said, 'I'll teach you.' I ended up back in the hospital, and they had to replace the stitches because I was hemorrhaging. I remember that ether cloth going over my face, and then they sewed me up again. I could hardly walk."

VERNON'S ACTIONS WERE TRUE to the pattern followed by many batterers. Studies show that one in five battered women in Canada are abused during pregnancy, and that 40 per cent of abused women report that the *first time* they were abused was during pregnancy.[6] In 2004, Health Canada reported that women abused during pregnancy were four times more likely than other abused women to have experienced serious violence, including being beaten, choked, threatened with a gun or knife, or sexually assaulted. Similar numbers are reported in the United States, and according to a University of Michigan report, sexual assaults can include forcing vaginal, oral, or anal intercourse against a woman's will; biting breasts or the genital area; shoving objects into the vagina; or forcing sexual acts with other people or animals.[7] About 18 per cent of the women abused during pregnancy report suffering a miscarriage or other internal injuries as a result of the abuse.[8]

Why do abusers go after vulnerable pregnant women? According to some experts, an abuser may become jealous at having to share his partner's time and attention with a baby, or become angry about the added responsibility of having a child, or worry that a health care provider might influence his partner, or dislike a woman's changing body appearance in late pregnancy. It's not unusual for abusers to target a woman's breasts and belly for punches or kicks meant to harm both mother and child.[9]

BILLY STAFFORD WAS A CLASSIC BATTERER. After Jane gave birth to the only child they had together, she began to hemorrhage, as she had done after a previous delivery, and on her doctor's recommendation underwent a tubal ligation. The day after the operation, just three days after the birth, Billy—who had been at sea working on the fishing boats—came to visit her in the hospital.

"You got what you wanted, didn't you?" he said. "Well, old woman, you can damn well look after him. He's all yours. I've been on a party since I got in Saturday morning, and now I'm going back to party some more."[10] He also told her that her operation, which he disapproved of, "makes you no fucking good anymore."

Unlike Vernon, Billy didn't rape his partner when she came home from the hospital with the baby, but he was surly and quick to anger when she made a simple, logical request. "They told me not to do any lifting or strenuous work for six to eight weeks," she told him. "I've still got my stitches in. Can the baby and I stay at your mother's for the next two weeks while you're out to sea?"

"To hell with that idea, old woman," he said. "It was you agreed to that operation, not me. So you just get your ass home and get back to keeping house and looking after that bastard you got there in your arms."[11]

Jane was a spotless housekeeper, but when they got home after her time in the hospital, she walked into a disgusting mess, including stacks of dirty dishes in and around the sink and overflowing ashtrays. "There were booze bottles and cigarette butts all over the place. Your feet stuck to the floor where booze and pop had been spilled, and the bedroom smelled like a pigpen. Bill had been drunk-sick and vomited over the bed and floor and just left it there."

"Well, what the hell are you waiting for?" Billy sneered. "Put that little bastard in the crib and get busy."

There was no running water in the house. Water had to be drawn from a well, carried into the house in a bucket, and heated on a wood stove. There was no washing machine and the laundry had to be done manually. Jane begged Billy to get the water, but he refused. "What in fuck is wrong with you? Crippled or something? Get your own fucking water."[12]

ELLA WAS NO STRANGER to backbreaking work either. When she got back from the hospital after getting her stitches repaired, there was no heat in the house. "It was cold, so I had to go out and get a bucket of coal, and I had to chop wood and take it in and start the fire. There I was in pain with a new baby, and no heat in the house. Vernon said it was my job to take in the buckets of coal and it didn't matter if it was at night or if it was cold. Most of the time, I had no choice because he wasn't home anyway. Lots and lots of nights, he stayed away. I didn't know where. So my job was to keep the house warm. And he would threaten to beat me up if I didn't do it."

Ella was now spiralling into an increasingly dangerous cycle of betrayal and emotional and physical abuse meted out by the man she had once believed was deeply in love with her. It got worse when, after several months on the job at the Allan Shaft in Stellarton, Vernon had both legs broken in an accident. "He became very hateful," said Ella. "His whole personality completely changed. He was nice for such a short time—then he blamed everything on me."

The accident gave Vernon all the justification he needed to insist that it was Ella's job to take in the coal and keep the house warm. "He used to make me chop wood for the Quebec heater in the kitchen. It heated the whole house. We'd get a ton of coal—a shunt of coal from the mine—and because he used to work there, it was free. But I had to haul it in."

Added to that were the tirades, insults, and beatings. "Vernon wore workboots, and he would suddenly just kick me," said Ella. "He kicked me in the stomach and legs with those boots, and it was very painful and very hard to move, but he didn't care. And he would punch me in the back or hit me in the arms. My arm would be so sore I could hardly move it. I always had to wear long sleeves and I could never wear shorts because my legs were always bruised and swollen. He could do what he wanted, and I couldn't stop him."

The slightest miscue or misstatement would trigger Vernon's anger.

"Is there nothing to eat in this house?" Vernon asked in one incident.

"But you didn't buy any food," said Ella, looking through the cupboards. "Here—I found a can of soup."

"Well, I'll have that."

"But what about the rest of us?"

"I don't give a shit about you."

"Well, you could at least share it with the baby."

"No way. Get out of my face, you fucking bastard."

Ella heated the soup for Vernon, and she and Estelle went hungry as he ate it in front of them. When a similar situation arose a few weeks later, she was so angry because her daughter was crying that she threw the can of soup out the door. "You can't do that," he shouted. "It's mine. I bought it."

Ella was forced to retrieve the soup. "And then he grabbed me and just pounded me, and pulled my hair so hard some of it came out by the roots. I had long hair and he'd pull it and drag me by it. But he never hit me in the face. He was a lot taller, and he would stand over me, grab me, and pull me right up to his face and say, 'You're a fucking bastard and one day I'm going to kill you. I don't need you.' He said that nearly every time he got mad."

Vernon didn't lack imagination when it came to devising ways to torment Ella. It was almost a compulsion with him.

There was a small garden between the house and the driveway, and Jimmy Ince would come around to tend it when he was sober. One day Vernon came in from the garden and "he came up behind me and dropped a handful of worms under my top. I could feel them crawling and squirming down my back. I just screamed. He knew I was terrified of anything that crawled. I ran into the bedroom and tore off my clothes and there were worms and dirt all over the floor. He thought it was so funny. To this day, I can still feel those worms."

After another of Ella's beating-related trips to the hospital, she returned home and was ordered by Vernon to "start the vegetables" to complement a cooked pork roast he said his mother had given them for supper. "He liked cold pork and hot vegetables," Ella remembered. "I didn't look at the meat right away. I remember it was wrapped up in bread wrap with newspaper on the outside. Estelle was sitting in her high chair, and I mashed up the vegetables for her and put some on a plate for him."

"I don't want any," he said, pushing his plate away. Ella didn't understand. Then she went to the counter to slice off a piece of pork for Estelle. "But I jumped back when I saw what was in the package. The meat was green and crawling with maggots.[13] Then he wheeled around and threw me on the floor and tried to force some of the meat into my mouth. I got physically ill, and then he tried to force it on Estelle."

Ella jumped up and pulled him away from the baby. "You eat it!" she screamed.

"I don't eat garbage," he laughed as he walked out.

Ella never believed that Vernon's mother sent them that roast. "She's long dead and gone, but I know she would never do something so horrible. She always thought the world of Estelle and the other kids, and I give her credit for that. I just couldn't see her doing that."

ELLA NOW FIT THE CLASSIC PROFILE of a battered woman, trapped in a fearful, walking on eggshells environment with daily verbal and physical abuse designed to demoralize and degrade her. Passive, with no feelings of self-worth, she stayed because she feared her husband would kill her or her child if she tried to leave. Her isolation and lack of money exacerbated her despair. "I couldn't tell my parents. I couldn't tell my relatives. The few times I did get home, everything was smooth and happy. It was like I lived in two worlds—a happy world and a bad world—and I always had to go back to the bad world because I couldn't tell my family. I was too ashamed. Nobody in my family had a car, and the only way I could see them was by bus. I think they ran every hour or two, but I had no money for the fare, even though it was only ten or fifteen cents. I was small and I would have to walk two miles if I wanted to visit them. And I would have to carry Estelle unless I could get Vernon's mother to take me. But if I did that, I was afraid he would find out and there would be more beatings. He wouldn't give me money for anything, but he always seemed to have some for gambling, partying, or liquor."

Ella found a tiny island of tranquility in the friendships she developed, during Vernon's frequent absences, with two neighbours, neither of whom was related to the Ince family. Mrs. Bain lived across the street and Dorothy "Dot" MacNeil lived three blocks away, at the end of Maple Street.

Most people knew Mrs. Bain—she was one of the few people around with a telephone. "Mrs. Bain was a dear widow who cooked and baked, and her home was beautiful," said Ella. "The kitchen sparkled with white enamel walls and sheer white curtains on the windows. She lived with her daughter, who was in her forties and worked in an office. The daughter had the phone installed in the house because her mother was in her mid-seventies, and if there was a medical emergency, she could call for help." But Ella was too ashamed and too proud to tell the older woman what she was going through.

It was different with Dot and her husband, Daniel "Danny" MacNeil. Ella had met Dot at Olive Fleming's small store in the front of the Maple Street house, and they often talked. Dot was intelligent and outgoing, and she took an immediate liking to this waifish young mother with the sad eyes. She gained Ella's confidence and gradually learned about life in the rooms behind the store. Dot had her own feelings about Vernon Ince—she was the sister of Helen Betts, the fifteen-year-old girl who had had Vernon charged after he kicked her in the stomach.

Both Dot and Danny MacNeil are now dead, but their daughter Danna currently lives in a small city north of Toronto and knows Helen's story. "Vernon's family stopped speaking to Aunt Helen, and I guess they were ticked off with my grandparents because she had him charged. I guess they thought, 'How dare they do such a thing?' They never really admitted what a bastard he was. And Ella was terribly abused. He was rotten to just about everybody. I think his mom spoiled him terribly. Vernon was a very good-looking man, but my mother always thought he was so nasty it made him look ugly."

Danna MacNeil was just seven years old the last time she saw Ella, but she has very specific memories of her, and through the years she and her parents often talked about Ella and what she went through with Vernon. "I can remember her crying at our house, sitting at the kitchen table telling my mother that he was going to sell off her furniture. I don't know if he was going to sell it for booze liquor or what. My mother went down and spent the day there sitting on the chesterfield so he couldn't sell it. And he wouldn't dare touch my mother, because my dad would have killed him."

Danny MacNeil was taller than Vernon and about the same weight. Affable but tough, as a young man Danny had been in the merchant navy and was a prospect for the NHL's Boston Bruins until he'd broken his foot. When he found out about Vernon abusing Ella, he wasn't afraid to confront him. "To his face, my dad called him a coward, a rotten bastard, and a woman beater and threatened to kick the shit out of him," said Danna. "Vernon was afraid of him, but then he would get drunk and get the courage to go after Ella. She was always afraid to say he was abusing her.

"My parents just loved her and they felt heartsick for her. When you think back to those days, she was surrounded by his relatives. There was no Children's Aid, no battered women's shelters—no backup at all. The difference today is that women have options. When I look back at Ella, I wonder how she survived at all. And she was so young. I can remember as a seven-year-old seeing three or four bald spots on her head where he had pulled her hair out. And she had this nervous habit of flicking her hair with her hand to cover the spots, but it got to the point that she couldn't cover them anymore."

VERNON DIDN'T WANT HIS FATHER coming around the house. "Vernon didn't like the idea of his father talking to me or me talking to him, because Vernon was his mother's boy," Ella explained. "Jimmy was a very kind man, and he would do anything for me. He liked me as a daughter-in-law and we got along well. He was a very smart man and a good worker. If he was there and I was about to wash the stairs or something, he'd say, 'Don't touch that—I'll do it.' That's the kind of person he was. And he was very good at gardening."

Ella was helping Jimmy plant his garden one day when he started talking about his wife, Dorothy May. "He said he had gone through a lot, but he still loved her. He said she got him drunk and promised she would leave Big Ray and go back to him if he signed the house over to her. She had already had a lawyer draw up the papers to transfer the house and property. After the paperwork went through, she told him she'd changed her mind."

Doug Ince said his father ceded the house to his mother when they separated. "Mother got angry over the drinking, and they used to get into fights about it. But he thought a lot of her and he was good to her when he was sober. He shouldn't have been drinking, because he would go a little haywire. He would get angry and mouthy sometimes. At home, he'd break out on a drinking bender for a while and then quit for a few months. It was the same in the boarding houses: a bender and then quit for a few months. That's the way he was. I got along all right with him, drunk or sober. I'd get mad at him, but I'd never lay a hand on him—never harm him."

Vernon Ince was not so gentle with his father. "Well, they had their ups and downs," says Doug. "The old man was trying to steal liquor on him, I suppose. You couldn't hide liquor from the old man. Vernon had it hidden in the coal house, and the old man found it. They got in a little...tussle over that."

On one occasion, it was more than a tussle. Vernon used to play poker in the garage behind the house on Sundays. "Vernon fed him drinks and got him drunk," said Ella. "He didn't like his father interfering with him and his mother. On the pretense of the poker game, he got him into the garage and chained him to a pillar like a dog. The chains were already in place, so he must have planned it all in advance. He put locks on the chains and left his father there and told me not to go near the garage."

Vernon didn't come home that night, and Ella couldn't sleep for worrying about her father-in-law. When Vernon didn't return the next morning, she was convinced he was leaving his father to die. "I had no keys, but I got brave and went to the back of the garage and pried off two boards. I was able to sneak in and found him standing, but slumped over, with his head hanging down." She gave him beans or soup from a can and some water and hot tea. "His hands were tied behind his back and there were chains around him. I couldn't untie him and I had to spoon-feed him."

"Oh, thank God you're here," said Jimmy.

Ella left, carefully replacing the boards so Vernon wouldn't notice. "He had threatened to kill me if I went near the garage. I really started to believe he was crazy. God knows what would have happened if he'd come home and caught me."

She went back to check on Jimmy the next day, but he was gone. She never did find out how he was freed.

Vernon returned a couple of days later.

"Where the hell did my father go?" he asked.

"I have no idea," said Ella.

"You must know. You must have heard him hollering."

"Why would he be hollering?"

"None of your fucking business," he said.

WHEN VERNON WASN'T AT HOME, he usually wasn't far away. He was spending more time at his mother and Big Ray MacDonald's place, helping with the bootlegging business. "They were all bootleggers," said Ella. "Food was even more scarce for us because he would stay away night after night playing poker and selling liquor for his mother. The poker games were a front for the bootlegging."

Dorothy May's bootleg operation gained a reputation for attracting a fairly prominent clientele. "The chief of police, the chief magistrate, some lawyers, the undertaker, and some off-duty police officers from surrounding towns used to drink at her place," said Ella. "She was becoming famous. My family was upset that I was involved in this situation. They found it embarrassing. She was raided more than once, but I believe the chief of police arranged the raids because he was trying to make it look as if he were doing something to stop her."

Raids by the RCMP, however, were another matter. In one of them, Ella claimed, the chief magistrate escaped through a window, but the chief of police and several others were arrested and charged with gambling in a public place. "The chief was almost fired," she said.

After the raids, to take the pressure off his mother's operation, Vernon Ince began selling liquor and beer out of his own residence. "They tried to force me to front for them to take the heat off," said Ella, "but I refused. I wasn't brought up like that. And I said, 'You can kill me first,' and Vern almost did. People would come knocking on the door for liquor all through the night. I refused to answer the door, and every time I refused, I was beaten."

The RCMP quickly figured out that Vernon was now selling alcohol illegally in the Asphalt and swooped down, but they raided his brother's apartment by mistake. "I was pretty upset when they came to my place," said Doug. "I didn't know what the hell was going on. My mother was just up the road. And here they were looking for liquor that Vernon was more or less keeping for my mother so she wouldn't get caught. I got cocky with them when they found out they had the wrong place. But a few days later, they came back to the right place."

Because Ella refused to help bootleg, "He wouldn't provide us with anything. I was always worrying about food and where I was going to get the next slice of bread. I would say to my mother, 'Oh, it would be so nice to have some of your homemade stew—I really miss your cooking,' and down they'd come, you know. I had to make up excuses like that so the kids and I wouldn't starve."

TWO YOUNG GIRLS HAD FIRST-HAND knowledge of what was going on in the house on Maple Street. Bessie Smith was Ella's first cousin and Betty Lou Boutilier was Vernon's first cousin. Both girls were eleven years old when Ella and Vernon moved to the Asphalt. They are now in their late sixties, with understandably differing perceptions of what was happening.

"Doug's mother and my mother were sisters," said Betty Lou, now retired from Michelin's Pictou County tire plant. She says that when Dorothy May separated from Jimmy Ince, Vernon moved in with her family and lived with them until he married Ella. "He was with us about two or three years," she says. "He was kind of brought up like a brother to me. His mother was living with Big Ray. So his home was broken up. He was a very quiet boy. I never saw him get mad. He was always pretty close to his mother. His father, Jimmy, used to visit us. I liked the old fellow."

Betty Lou knew Ella from the time she started going steady with Vernon. "I was at the wedding," she says. "I was just ten going on eleven. My older sister Dorothy stood for Ella. You can see her in all the wedding pictures."

Both Bessie and Betty Lou did babysitting for Ella during the two years she and Vernon lived in the Maple Street house. Two things they do agree on is that they didn't babysit so Ella and Vernon could go out together and that Vernon was seldom there. "I never knew them to go out together, and I didn't see them together much at all," said Betty Lou. "It was usually her going somewhere, skating or dancing. He wasn't there very often when I was there. She would call and ask me to babysit. I don't think Vernon ever asked me to babysit. He was always away somewhere, and I never asked where."

Ella was a free-spirited seventeen-year-old who, in less than a year, had been transformed from a fun-loving, popular teenager who liked to sing, dance, and fly around a rink on skates to a bewildered wife and mother with a mostly absent husband who physically and mentally brutalized her whenever he did show up.

As incongruous as it may seem, her will wasn't quite broken, and her way of fighting back was to cling to one of the great passions of her young life: skating at the local indoor rink just a few blocks down Acadia Avenue on Stellar Street.

The Stellarton Memorial Rink—the first rink with indoor artificial ice in Pictou County—was built and opened in 1947 to honour local soldiers killed in the First and Second World Wars. Ella had been a regular from the day it opened. She loved skating to the music, and most of all she loved speed skating with her special "racer" skates. With Vernon usually away, she decided that, once Estelle was two or three months old, she could get Bessie or Betty Lou to babysit for her while she slipped out to skate.

"Ella was young, and she wanted to get out," said Bessie. "And if he was out all the time, then she needed to get out too. But she was a good mother. It was often after school that I babysat. And she'd go off to skate in late afternoon or sometimes in the evening."

"Ella was a liar," says Betty Lou, "but she said it so pleadingly that you couldn't help but believe her. She made you believe her. She would lie about Vernon not being home—well, lots of times he wasn't home—and not giving her any money." Betty Lou admits, however, that she never once saw Vernon give Ella money.

"And I never, ever heard of him hitting her," she said. "I'm not saying he didn't, because you never know. For years, I was badly abused myself, by *my* husband, until I divorced him. He was an alcoholic."

On two or three occasions, Vernon *did* come home when Bessie was babysitting. "He was basically pleasant to me, but he just had a terrible temper," she said. "And he would come home from work, maybe from the mines or somewhere, and Ella wouldn't have any supper ready, that type of thing, and he was just wild—quite angry, you know. He had a hair-trigger temper. I just remember the anger if supper wasn't ready. I remember I wanted to leave because I was scared."

As her relationship with Vernon deteriorated and he stayed away more, Ella suspected he was seeing other women. She became more daring and went to a couple of public dances. Whether she was naïve or she was being defiant, she asked Vernon's cousin Betty Lou to babysit Estelle for her.

"A girlfriend came down with me to babysit," said Betty Lou. "We were only twelve or thirteen, and she was going to a dance and she left about 8 or 8:30 and never came back until after 1. The house was such a mess that we worked that whole time cleaning it up. There were dirty dishes everywhere. I think we even had to wipe down the walls. And we even washed Estelle in the kitchen sink. A man came to the door with Ella—I guess to see her home safely. I don't know where Vernon was. He could have been working backshift, he could have been hunting, he could have been fishing, he could have been playing poker—everybody knew he played poker."

BIRTH CONTROL WASN'T SOMETHING that Vernon Ince thought about much. And in January or February of 1950—just weeks after the birth of Estelle—Ella began experiencing morning sickness and realized she was pregnant again. Her reward for informing Vernon was a severe beating.

"I don't want another goddamn brat," he said. "That will teach you a lesson—don't get pregnant."

"He kicked me in the stomach with his boots, and I ended up in the hospital with a miscarriage," said Ella. "Later, he said he was sorry and said he would come to pick me up when they discharged me. It was in March and it was cold. I waited in the lobby for hours, but he didn't show up, so I got brave and called a taxi. I had no money, so I went to the lady [Olive Fleming] in the store at the front of the house and she paid for the cab. When I got home, it was dark and it was suppertime, as it got dark early in the winter. The house was freezing cold and there hadn't been heat in it for days. Then my mother-in-law arrived with Estelle and told me to get some heat on. I went out and chopped wood, got a bucket of coal, took it into the house, and got some heat on for the baby.

"By this time, the baby had caught a cold from the damp house. Vernon arrived two days later and blamed me and beat me up again. He said I wasn't capable of looking after the baby or she wouldn't have come down with a cold. I told him it was because of the cold, damp house, but he wouldn't listen."

Ella felt only despair and monumental weariness when she learned in the early summer of 1950 that she was pregnant once again.

AT THE END OF JULY 1950, DOUG INCE got married, and it was decided that he and his new wife, Susan, would take over the apartment Ella and Vernon shared, and they in turn would move to the three-room apartment at the back of the house, giving them more room for their growing family. Doug Ince says the move was made around the end of August. Ella and Vernon now had a kitchen and living room downstairs and a bedroom upstairs. Ella's second child, a boy they named Donald, was born in Aberdeen Hospital on March 1, 1951.

It was soon apparent that caring for a babe in arms and a toddler while being brutalized by a drinking, gambling, womanizing husband was an impossible task for anyone, let alone a girl barely out of childhood herself.

"The baby didn't stop him," said Ella. "He would hit me for any little thing. I could never wear a dress. I had to wear jeans to hide the bruises on my legs. He was careful never to hit me in the face. I didn't want Mom or Dad or anyone to know. I figured I made my bed and I would have to lie in it." Jane Hurshman had used similar words when she discovered she was pregnant the first time: "I was pregnant, and when you were pregnant, you got married—you make your bed, you lie in it, and make the best of it." Ella said, "Pride would not let me admit I had made a serious mistake, and I was really afraid."

Feeling she had nothing left to lose, she told Vernon she was going to leave him. He went into a rage. "He just beat me up harder and harder and harder." Ella was several inches shorter than Vernon and less than half his weight. On that day, he grabbed her by the neck of her shirt, as he often did, and pulled her close, yanking her hair to force her face up toward his.

"You fucking bitch, you're not going to make a fool of me with my family," he said. "I'll kill you if you try to leave."

"He said that I wasn't going to embarrass him with his family, because none of them had ever been divorced," said Ella. "His mother was separated and living with somebody else, but I guess that didn't count." Ella was terrified and had no doubt that Vernon would follow through with his threat if she attempted to leave him.

Billy Stafford's first wife, Pauline, and a subsequent common-law wife had both fled to other provinces after he severely abused them and their children. But he wasn't about to let Jane leave him. The defining moment for Jane came when, from his bed, Billy fired a .22-calibre bullet just above her head as she was bent over putting wood into the stove. Her heart beat wildly and the blood drained from her face. "If I had stood up, I'd be dead. I really thought I was going to have a heart attack."

"Don't worry, old woman," Billy chuckled, "if I'd wanted to hit you, I wouldn't have missed." When the shock and fear subsided, Jane stared at him as he lay laughing, the rifle across his thighs.

"I'm going to leave you," she said firmly.

"You can leave me anytime you want," said Billy with a derisive laugh. "But I told you before, I won't be a three-time loser. If you go, you'll be coming back and you'll bring that little bastard with you, because I'll start shooting that precious family of yours one by one until you return."[14]

Jane's friend Andrea (Wamboldt) knew Billy's first wife. "He never got over Pauline leaving him, which is why he threatened Jane," she said. "I heard him say to Jane many times, 'Old woman, get it out of your head. Don't think you're leaving me, because I'll kill you.' And Jane was *really* afraid of Billy. She was scared, really frightened. I was very scared of him."[15]

ELLA HAD LONG AGO STOPPED WONDERING where her husband was when he would disappear for several days at a time. His absences meant peace and quiet and respite from his brutality. But one night she chanced his wrath and asked him where he'd been for the past two or three days and nights.

"I have a new girlfriend, and I'm living with her and her mother," he announced. "What are you going to do about it?"

Ella was silent.

"Her name is Florence," he said. "But don't worry—I've got enough to go around for everybody."

Ella had sensed for some time that Vernon was seeing other women, and after his disclosure about Florence, he became more brazen and began bringing women home.

"He had an old-fashioned grey and brown gramophone for playing records, and they would party and drink and carry on half the night," said Ella. "There was only the one bedroom upstairs, and I was there with Estelle and Donny. There was no door at the top of the stairs, so you could hear everything—the blaring music and the giggling."

"Don't come downstairs and keep those goddamn kids quiet," Vernon would shout up to her.

On one of those nights, Ella needed milk for the children and called to him, asking if he would prepare a bottle since she wasn't allowed downstairs. He cursed, charged up the stairs, grabbed her by the hair, and started punching her arms, back, and chest. "Keep the fucking brats quiet," he said. "You're not getting any fucking milk. And if I have to come up here again, I'll throw you down the stairs."

"But the children were hungry and couldn't sleep with the music blaring," Ella remembered. "They were crying and screaming, and he came upstairs again. He didn't touch them, but he grabbed me by the hair and pulled me from the bed."

"Come and see my beautiful girlfriend," he said.

"He pushed me to the top of the stairs, and I was crying and very upset. I took two or three steps down, then he gave me a hard shove from behind, pushing me down the stairs. I couldn't get up. I thought my leg was broken. Then he came down and began comparing me to his girlfriend. What a mess I was, lying in a crumpled heap on the floor. He stepped over me and they left the house laughing. It was the middle of the night and no one else was in the building. I had no phone and no way to go for help. I was in pain all night."

When Olive Fleming arrived at nine o'clock the next morning to open the store, Ella called out to her. "She had a key for the door between the store and the house. She called Dr. McKenzie and took the baby and fed her for me. The doctor took me to the hospital, and they had to rebreak my leg and set it. Now I had to use crutches and it was impossible to get up the stairs because there was no banister. The doctor questioned me, but I wouldn't tell him what happened. He kept questioning me, and I said I fell. He knew that all the old bruises on my legs and body didn't come from a fall down the stairs. Vernon had warned me that he would kill me if I ever told, and those boots were imbedded in my mind. I couldn't tell anyone. Estelle was at the age where she was getting into everything, and I was worried because I couldn't chase her."

Ella said Vernon's mother tried to help out by paying a young woman to look after the baby and do the housework. "Her name was Tina and she was about eighteen. At least we had some food in the house while she was there. Vernon turned on the charm with her, and they became attracted to each other. Then they started fooling around on the couch in front of me so he could show me what a good man he was. I was so embarrassed, but I couldn't do anything about it. And at night, he took her to my bed and I had to sleep on the couch."

"This is the perfect situation," announced Vernon, "but it's costing me money to keep you and those brats."

"Him saying that scared me even more," says Ella. "The death threats became very real in my mind, and I expected to get killed at any time."

Danna MacNeil said her parents knew something about Vernon's other women. "I remember them talking about him bringing his girlfriends home when she was there. He would make her wait on them. And he would get mad and beat her if she made him breakfast with two pieces of bacon instead of three. He was looking for any little thing that she supposedly did wrong so he could beat her up. I don't think she realized what real danger she was in."

THE ONE BATTLE THAT VERNON couldn't win with Ella was to force her to sell his mother's illegal alcohol. No matter how often he beat her, he couldn't break her will. But he tried his best one cold night in late May or early June 1951 when a customer looking for bootleg liquor knocked on the door of their apartment. Ella was already in bed with the children. "Vernon was home for a change," she says. He ordered her to answer the door. "He was downstairs but refused to answer the door himself, and there was no way I was going to answer it. I knew it was somebody looking for liquor."

Vernon charged up the stairs and into the bedroom. He dragged her out of bed and down the stairs in her nightgown. "You won't listen to me, you fucking bitch," he screamed, "you're out of this place, now."

"He threw me out the door with bare feet and in my nightgown," said Ella, wincing at the memory. "I had no jacket or shoes.

I didn't even own a housecoat. I was shivering and I didn't know what to do. I couldn't go to Mrs. Bain across the street because she and her daughter would be sleeping and I didn't want them to know what I was going through." And the last person she would run to was her Aunt Tina just down the street—the shame would be too much, almost worse than death.

Instead, she ran the three blocks along Maple Street to Dot and Danny MacNeil's house. "They were really the only friends I had except for Mrs. Bain," said Ella. "I fell many, many times before I made it to their doorstep. I pounded on the door, and Danny came out and picked me up and carried me into the kitchen."

"I remember it was really cold out," said Danna MacNeil, "because my dad put a coat around her when he took her in." Dot and Danny rubbed her legs and feet with flannel cloths soaked in oil and hot water. She stayed the night with them, and in the morning, Danny drove down to the house and pounded on the door until Vernon opened it.

"If you ever touch her again, you're a dead man," said Danny. "And it will be me doing it. Don't ever throw her out like that again—she's not an animal."

The children were by now at Vernon's mother's house, and Danny drove Ella to Dorothy May's, where they picked up the baby. Dorothy May said she would look after Estelle for a while. Danny then drove Ella and the baby to Ella's parents' house in Westville. "Danny went to see my mother and told her what had happened, and he told her about the abuse I was going through."

Danna MacNeil says her father was convinced Vernon would eventually kill Ella. "He didn't think she was mature enough, at that age, to realize how dangerous it was. She was scared, she was terrified, and he was hurting her, but she didn't realize what he was actually capable of. My dad said, 'That bastard's going to kill her.'"

7

The Deer Hunter

Jared Andrew Osidacz, 8. Brantford, Ontario. Jared was stabbed to death by his father at the home of the father's girlfriend and her eight-year-old daughter. The girlfriend and her daughter were also stabbed but survived and were taken to hospital. Approximately an hour later, police shot Andrew Osidacz to death at another residence where he was holding his ex-wife, Jared's mother, at knifepoint. Osidacz had been convicted in 2003 of assault on his ex-wife. He was ordered to do seventy-five hours of community service, to give $300 to Nova Vita Women's Shelter, and to participate in rehabilitative programs. Osidacz had been ordered to have no contact with his wife, but a family court order for access made an exception for contact with Jared. (March 2006)

P EARL ARMOUR COULD NOT BELIEVE WHAT SHE WAS HEARING. How much Ella actually told her back then will never be known. Bessie Flanders (Smith) said she heard her mother and Pearl wondering if Ella was being abused, because the vibrant young woman they had known in the past often looked frail and wasted. "They thought something might be going on, but they had no idea it could be that bad," said Bessie.

Ella remembered, "There were a lot of times when I could hardly walk and my mother would say, 'What's wrong with you? Do you have a sore stomach?' I would tell her I had a touch of diarrhea or maybe was getting the flu—I couldn't tell her the truth. I loved my family so much, and I was so ashamed of what I got myself into.

"She had always suspected something was wrong. But she didn't know until I left Vernon and went home to live. And then they wouldn't give Estelle back to me. His mother was looking after her, and Vernon said he had rights and I wasn't getting her."

Pearl and Recky were furious with Vernon, and some wondered at the time if the old soldier might have done more than just fume about it if he had not been in such poor health.

But within days of Ella's retreating to her parents' home, Vernon Ince was suddenly contrite and reformed—his charming old self, the man Ella had fallen in love with. "He didn't go back to the mines after his legs healed," said Ella. "Now he was a happy-go-lucky guy who got a job driving truck with no heavy labour. He became Mr. Nice Guy, and even dared to show up and apologize. My parents asked him, 'Did you straighten out?' and he said, 'Oh yeah, I'm not the same guy. I'm straightened out and I'm happy.' And he was being nice to me and apologizing and saying it would never happen again."

ACCORDING TO A THEORY FIRST PROPOSED by Lenore Walker in her 1979 book *The Battered Woman,* and in the parlance of domestic violence, Vernon Ince was in the "loving and contrite" stage of the cycle of violence. The website for Abuse Counseling and Treatment (ACT), which works closely with the Florida Office of the Attorney General, says that, generally, "Battering does not occur constantly, but rather in a cycle." The cycle consists of three phases: tension-building, acute battering, and love and contrition, often referred to as the "honeymoon" phase.

In the tension-building phase, there is increasing physical and emotional abuse, which the woman attempts to control with coping techniques "such as avoidance, placating, or 'giving in.' These are 'stop-gap' measures, however, and do not work for long, if at all."

As the tension reaches an unbearable level, the acute battering phase begins. In this second phase, the battering is "much more serious and intense" than in the first phase and may result in serious injury to the woman. "There is no escape once the battering has begun; only the batterer can end the incident."

After severe battering, the couple moves into the honeymoon phase. ACT says that in this phase, "The abuser realizes he has gone too far" and "typically exhibits loving, kind behavior while apologizing and promising that it will never happen again."[1]

The cycle theory certainly describes Ella and Vernon's relationship. But in the past few years, there's been considerable evidence that the honeymoon phase is not typical in most abusive relationships. There was certainly no honeymoon period for Jane Hurshman. The most she got out of Billy after his first beating was a promise the next morning that it wouldn't happen again.[2] It took him only a few days to break that promise and accelerate his abuse. Nor did the theory apply in Kathleen Waits' first-person report on the battering victim called Mary.

"First and foremost," said Waits, "Mary never experienced the 'cycle of violence.' Russ was never contrite or loving after a severe beating. He never apologized, and...acted as if he had done nothing wrong. We now know that the loving and contrite phase is absent in many abusive relationships. In others, it may occur after the first severe battering, but then disappear. Yet some experts in the field continue to push the cycle of violence as an essential element of violent intimate relationships."[3]

Waits and other experts say that even if the honeymoon phase is exhibited once, it can't be a "cycle" if it never happens again. It happened once in Ella and Vernon's relationship, but it would never happen again.

AFTER THE TERROR SHE'D BEEN THROUGH, Ella didn't believe Vernon at first. But he persisted for three months, and at last she relented. Mostly, though, she wanted to regain custody of her daughter. "So my parents said, 'Try going back if you want, but at the first sign of trouble you can come home.'" Ella thought about it and decided it was worth the gamble to get Estelle back.

Vernon appeared almost sheepish when he arrived to pick her up in September. On the drive to the Asphalt, she laid out her ground rules: "Let me tell you something—I am not going to live like I did before. You are either going to be an honest man and a good husband or I'm leaving." Vernon agreed, and, "He was very nice for a while—including the sex. Just like the guy I first met."

Ella didn't like gambling or poker, but she enjoyed playing cards for fun. They had played a lot of cards when they were dating and early in their marriage, often with his family. Now they were doing that again. "But I was always on guard," said Ella. "I didn't really think it would last and it didn't. It started again just two or three weeks later."

Ella hesitantly confessed to Dot and Danny MacNeil that she had decided to return to her husband. "They knew all that had happened before she left him," said Danna MacNeil, "and then when she told them she was going back to him, I remember my father being very, very sad because he knew what Vernon was really like."

Before long, Vernon was back to selling bootleg liquor, ignoring Ella's pleas to stop for the sake of the children. He refused to stop because he was in partnership with his mother, and he beat Ella for interfering with his business.

About a month after she came back to Vernon, Ella's cousin Dorothy and Dorothy's husband, Tin Watters, moved into a rented house in the Asphalt around the corner from Ella. Dorothy and Tin had been married on August 2, 1950, less than fifteen months after Ella had married Vernon. For all the talk about Ella being so young and dating "an older man," Dorothy and Tin went together for four years before they were married, and "I was only fourteen when I met him," Dorothy laughed. "It wasn't uncommon back then." When they married, Tin was nineteen and Dorothy was a couple of months shy of seventeen. Before moving to the Asphalt, they had lived with Dorothy's grandparents out in the country, between Westville and Stellarton. They were oblivious to the tribulations of Dorothy's once vibrant cousin. "We didn't know anything about Vernon being so nasty with her," said Dorothy. "Ella never told me, or anybody, what was going on."

In those fateful two or three weeks in September, when Vernon was faking "his old self," Ella once again became pregnant, and once again her husband greeted the eventual news with a kick to the belly. "When I told him I was pregnant, he got very angry. I said it wasn't my fault, and he said everything was my fault. I ended up in the hospital again, and I almost lost the baby.

"But he was all nice when he came to visit me in the hospital, and he said he was sorry and would never do it again. By then, I had absolutely no feelings for him. There was nothing there. He was like the devil in sheep's clothing. That's how I looked at him. My family was very upset. And all I could think about was that happy upbringing I had and that other part of my life with him—which was hell." She believed Vernon came to the hospital to apologize because more people, including her family, now knew what he had done.

R. LUNDY BANCROFT, FOR MANY YEARS a counsellor and supervisor in programs involving more than 1,500 abusive men and hundreds of their victims, warns that it is difficult to profile a batterer psychologically and generalizations about them have to be made with caution.[4] Bancroft says that, other than a batterer's wife and children, people "do not generally perceive him as an abusive person, or even as an especially angry one. They are as likely to be very popular as they are to be 'losers.' Most friends, family, and associates in a batterer's life find it jarring when they hear what he has done, and may deny that he is capable of those acts.

"He is manipulative, he misleads people inside and outside of the family about his abusiveness, he twists arguments around to make other people feel at fault, and he turns into a sweet, sensitive person for extended periods of time when he feels that it is in his best interest to do so. His public image usually contrasts sharply with the private reality."

ELLA FELT TRAPPED BY HER PREGNANCY and began thinking about escape for herself and her small children. By the first weekend of November 1951, Vernon had provided more incentive. That Saturday, Ella paid a bill for $30.40 in furniture at Eaton's with some "liquor money" she found in the house. When Vernon found out, he knocked her to the floor, kicked her, and pushed her down a flight of stairs, because, he said, that money belonged to his mother.

THAT YEAR WAS A GOOD ONE FOR hunting deer in Nova Scotia. The deer population had been steadily rising. It would peak three years later, crash in the sixties, rebound in the eighties, and crash again in the nineties, but nobody was thinking about future ebbs and flows when the provincial government handed out 55,785 licences for the forty-five-day hunting season in 1951. Each hunter was allowed to kill two animals, male or female, and when it was all over, 42,343 of them would make it from the bush to the table.[5]

Vernon Ince and his pal, Malcolm "Mort" Brown, were two of the hopefuls going after their limit that year, as they did every hunting season. Their cozy "camp"—local lingo for a cottage or cabin—was only an hour or so away. The camp was owned by Mort's half-brother, a pilot who spent most of his time around Moncton, New Brunswick, and usually showed up only once a year. When the brother wasn't around, Mort and his friends were welcome to use the place, as long they looked after it.

Doug Ince's neighbour, Mel MacLean, is not a hunter, but he is a keen observer and a thoughtful man who says the boys' trips to camp were sometimes for more than deer. He doesn't judge, but he does ask, "Why would you go hunting with a white shirt?" and then answers his own question. "About twenty-five or thirty miles from the hunting camp, there was a place called Country Harbour where there was dancing. They would hunt most of the time, but probably on Saturdays they'd go to Country Harbour for the dance, and that's why the white shirts went with them."

This was to be Vernon's third season with the cherished .30-30 Winchester his brother had bought for him in Ontario. "He was a good man in the woods," said Doug. "Very careful. He just hunted deer, not other animals."

Vernon and Mort planned to leave for camp at the end of the first week in November. There were plenty of warm blankets at the cabin, but Mort had purchased a new sleeping bag and was anxious to try it out. Vernon decided he should have a sleeping bag too, so in early October he sent Ella down to Eaton's mail-order office to order one. She also ordered razor blades, a hunting knife, and a flashlight.

"He never took me to the camp," said Ella. "But I heard him and his buddies talking, and it was fully furnished with bunks, stove and fridge, fishing boats, and lots of food and dishes and blankets—everything. But he said he still needed all this hunting stuff, and I said, 'Listen, I never have a dime. The kids and me hardly have any clothes except what my parents or my aunt give us, and they're getting tired of that. Look, I'm back to no food in the house and no clothes for the kids—the same situation as before.'"

Vernon ignored Ella, and when the items arrived, he gave her the money to go to Eaton's and pick them up. "I decided to stand up for myself," said Ella. "The kids needed food and clothing more than he needed that sleeping bag. It was November and getting colder. Estelle had grown out of her coat and she needed a winter hat. So I paid for the hunting knife and the other items but kept the money for the sleeping bag. It was $29.95. He didn't need it, so I sent it back."

VERNON AND MORT PLANNED TO leave on the hunting trip around noon on Wednesday, November 7. They would drive to the camp in Vernon's '34 Chevy. The car was seventeen years old and needed a bit of work to get it ready for the trip. Mort came over in the morning to help Vernon work on it in the driveway.

Pearl Armour also arrived at the Inces' that Wednesday morning to help Ella with the laundry and housework. Her daughter needed the help because she was still in considerable pain from Vernon's vicious beating the previous Saturday, the same day she'd picked up the knife and the other items but told him the sleeping bag had yet to come in.

As he began loading the car for the trip, Vernon ordered Ella to return to Eaton's to pick up his sleeping bag. "It has to be in by now," he said. "And if it's not, I want my money back." Ella was in a panic. She had hoped he would forget about the bag. She went to the Eaton's mail-order office and asked for help from Lois Kellock.

"If my husband comes in and asks about the sleeping bag, can you please just tell him it won't be in for a few days?"

"I'm sorry, I can't do that," said Kellock.

Ella was tense when she returned home. "It's still not in," she told Vernon, who was loading groceries, liquor, and supplies into the car with Mort.

"Well, did you get the money?" he asked.

"No. The regular girl wasn't there to sign the cheque."

"Well, you go and get the goddamn money." Ella left, but once again returned without the money. Vernon glared at her and went across the street to Mrs. Bain's house, called Eaton's, and learned that the sleeping bag had been returned and Ella had the money. He came back, screaming at her and demanding his money. Trapped in her lie, Ella stuck to her story and said there must be some mistake.

Vernon controlled his rage and smugly said he and Mort would drive her to Eaton's so she could get his money. She went in alone, but when she returned to the car empty-handed, Vernon said they would go back in together while Mort waited in the car. Ella was desperately hoping the clerk would appreciate the situation and go along with the story in front of Vernon.

"So the sleeping bag will be in next Saturday?" she asked Arlene Kellock, sister-in-law to Lois.

"No," said Arlene. "As you requested, I sent it back when it arrived."

"Oh, I don't remember that."

Vernon was seething but said nothing until they were outside.

"I knew you were lying. I'm going to fucking kill you. Where's my money?"

On the way home in the car, Vernon, who was driving, twice tried to strike Ella, but the blows were blocked by Mort Brown. "Don't do that to her," Mort said to his friend. Vernon's verbal harangue continued. "What did you do with the money? I'll fucking kill you if you don't get it." So Ella came up with a new story and told him she'd loaned the money to Peter Keating.

"I made up that story because I thought Peter would be at work and Vernon wouldn't be able to check it out until he got back from hunting. I thought I could stall him off until then." Unfortunately for Ella, Keating wasn't at work that Wednesday, and Vernon spotted him on the street while they were driving home.

"Didn't I give you a loan of $30?" asked Ella when they pulled over to talk to Keating.

"No, Ella, you didn't," said Keating, who later admitted Ella seemed nervous and frightened.

"See, Peter won't lie for you," said Vernon.

He continued to berate her all the way home. When they arrived back in the driveway, the car was already packed and ready to go, but with all of the arguing and driving around, it was now past their planned noon departure. Ella went directly into the house while Mort and Vernon updated their plans. Mort said he was going home for lunch and they would leave when he returned.

In the house, Pearl Armour was operating the washing machine when Ella came in and began making lunch. Estelle, whose second birthday was the next day, was playing in the kitchen and eight-month-old Donald was in the pram.

Vernon came into the house and continued his tirade. Pearl was concerned with his cursing and verbal abuse of Ella, particularly in front of the children.

"I want that goddamn money," he shouted.

"I told you, I gave it to Peter," said Ella.

"You're a goddamn liar. He said you didn't. And you couldn't get him to lie for you."

Vernon wouldn't let it go, and he told her to come out to the car so he could drive up to Keating's place and settle the issue once and for all. He grabbed her, dragged her out to the car, and struck her on the cheek. Pushing her into the front passenger seat, he slammed the door and went around to the driver's side. "I'm going to take you up there, and if he doesn't have the money, there's only one of us coming back, and it's not going to be you. And nobody will find you."

Keating's place was about half a mile away, in a wooded area on Old Foxbrook Road. "I knew he meant it," said Ella. "It was all trees and brush. He planned on killing me out there. Keating was an older man who used to play cards and drink at Vernon's mother's place, so he wouldn't tell. I'd just disappear."

When Vernon reached into his pocket to get his keys, Ella made her move. "I have to wash my face," she said, jumping out of the car and running for the house.

OLIVE FLEMING AND HER HUSBAND, Charlie, had operated the small grocery store in the front of the Ince house on Maple Street since taking it over from Dorothy May, who used to run it when she was still with Jimmy Ince. Now it was the Flemings' store, and they paid rent to Dorothy May, who still owned the building.

The door between the Inces' apartment and the Flemings' store was blocked off, but there was a small opening where the lock had been. The only sound barrier was a calendar that covered that opening on the store side of the door. So from the store it was impossible not to hear what was going on between Vernon and Ella.

"The woman who ran the store wouldn't see anything, but she'd hear it all," says Doug Ince. "She would know every word that was said. Even if you were in there trying to whisper, they could hear you. It wasn't a solid door, it was hollow, and you could hear right through those things."

Over the two-year period since Ella and Vernon had moved in, Olive had often heard them quarrelling, and Ella had complained to her many times that the children needed clothes.

On this Wednesday morning, Olive had opened the store at 10:30 a.m. as usual, and she could hear the voices of Ella and her mother in the apartment when she first arrived. Then, a short while after opening, she saw Ella go by the store in Vernon's car. She was in the passenger side and Olive presumed Vernon was driving. A while later, the car returned and was parked almost in front of the driveway that ran parallel to the house along Acadia Avenue. At intervals during the morning, Olive could hear Vernon and Ella in the house, quarrelling loudly over money and the sleeping bag. And then his voice, insistent, ordering Ella to accompany him somewhere (to Keating's), and her refusing to go. From the store window, a few minutes later, she saw Ella, wearing slacks and a sweater, running from the car with Vernon in pursuit.

Doug and Susan Ince's two-room apartment—the one-storey add-on to the existing building—was much more soundproof than the other apartment. With the radio on, Susan wasn't aware of the real-life drama that Olive Fleming heard unfolding through the flimsy door separating the store and the rear apartment. "I had been busy all morning in the kitchen, rolling dough to make pies," said Susan. Through her small kitchen window overlooking the driveway, she had seen Vernon and Mort Brown working on the car but didn't notice anything out of the ordinary, other than some "awfully loud talking" from her brother-in-law's apartment. Later, she saw Ella and Vernon walking along the driveway toward Maple Street.

When Ella ran back into the house, she was crying and there was a red welt on her face. She slammed the door, but Vernon yanked it open seconds later and rushed in behind her.

"What happened to her?" asked Pearl, glaring at Vernon.

"I did it," he said, his face flushed with anger, "and I'll knock her fucking head off."

"Don't be like that, Vernon," said Pearl, who was now holding Estelle in her arms.

But Vernon lunged for Ella. "You are coming with me if I have to drag you," he said, seizing her by the hair and pulling her out to the porch. There, he held her down with one hand on her thigh and began banging her head against the floor with the other.

"Give me my money or I'll kill you," he shouted.

"He was swearing like a lunatic, and she was crying and awfully scared of him," Pearl would later testify in court. "He was pounding her on the head and pulling her hair. I called to Mrs. Fleming to get the police or the Mounties because Vernon was killing Ella. I tried to get his fingers out of her hair but couldn't budge them."

When Pearl, holding Estelle, tried to get past Vernon to call the police, he released Ella and went after Pearl. With that, Ella was able to free herself and run into the house. Susan Ince, for a second time, saw Ella running along the driveway toward the house with Vernon in pursuit. The door slammed shut behind Ella, the catch in its "snap-type Yale lock" engaged, and she was locked in, leaving her mother and Estelle with Vernon on the porch. Susan Ince then heard what sounded like a "scuffle" in the porch.

Inside the house, Ella was searching for an escape. There was only one door and it was locked, with Vernon raging at her on the other side. She went to the living room to see if she could get out through the window. "I tried to open it, but it wouldn't budge." Then she saw Vernon's .30-30 Winchester leaning against the wall and several bullets visible in the pocket of the case beside the gun. She had never loaded or fired the gun before, but she had seen Vernon load it many times.

Meanwhile, Vernon ran from the porch to his car and pulled the keys out of the ignition. On the key ring was his key to the Yale lock on the apartment's main door, which led to the kitchen. He was screaming at her as he unlocked the door. Inside, Ella was slipping a shell into the chamber of his rifle.

"I was just going to fire it to scare him," she said. "He was yelling and screaming at me, saying, 'When I get in there, I'm going to kill you.' I was panicking more and more. He was calling me a fucking bitch and saying, 'I don't need you—I've got better women than you.' He was just a monster."

In the store, Olive Fleming heard Vernon slam through the door into the kitchen, where Ella was now standing with the rifle pointed at him.

"Stay away from me," she said. "Leave me alone!"

"You haven't got guts enough to pull the trigger," said Vernon, lunging at her.

Ella jumped back into the living room and the gun went off. She would have no memory of pulling the trigger or the sound of the shot. Nor did she realize that her mother, holding Estelle, was standing directly behind Vernon.

Vernon was crouched and springing at her when Ella fired from no more than a foot away. The bullet made a small, neat, almost innocuous hole in the right side of his chest, but inside there was catastrophic damage. The bullet tore through his body, fractured several ribs, and lacerated his right lung, causing extensive bleeding. There was a much larger wound where it exited Vernon's back. When it struck his ribs, the bullet fragmented into several pieces, some of which struck Pearl Armour around and just above her eyes.

Vernon grasped his chest with both hands, said, "Ella, oh Ella," and managed to stand and run past Pearl and Estelle out to the driveway.

ON THAT WEDNESDAY, JUST AFTER 1 p.m., Dot and Danny MacNeil's seven year-old daughter, Danna, was returning to school after lunch at home. She was alone. Her route took her along Maple Street to Acadia Avenue. She was in front of Olive Fleming's store when she heard the noise.

"I was right in front of the building, and it was a very loud sound and it stunned me," she recalled fifty-five years later. "I didn't know then, but it was a gunshot and the sound was magnified because it was so quiet. I can still picture the building. It was like cedar shakes and it was painted black. And I remember the small addition to the right [Doug and Susan's apartment] if you're facing it, and Vernon and Ella lived behind that at the back."

With the sound of the shot, Danna MacNeil stopped on the street, at the top of the driveway. "And he came running toward me from the back of the house, and I remember it was so quiet. It was surreal. There was no noise. There were no people, nothing—just him bursting through the door and running. He was wearing a light shirt and dark pants."

Susan Ince heard the shot and through her bedroom window saw Vernon come around the house and up the driveway. "And I could see him bent over. He wasn't really running—just walking, but hurrying." She went to her door as he was rounding the front corner of the house.

The noise of the rifle shot, so close, startled and frightened Olive Fleming, who was standing a few feet away behind the door that separated the store and the apartment. Her ears were still ringing when she picked up the keys for the store and headed for the front door.

As Vernon approached the front of the building, Danna MacNeil said, he veered from the driveway and tried to knock on the first door he came to—at his brother's apartment—and then the door to the store. Susan Ince and Olive Fleming opened their doors almost simultaneously and heard Vernon mutter, "Get a doctor," then turn to face the street.

"Vernon just fell on his face right as I opened the door," said Susan Ince. "There weren't many phones back in those days, and the lady from the store came out and ran across the street. Mrs. Bain had the phone."

Danna remembered that Vernon had his hand over his chest, and at first she didn't see any blood. "And then I noticed blood coming out of the side of his mouth. He tried to say something, and then he fell right in front of me. I just froze. He was just inches away. The thing that stays in my head was this red blood rising up, like puffy foam, out of his back through his shirt. It was awful, but I was mesmerized by it. And the next thing I remember was my father running down the street and telling me to stand to the side."

Within minutes of the shot being fired, the quiet, empty street quickly filled up with dozens of onlookers. "The kids were coming or going from school at lunchtime, so there was quite a crowd," said Susan Ince.

Ella had followed Vernon out of the house a few seconds after firing the shot and saw him lying on the sidewalk with blood on his back.

"She was just dazed," said Danna MacNeil. "She was absolutely stunned. I was only seven, but I remember she was wandering back and forth on the driveway. She came up to him, but not too close—maybe five or six feet. I don't think she was even aware of me. People were coming out of their houses and gathering around, but nobody talked to her. Then my dad went to her and whispered something in her ear, and she went over and sat on the running board of a car and he stood by her until the police arrived. She was bent over with her head in her hands, and by her body language, she looked all pulled in. She must have felt just like a nothing, having shot him, and everybody hanging around and not talking to her."

Danny MacNeil told his daughter later that he had cautioned Ella not to say anything to anyone until she spoke with a lawyer. "And I think he phoned a lawyer for her."

Susan Ince saw Pearl with Estelle and there was blood on both of them. "I remember taking Estelle into the house to wash the blood off. I wanted to see if she was okay. Fortunately, she wasn't hurt. I think Mrs. Armour and Ella went around back. And Vernon's mother came from up the street, but I don't know if Vernon had been removed by then or not."

Danna's last memory of the scene was of the doctor and the police arriving at about the same time. "I was on the other side of the car where Ella was sitting on the running board, and my dad was with her. And then somebody took me away from there."

At home that evening, Danna's parents, worried about lasting emotional effects the shooting might have on their daughter, asked Danna to recite in detail what she had seen that day. "And I told them, and then my father said, 'Okay, now we won't talk about it again,' and we never did until I was in my early twenties, when one day he asked me if I remembered it. I had literally put it out of my head, but he was surprised when I remembered every detail."

Now retired and living with her husband in Newmarket, Ontario, Danna said the experience of that day "wasn't something that changed my life, but it stayed with me forever. It's as clear in my head right now as it was when I first saw it."

DOUG INCE WAS DIGGING COAL on a slope about three-quarters of a mile below the surface in the Albion Mine when the underground manager approached him. "You're wanted at home," he said. "I hope everything's all right."

"That's all he told me," said Ince. "I didn't know what was going on. I had my own car and I drove home. There were people there, and my aunt told me, 'Ella shot him.' I thought he was just wounded, but then I heard that he was dead." He said that Vernon's death was particularly devastating for his mother. "That killed her. They were really close. They gambled together and both of them just loved to play cards, and Ella loved to play cards herself. Oh Jesus, yes, she would stay up all night playing cards. She loved playing cards as much as anyone."

Ella's cousin, Dorothy Watters, said news of the shooting spread quickly around the neighbourhood. "I think somebody called me just after it happened." Her husband, Tin, was working the day shift in the mines and didn't find out about it until he returned home at about 3:30 p.m.

"Dot told me about it as soon as I walked in the door," he said. "The neighbourhood was in an uproar. Everybody was saying, 'Ella shot Dickie.'"

Vernon's cousin, Betty Lou Boutilier, had been home for lunch, "and had just got back to school and I was deathly sick. I'll never forget that day. I rushed out without asking, and then I returned white as a sheet."

"What's wrong?" asked the teacher.

"I don't know. I was just sick all of sudden."

"Do you want to go lie down in the nurse's station?"

"No, I think I'd like to go home."

"Would you like someone to go with you?"

"No. Maybe the fresh air will do me good. I'll walk home."

Betty Lou said, "All the way home, I had this queer feeling. I don't think I'll ever forget it, and when I got to the railway crossing, they were just putting Vernon in the ambulance. And I went over and Sue [Susan Ince] was there, and she was pretty shook up and she said Ella shot Vernon and I couldn't grasp it all. And then I turned around and went home. It was like a premonition—getting sick like that."

At the time of the shooting, Mel MacLean was working at the Pictou County Dairy in Stellarton, near the railroad station. He delivered ice cream and butter in a small van. "It didn't even have a freezer," he said. "All you had was an ice box with dry ice in it. It would keep pretty good. They just called the orders in and we delivered it." On that Wednesday, MacLean was making a delivery to a small canteen in Stellarton when he saw Lizzie Porter walking down Acadia Avenue on her way to work at the post office. She lived near him on Coll Avenue, not far from Vernon and Ella's.

"Did you hear about the accident?" she asked as she approached MacLean.

"No, I didn't. What happened?"

"Vernon got shot."

"Vernon got shot?"

"Yeah."

"Who did that?"

"Well, as far as I know, Ella did."

MacLean had been home for lunch and returned to work just before the shooting. The delivery to the canteen was his first of the afternoon. He interrupted his schedule and "zipped right up" to the scene. "And everything was cleared up. There was no yellow tape like you see today. Nobody was around. It was like nothing had happened. So I just kept on doing my deliveries."

WHEN DR. J.B. MACDONALD arrived a few minutes after 1 p.m., Vernon was lying crosswise, face down on the sidewalk. There was no pulse, but there was air escaping from his right lung and through the wound in his back, accounting for the bloody "puffy foam" witnessed by Danna MacNeil. MacDonald dressed Vernon's wound and had an ambulance take him to Aberdeen Hospital, where he was declared dead on arrival.

Vernon's body was removed to the H.C. MacQuarrie Undertaking Parlour in Stellarton, where a coroner's jury was quickly empanelled before New Glasgow coroner Dr. D.F. MacLellan. After the jurors viewed the body, the inquest was adjourned till November 24 at the Stellarton Town Hall.

After Vernon's body had been removed, Dr. MacDonald examined Pearl Armour and found small bullet fragments around her eyes, with a larger puncture wound above the right eye. He sent her to the hospital for treatment. "She could have been killed too," Doug Ince pointed out. "I went to see her in the hospital. She had two black eyes from the shrapnel that hit her. She was a pretty lucky woman. Two beautiful shiners—I can see them yet."

Examining Ella later that Wednesday evening, Dr. MacDonald found a fresh bruise "which looked like fingermarks" on her thigh and observed that a piece of her scalp one inch in diameter was denuded of hair. He also discovered a sizable lump on the back of her head and old bruises on her shins and legs.

Ambulance driver Hillman Payne took some keys out of Vernon's hand before he was put into the ambulance. He handed the keys to Vernon's uncle, Bedford Field, who turned them over to Corporal George King of the nearby New Glasgow RCMP detachment. One key was for Vernon's car, and the other was for the Yale lock on the main door to the apartment.

King was the lead investigator in cooperation with Stellarton chief of police Sam Baker. When King first arrived, he found a pool of fresh blood where Vernon had fallen in front of the store, and there were bloodstains on the wide back step and on the porch leading to the apartment. King had several metal fragments removed from the wooden wall of the porch and from the kitchen door and wall that had been pierced in several places. Vernon's .30-30 rifle was found in the living room, with one expended cartridge in the breach. The gun case was near the rifle, and in the pocket were eight rounds of ammunition.

From a padlocked cupboard in the closet of the upstairs bedroom, King removed fifty-five quarts of ale, eight quarts of wine, and a partly filled bottle of rum—Vernon's stash of bootleg liquor. King also removed a one-quart bottle of gin from Vernon's car.

In a statement Corporal King took from Ella on the afternoon of the murder, she described some of the abuse Vernon had subjected her to and how Vernon had claimed he'd reformed, but when she returned to live with him, she discovered he was selling liquor for a living. She stated that she had asked him to give it up for the sake of the children, but he refused and beat her for "interfering."

Doug Ince said that King also discovered "two .22-calibre bullet holes in the floor or the wall—I can't remember which" of the upstairs bedroom in his brother's apartment. "They figured they were fired some time ago," he said. "They examined all the floors and the walls up there. Whether she fired them or Vernon fired them, I don't know." He said he and his wife never heard any shots, "But a .22 doesn't make much noise." Doug said his brother owned a .22-calibre rifle, which Doug himself kept after the shooting. "I have it to this day. The Mounties know that I kept it."

Danna MacNeil said her parents told her that Ella had complained that Vernon kept a loaded rifle in the living room of their apartment. "He teased her with it, and she didn't want it there. She was afraid. She was always at him about it, but he just laughed at her. I remember my mother telling me that. He kept it just to annoy her."

Provincial pathologist Dr. N.B.G. McLatchery, who performed the autopsy, later reported the bullet went into the right side of Vernon's chest, fractured several ribs, and lacerated the right lung, producing hemorrhaging. He died a few minutes after being shot. The shot was fired from no more than a foot away, and there was no alcohol in his system.

Meanwhile, Mort Brown had his lunch and returned to Maple Street eager to set off with Vernon for camp, confident they would bag a deer or two each. Instead, he walked into a crowd of sombre onlookers and learned that his deer hunter friend had been shot dead with his own beloved .30-30 Winchester rifle.

8

Expectant Inmate

Francine Mailly, 37, and her three children, Jessica, 12, Brandon, 9, and Kevin, 6. Ottawa. Francine and her three children were shot to death before the house was blown up and engulfed in flames. Francine was estranged from her husband, Francois, who was found dead on the lawn of the house with a .22-calibre gun beside him. A note outlining his plan to kill the family was found in his van, and Francine's family reported that he had often said that if he couldn't have her, nobody would. Francois Mailly had a history of contact with police as a result of domestic violence and other issues and was under a restraining order to have no contact with Francine at the time of the murders. He was also in anger management counselling and the Children's Aid Society had a file on the family. His family and co-workers were surprised by the murders and described him as a hard-working family man who loved his children. Her family talked about Francine's ongoing fear of her husband and the lack of police support for her. (April 2006)

CAPITAL CRIME HAS ALWAYS SOLD NEWSPAPERS, PARTICULARLY if the perpetrator is a woman, and especially in the days before television started providing live news coverage and a steady stream of lurid true-crime programs and police and court dramas.

Television was still two or three years away for most Nova Scotians when Ella shot Vernon, but while the story was covered locally, it did not generate extensive coverage in such wide-circulation dailies as the *Chronicle-Herald* (Halifax) or in newspapers out of the province. This had nothing to do with Ella or Vernon or the story itself. The province and the country had gone royally mad over the first visit to Canada by the young Princess Elizabeth and her husband, the Duke of Edinburgh. Three months later, her ailing father, King George VI, would die and she would ascend the throne. But the day Vernon was killed, the princess and her party arrived in Halifax by train in a raging Atlantic rainstorm that soaked the waiting crowd of more than thirty thousand. Even the royals didn't escape the torrent. "A canopy above their heads at the entrance to city hall, which had been collecting rainwater for almost two hours, suddenly tipped sideways just enough to give a healthy dousing to the Royal party and to horrified Mayor Gordon Kinley in his scarlet robes of office," reported Allan Kent of the *Toronto Telegram*. "Philip was struck squarely on the shoulder by the cascade and Elizabeth got full benefit of the splash."[1]

The princess and her consort were nearing the end of a thirty-six-day Canada-wide tour and drawing huge crowds wherever they went. Newspapers across the country covered even minute details with seemingly endless copy and page after page of photos. Advertising space was at a premium, and most merchants demonstrated their loyalty by welcoming the Royal Tour—even promoting their products was secondary. The Nova Scotia papers were no exception.

And another story of "royalty" vied for headlines that same day: the king of the crooners, Frank Sinatra, had left his "good wife," Nancy, and their three children to marry slinky screen siren Ava Gardner.

In the *Chronicle-Herald*, news of Vernon's death was relegated to a single-column, six-paragraph story on the front page of the second section. Squeezed to one side by a photo spread of the royal couple, the headline read, "Mother, 19, Held in Fatal Shooting."

ELLA'S COUSIN, THIRTEEN-YEAR-OLD Bessie Smith, and Bessie's mother were caught up in the fuss over the royal visit. "We were there that day for Princess Elizabeth and Philip," Bessie says. "My brother Alden worked for CP Telecommunications in Halifax, and we were standing there looking out the window in the upstairs office. I think it was just up from the train station, and it was pouring rain. While we were there watching, Alden got a teletype and he came back and told us Vernon had been shot, and we left right away."

Arriving back in Stellarton, they went directly to the Aberdeen Hospital to see Pearl. "Her face looked terrible," says Bessie. "She was really beat up and had two shiners."

THE DAY VERNON WAS KILLED, major Ontario newspapers were covering a case with eerie similarities. Lillian Thompson, a thirty-five-year-old mother of five, including a three-week-old daughter born in prison, was on trial for her life for killing her husband, Roy, in their Peterborough, Ontario, home.

Witnesses said Roy Thompson, a prosperous scrap dealer, had returned home after a night of birthday drinking and announced to

Lillian that he wanted to go to a party with neighbours. She said he'd had too much to drink and she didn't want him to drive. He became angry and quarrelled loudly with Lillian, who became so upset she said she would shoot herself if only she knew how to load the gun. He loaded it and handed it to her. "Why shoot yourself?" Roy Thompson asked. "Why not shoot me?" Then he laughed at her and said, "You're too yellow to pull the trigger." The *Toronto Telegram* reported, "He was buried two days later in quiet Little Lake cemetery and his wife was lodged in jail, a murder suspect."[2]

LILLIAN THOMPSON'S TRIAL ENDED the day after Vernon was shot when the judge instructed the jury to bring in a verdict of not guilty because there was no evidence to prove murder or manslaughter. As Ella came to realize the seriousness of her situation, she might have been consoled by the Thompson court decision. But Ella was oblivious to the Royal Tour, Frank Sinatra's new marriage, a murder trial in distant Peterborough, and, for a time, even the import of what had happened in her own life on that day.

She felt conflicting emotions. Her mind swirled with fragments of thoughts and conversations. She did remember two Mounties arriving after the shooting and "taking measurements—the height of me and the height of Vernon, and then the distance from the house to where he was. They asked me what happened and I told them exactly what went on. And then they took me down to the Stellarton jail. And that night I still didn't realize what was going on, but a feeling of peace came over me and I felt safe for the first time in years. Vernon was gone and he couldn't beat me anymore."

Jane Hurshman felt the same relief after she was charged with murdering Billy Stafford. He couldn't hurt her anymore and nothing else really mattered. "When I went to the correctional centre for those first few days, it was almost like being in a motel.

Somebody served you something to eat. You didn't have to get up. You had nobody telling you to do anything. Nothing they could do to me would have been worse than when I lived with him."[3]

When she awoke the next morning, Ella remembered Vernon had been killed, but she didn't understand why she was in jail. "If he died as the police said he did, it had to be an accident, so I couldn't figure out why they were keeping me there." It wasn't until later that day, "It finally sunk in." She was being held in custody on a charge of "occasioning grievous bodily harm." She also learned that her mother was in good condition after treatment at Aberdeen Hospital for minor shrapnel wounds around her eyes.

Ella was wary when she realized she was in the custody of Stellarton police chief Sam Baker, one of Dorothy May Ince's bootleg customers. Her anxiety eased somewhat when she was visited by a lawyer who said he'd been hired by her parents and was there to help her. Still, "I didn't say much, because I didn't know whether to believe him, and by then I didn't trust anyone."

The lawyer was working on the case with C.A. "Charlie" Manning, considered by many to be the best criminal lawyer in Pictou County. Manning was expensive, but Recky and Pearl Armour knew their only living child was in serious trouble and they wanted the best representation they could find. "Charlie Manning was the best criminal lawyer around here," said Mel MacLean. "Anyone in that kind of trouble, Charlie Manning was the one to get."

In midafternoon, Chief Baker announced another visitor, Ella's father-in-law, Jimmy Ince. Ella had always liked Jimmy, but she wondered now if he was angry over his son's death and was there seeking revenge. "I remember getting off the cot and I sat on the floor against the brick wall below the barred window. I was cringing and covering my head to protect myself, because I thought he might be coming at me. I'll never forget that."

Instead, Jimmy Ince approached her with open arms. "Then he took my hand and helped me up. I looked at him and I felt a warmth. He put his arms around me and hugged me and we both started to cry. We talked back and forth for a while, and then he said something I couldn't believe."

"You did something I should have done years ago," said Jimmy.

"It wasn't meant to be like that," Ella told him. "He was going to kill me and I didn't know what to do. I really couldn't take anymore." Ella said they cried together again before he left the cell.

IT WAS ALSO JANE HURSHMAN'S father-in-law, Lamont Stafford, who offered support after she killed Billy Stafford. Physically exhausted and emotionally drained after an all-night session of questioning, Jane had refused to budge from her blatantly transparent lie that the Mafia had killed Billy over a drug deal. She believed her two main RCMP interrogators were engaging in a game of good cop, bad cop, with one of them sympathetic and the other stern and aggressive.[4]

"I want to see Lamont," said Jane, fighting to stay awake and ignoring their questions.

"Look," said one of the frustrated officers, "I'm getting tired, you're getting tired, we're all getting tired. So why don't you tell us the truth so we can all go home?"

Jane remained silent. The officer persisted, telling her the people out in the area of Queens County, where she lived—many of whom feared Billy—were "celebrating Stafford's death. Why don't you confess so you can go home and celebrate too?"

Jane found it ironic that the police thought they could cajole her into talking. Under Billy Stafford's reign of fear, she'd been beaten into unconsciousness, shot at from close range, unspeakably degraded and humiliated, and had a knife held to her throat. She hadn't done much talking.

"I want to see Lamont," she repeated, believing Billy's father should hear first from her that she'd killed his son. The police relented and brought Lamont Stafford to the station. Jane met him privately for about twenty minutes, and then they were joined by her father, Maurice Hurshman, and the officer in charge of the division, Peter Williamson. They sat around a table, Williamson facing Jane. When he asked her a question rather gruffly, Lamont jumped to his feet.

"She's had enough of that garbage," he said. "If you want to talk to her, then you talk right to her." He sat down and turned to Jane. "Did you kill Bill?" he asked.

"Yes," Jane replied softly.

It was then that she gave a full statement while Lamont held her hand and consoled her when she wept. Williamson noticed that Lamont didn't seem angry or upset with Jane when she admitted killing his son. Shortly after she gave her statement, Williamson was overheard telling other officers that she deserved a medal for shooting Billy Stafford.

A DAY OR TWO AFTER THE LAWYER visited Ella at the Stellarton jail, she was transferred to the main county jail in nearby Pictou.

On the cloudy Friday two days after Vernon's death, *The Evening News* (New Glasgow) ran a full banner headline at the top of page 1, "Charge in Stellarton Death Not Determined." The two-column subheading said, "Mother of Two Shoots Husband, Injures Parent."

The story suggested that after uttering his last words, "Get a doctor," Vernon turned and may have been making for his car to drive for help, since the keys were found in his hand after he collapsed: "The car, a Chev, was still in front of the building today with the keys in possession of the Mounties. Yesterday they had examined and photographed the car and district from all angles."

The lead paragraph of the story reported, "The possibility of manslaughter or murder charges being laid in connection with the death by shooting of Vernon Ince was being considered by authorities today. But they weren't talking."

Later that day, RCMP corporal George King came to Ella's cell in Pictou and formally charged her with the murder of her husband.

"They had capital punishment then," Ella said. "That meant I could be hanged in the courtyard of the jail if I was found guilty."

Her fear of the gallows was genuine, but the reality that she was pregnant and the fact that no one had been hanged in Nova Scotia since 1937 made her execution an extremely remote possibility.[5]

After speaking with several witnesses, arresting officer and lead investigator George King soon learned that Ella was from a caring, respectable family and that her life with Vernon Ince had been horrible. "He knew what kind of hell I lived through," said Ella. "And I guess he felt I shouldn't be in jail. He was so kind to me, and I'll never forget that." It was King who informed her that Pearl had not been badly injured by the bullet fragments that struck her head and face. "I didn't even know how my mother was hurt until he told me that she was in the doorway behind Vernon when the bullet went through him."

THE INQUEST INTO THE DEATH OF Vernon Ince was held on Wednesday, November 21, 1951. Corporal King read into evidence the sworn statement Ella had signed on the day of the shooting. (The statement didn't include everything Ella had told him, however, which would result in legal manoeuvring later.) The twelve-man jury concluded that Vernon's death was the result of the gunshot wound to his right chest and recommended further investigation by the Attorney General's office. The investigation was largely complete, however, and the consequence of the jury's decision was the announcement that a preliminary hearing on the murder charge against Ella would begin on the afternoon of November 27, the following Tuesday.

The preliminary hearing opened on schedule at the Stellarton courthouse before Magistrate William A. "Billy" Richardson, who had spent his early years in Westville and as a young man had been known throughout the province for his skills as a baseball pitcher.

A graduate of Dalhousie Law School, Richardson had returned to Pictou County in 1930 as magistrate for the town of Stellarton.[6] Behind his back, he was known as "Stoneface," particularly by those who appeared before him to be judged. "They called him that because he was so hard he wouldn't even look up at you," says Mel MacLean. "He would just read off the charge, and you would say guilty or not guilty, and if you said guilty, he'd say, 'The fine will be' such and such and he'd never look at you." Doug Ince said Stoneface was "a tall, skinny guy, over six feet, and he'd keep his head down, and sometimes it seemed like you were guilty before you stepped up there."

Ella believed that because Richardson played poker and drank at Vernon's mother's place, she "didn't stand a chance." Doug Ince says he never saw the magistrate or Chief Baker buy liquor from his mother. "They could have—who would know?" But he's certain that they didn't play poker there. "She [Dorothy May] played poker, but not with those people," he says. "It was more like a family thing—my mother, Vern, my uncle, and my grandfather and grandmother. I think Reggie Myers was the only stranger that I know who ever played poker with them. He was quite a gambler,

Reggie. He made his living gambling. Billy Richardson played cards at different places—that was when you weren't allowed to play for money—but they [the police] would never raid that place because they'd know he was there. He liked to gamble, but he would play where there were guys that had some money to play with. He wouldn't bother with my mother's little penny ante games."

But Ella was adamant and insisted, "The chief of police used to gamble and buy liquor at Vernon's mother's place, and the magistrate the same thing. Anybody who was anybody used to show up there, including off-duty cops from outside the county. The only one who didn't drink there was MacQuarrie, the undertaker."

But it is unlikely that Richardson affected the outcome of Ella's preliminary hearing. Its purpose was to assess the evidence and determine whether the case warranted going to trial or should be dismissed. In the absence of unexpected or dramatic new evidence, a magistrate or judge would usually go along with the prosecutor and police and order the case to trial.

As he had testified at the inquest the previous week, Dr. Joseph MacDonald told the preliminary hearing that it was his opinion Vernon Ince died of massive hemorrhaging caused by a bullet wound to the chest. Pathologist Dr. McLatchery repeated his autopsy analysis. New Glasgow photographer Orin Hanright identified several photos he had taken at the scene of the shooting and of Vernon's body at the funeral home.

In all, fifteen witnesses testified, including Olive Fleming, Susan Ince, Mort Brown, Peter Keating, and two employees of the Eaton's mail-order office. In the typically stilted language of the day, the Halifax *Chronicle-Herald* reported that the prosecutor "questioned the witnesses relative to the happenings of the alleged gunshot death of Vernon Ince at his home at Asphalt Crossing Nov. 7." The hearing was then adjourned until December 7 to permit the court clerk to transcribe the evidence heard so far.

On December 7, in an unusual move for a preliminary hearing, Charlie Manning called Ella to the stand. She testified to the abuse she'd been subjected to by Vernon and explained how she fired the rifle in desperation as he lunged at her. Manning then cited several similar cases and said the fatal shooting was an act of self-defence "with not one iota of malice." He said the charge against his client should be dismissed because the Crown had failed to prove the malice necessary to support a murder charge.

Crown prosecutor E.M. MacDonald countered that the charge against Ella was valid and that there was sufficient evidence to warrant a committal to stand trial. He said Vernon died of a gunshot wound and only three people were present at the time—Ella, her mother, and the deceased. He didn't mention that Olive Fleming had been in her store just feet away, listening to every word and sound.

Magistrate Richardson agreed with the prosecutor and ordered Ella held in custody until her trial at the next sitting of the Nova Scotia Supreme Court in Pictou in May 1952. That meant the nineteen-year-old pregnant mother of two would remain in jail for the next six months, at the end of which she would be dangerously close to her delivery date.

Manning's contention that the Crown had no evidence of malice did not go unnoticed by the RCMP, who quickly realized that a charge of manslaughter, as opposed to murder, was more likely to succeed. They decided to make a personal approach to the incarcerated defendant when her lawyers weren't around.

Ella said two RCMP officers from headquarters in Halifax arrived at the jail, "and tried to get me to sign a document. I remember one of them so well, a sergeant, because he had one brown eye and one blue eye. He was extremely nice to me and told me my lawyer wasn't doing anything to get me out of jail. 'You might as well get used to being in jail,' he said. "Because after you go to trial, you're going to be in prison for a long, long time.'"

His words were frightening, but Ella initially thought he was there to help her. "I feel sorry for you," he said, "but I have papers here that, if you sign, I can arrange bail for you right away and drive you home to your parent's place. You won't have to stay here until your trial date. Wouldn't you like that?"

"Yes, I would," said Ella.

The sergeant's offer sounded enticing, but she remembered Charlie Manning's strict instructions: "No matter who approaches you to sign something, particularly anyone with authority, always refer them to me and don't sign anything."

Ella thought about her situation for a moment and decided she had to trust somebody. She decided that it would be Manning. "I don't know what to do," Ella told the Mounties. "I should talk to my lawyer, because he told me not to sign anything unless he was with me. So I guess I can't sign it. But maybe you can talk to him and it will be okay."

The officers' attitude changed abruptly. "They got mad at me and left. They never went to my lawyer, and I found out later that they had been in such a rush to lay a charge after the shooting that they laid the wrong charge. The papers that the sergeant wanted me to sign would have reduced the charge to manslaughter from murder. That would have taken the police off the hot seat and I would have only got two to five years if I pleaded guilty. It was a big decision on my part, because I could have been given bail and gone home for a while."

It will probably never be known who should have been on the "hot seat" for filing the murder charge against Ella Ince. Technically, it would seem to be Corporal George King. He was in charge of the New Glasgow RCMP detachment, he led the investigation into the shooting, and he laid the charge against Ella. But, as was the practice in Nova Scotia at that time, he was following instructions from headquarters in Halifax, either the county Crown prosecutor—MacDonald—or the provincial Attorney General's office.

THIRTY YEARS LATER, up in Queens County, Nova Scotia, Jane Hurshman's lawyer, Alan Ferrier, was galled that there would be any trial at all for his client. The battered wife syndrome was not yet an accepted defence in Canadian law, and he and Jane were prepared to enter a plea of guilty to manslaughter, because Billy Stafford was asleep in his truck when she shot him. The claim of self-defence would therefore not apply because the threat against Jane wasn't "imminent."

Ferrier believed the decision to proceed with a charge of first-degree murder was absurd, considering that one senior RCMP officer had said she deserved a medal and she'd probably saved at least two police officers' lives. But, "The difficulty with first- and second-degree murder is that the minimums are established and the judge has no control over that. Jane was charged with first-degree murder. She was looking at twenty-five years without parole. It's absolutely absurd to consider that kind of punishment for her reaction to an enduring life of violence over five years that none of us would tolerate for five seconds."[7]

The jury, which in Jane's case understood justice better than the Attorney General or the legislators did, acquitted Jane of murder and set her free. The Crown won its appeal on the "imminent threat" argument but accepted her plea to manslaughter on the second time around. She was sentenced to six months in prison but served only two, during which she was out of the prison for about eight hours attending classes in nursing on weekdays. The tragedy was that she had to go through two years of legal proceedings and publicly reveal on the witness stand, in front of a full courtroom, the degrading and sadistic abuse she suffered.

After her release from prison, Jane became an advocate for battered women, and the first time she spoke was to a criminal justice workshop in Lunenburg County in February 1985. On the evening of her address, there was a dinner at which the province's Attorney General, Harry How, was the guest speaker. "He is the same guy who ordered my appeal [after her acquittal]," Jane wrote to a friend. "When he stood up and introduced himself, I got up from my table and walked out."

At about 10 p.m. that night, a woman from the provincial parole service telephoned Jane in her room and asked if she would meet How at the hotel's main entrance. He had listened to taped evidence from Jane's trial and told a reporter, "The provocation was absolutely inconceivable in its brutality and degradation." But he said that he had to go ahead with the appeal, "Because self-defence only covered an immediate action or confrontation. It didn't take into account the accumulation of provocation. I searched in vain for any precedent in Canadian or British law. The law hadn't caught up with the growing phenomenon of wife abuse. Society's attitude in Liverpool [where her jury trial was held] was that this lady had suffered enough—beyond human endurance—but the law provided no defence."

Jane hesitated, then decided to meet How. He apologized for granting the appeal, but said that he'd had no choice. Jane said they talked for a time, "And then, right out of the blue, How said, 'Now, Jane—off the record—I want to say, that cocksucker should have been shot a long time ago.'"[8] Jane told a friend that those were How's exact words and that she was "shocked, amazed, and flattered" by them. "It gave me a new outlook on things."

In the Ella Ince case, however, Charlie Manning didn't want the murder charge reduced to manslaughter because he was supremely confident that the Crown couldn't prove capital murder, and that on that basis he could win an outright acquittal.

IN MEDIEVAL ENGLAND, EACH administrative district, or shire, designated a town to host its courts and sheriff, and a castle was usually built to house and protect them.[9] That tradition took root and survives to this day in Nova Scotia, where each of its counties has a designated "shire town," or county seat. On its masthead, the *Pictou Advocate,* which provided extensive coverage of Vernon's shooting and Ella's arrest and court appearances, proclaimed itself "Published In The Shiretown of Pictou County." And at the end of the preliminary hearing, the newspaper reported: "Mrs. Ince's trial is expected to be added to the docket for the early spring sittings of the Supreme Court at Pictou. In the meantime she is being held at the Shiretown." To the locals, "Shiretown" meant the Pictou County Jail.

"The jail was right next door to the courthouse," said Ella. "My cell was on the second floor, and for most of the time I was there, I was the only one in it. The rest of the cells were for men, and they were all downstairs."

The incarceration of Ella Ince was unusual in the penal history of Pictou County. That she was an abused, pregnant, teenaged mother of two—theoretically facing the hangman's noose—no doubt played in her favour. But the province's quirky, almost feudal prison system was also a factor. Nova Scotia's county-based system of government had been in place before most other Canadian provinces existed. Each of its eighteen counties built and operated its own schools, courthouses, and jails with minimal oversight from the province. While all the other provinces had provincial and county jails, Nova Scotia was the only one without a provincial jail system and the last to develop one.[10]

A 1997 report said that, for most of the twentieth century, conditions for staff and inmates in the old county jails "violated each of the human senses of touch (concrete and steel), sound (metal clanging), sight (jail colours, concrete, steel), smell (cigarette smoke) and taste (deep fried everything)."[11] In 1933 a Royal Commission on Jails and in 1958 an independent consultant had both called for a complete overhaul of the county jail system, but both sets of recommendations—essentially the same as those made every year between 1901 and 1913 by George Sinclair, Nova Scotia's first Inspector of Humane and Penal Institutions—were largely ignored.

Sinclair had said the system was inadequate, noting a lack of management expertise and "a lack of essential services, deficiencies in safety and security, and the idleness of the inmates."[12] But inmate Ella Ince wasn't idle, didn't lack essential services, and didn't face a steady diet of deep-fried foods. She remembers Warden MacLeod, who lived in an apartment in the jail with his wife. "I was mostly in that cell alone on the second floor, and I didn't eat the food the men ate in the cells downstairs. Whatever Mrs. MacLeod cooked for her and her husband, she always made enough for me."

Pictou's only town constable, Donald Wright, said MacLeod "was probably the jailer as well as the warden at the time. The jailer lived right there, and it was kind of funny because some of them used to get the inmates to babysit their kids, run errands for them..." He said for prisoners like Ella, "It was just like living at home."

Ella said Mrs. MacLeod was friendly. "She used to come and sit and talk to me, and she even taught me to knit. I guess it was very unusual, but I was provided with sheets, pillowcases, blankets, a table and chairs, tablecloth, plants, silverware, and a radio. I was also given the daily paper to read. I was the only prisoner with all those privileges, probably because I was the only woman. Except for the ones who were in my cell with me for a short time, I didn't see any other prisoners the whole time I was there. They were in a different part of the building."

Ella's cell had a single window that opened behind the bars. "I could look out," she said. "It was facing the street, and every weekend, people used to come down there in their cars. They would park and I could talk to them out the window. They came to give me their support. I think that's what helped keep me sane. When I was alone too long, I would get depressed thinking about my parents and my children.

"Monday was visiting day and a lot of people would come to see me—sometimes too many for the time allotted." But the MacLeods would abandon the rules and allow Ella to see all those who showed up at the jail. "I kept a record of everyone who came to see me on visiting day, and by the time I left there, the total was 111—not counting my family. My mother came quite a bit, but my dad couldn't make the trip because he was so ill. My mother didn't drive, so she always got a ride. It was a short drive to the jail from Westville."

Fifty-five years later, Ella's cousin, Dorothy Watters, still has clear memories of visiting Ella in the Pictou jail. "My mother drove and my grandmother went with us, but they didn't go in. They stayed in the car and I went in alone. It was on the second floor and I just followed the guy in. It was a long hallway and her cell was at the end. I didn't notice any other cells. There was a window, but it wasn't a big cell—not a heck of a lot bigger than my walk-in closet. I wasn't allowed into her cell, but we talked between the bars of the jail door. It was very upsetting. I think it was just before Christmas, and she was sad."

Ella's spirits lifted at Christmas when she was showered with gifts, "And Mrs. McLeod gave me a small tree, decorated, with a set of lights on it, and they served me Christmas dinner with all the trimmings. They were very, very good to me."

Her story had been picked up by the wire services and had appeared in many U.S. newspapers, particularly in New England. "I guess the news media had a field day with it," said Ella. "They didn't open my mail in the jail, and gifts and money came to me and my parents from all over the U.S. and Canada. Enough money was received to pay for my lawyers and all the other expenses, and there was still about six thousand dollars left over. I think we received about eighteen thousand dollars in total. And I got enough presents to sink a battleship. I even got cases of oranges and grapefruits from Florida. It was an anonymous gift, and it came to my parents every Christmas for the next four or five years. My God, it was amazing."

In addition to perks and friendly jailers, from the first day of her incarceration Corporal King took a special interest in the Shiretown inmate he had arrested. In Nova Scotia, each city or town could decide if it wanted to be policed by its own force or by the RCMP. Stellarton, New Glasgow, and Westville opted for their own forces, while Pictou chose the RCMP. "I guess the town figured the RCMP would cost them less," said Donald Wright, Pictou's sole non-RCMP constable. Although there was an RCMP office in Pictou, Corporal King's detachment was thirteen miles away, in New Glasgow. He first showed up at the jail to escort Ella to a viewing of Vernon's body before his funeral.

"The Mountie, King, took Ella to see Vernon's remains laid out in the parlour at my aunt's place—my mom's sister, Lilly Boutilier," says Doug Ince. "It was just across the street, and MacQuarrie brought the body in a coffin and set it up there in the front room. King was a nice man. He's the fella that come to me and said, 'I know you have the .22, Doug.' But he said, 'I'll say no more,' and he left with that. He was a heck of a nice guy—a gentleman."

Ella says she felt compelled to see Vernon in his coffin and experienced a rush of "mixed emotions" when she did. "It was strange to see him lying there so quiet while I was still in pain from the beatings he gave me. I don't remember talking to any of his relatives, and it was a relief to leave there."

King began appearing regularly at the Pictou jail, offering to sign Ella out in his custody. "He wasn't supposed to do that, but he would come and sign me out and take me home to Westville so I could see my parents and my children. He was a real gentleman and I appreciated his kindness." But she soon recognized she was being wooed and his interest was based on something more than any residual guilt he may have felt for laying the murder charge against her. "He was always in plain clothes when he signed me out, and after visiting my parents he would drive to Digby or Antigonish for dinner. We never had dinner in any local restaurants, I guess because people would recognize me."

As a pregnant mother with two small children there was considerable public support and sympathy for Ella and there was little criticism of her cushy confinement. She was appreciative of the preferential treatment, but alone in her cell at night she was often stalked by fear of what was to come in the courtroom and perhaps beyond. Soon, however, she wouldn't be alone in her cell at night.

9

Cellmates

Dale Cheryl Mapstone, 29. Toronto. Mother of two. Dale was stabbed to death in front of her 10-year-old son, Treyvon, who tried to save his mother's life by jumping on the assailant's back before running to a neighbour for help. Dale's boyfriend, Vaughn Maxwell Wilson, was charged with second-degree murder. (April 2006)

AS ELLA BEGAN HER SIXTH MONTH IN CUSTODY, THE SNOWS were gone and her belly bloomed along with the spring flowers outside the adjoining courthouse. The warden's wife, Rose MacLeod, pampered her more than ever, and a doctor made regular visits to monitor her pregnancy.

Meanwhile, Ella was fighting another legal battle, this one outside the courtroom, over the custody of her daughter. Estelle had been living with Vernon's mother since the shooting. Lawyer J.B. Baker, who was working with Charlie Manning on the case, had a letter delivered from Ella to Doug Ince's wife, Susan, "or any other person who may have custody of my daughter Estelle. This is to authorize and direct you to hand over the care and custody of my daughter to my solicitor, J.B. Baker, so that he may place her with my mother or one of my aunts in Westville as he sees fit." The letter was signed by Ella and witnessed by Rose MacLeod.

Bessie Flanders (Smith) remembers her mother and Pearl reading a copy of the letter. "They were all very upset that they didn't have Estelle with them," she says. Doug Ince says his mother "was looking after Estelle when Ella was in jail. She also looked after her when Vern and Ella were separated for a while. She was always good to those kids." Good or not, Estelle was returned to the Armours and reunited with her brother, Donny.

Anxiety over her daughter wasn't Ella's only concern as she sat patiently in her cell. Two weeks after she welcomed in the new year of 1952, the Pictou Coalfield lived up to its reputation as one of the most unstable sites on the planet. A violent explosion ripped through the MacGregor Mine in Stellarton, killing nineteen and injuring two others. Five of the dead were from Westville, including a close friend and neighbour of Ella and her parents and two of Harry Muir's relatives.

Whenever there was a fire or an explosion in the mine, a loud whistle sounded across Stellarton. "You could hear it in the schools—you could hear it everywhere," says Danna MacNeil. "I remember the kids started to cry. My mother was out hanging clothes on the line, and she started to cry too. She went down to one knee and then remembered my father hadn't gone to work... He had smelled something in the mine the day before, and he said, 'I'm not going to work.'"

A few months after the explosion, the MacNeils moved away from Nova Scotia for good. Tin and Dorothy Watters did the same. Tin had been on his way to work at the mine when it exploded. "After that, I told my father, 'Look, old fella, that's it for me—I'll never go back into a coal mine again.' And that was in January 1952."

Then, less than a month after the MacGregor explosion, Ella's popular "uncle with the Buick" died of a stroke at the age of 63. Married to Pearl's sister Tina, Alexander "Alex" Levi Smith was treasured for driving various relatives to weekend outings or hosting large family dinners at their place in Stellarton, and was often at the Armours' in Westville for a meal and music after church on Sundays.

"After my father's death, we moved from Stellarton back to Westville," says Bessie. "My mother didn't drive, so we had to take the train with Pearl to visit Ella in jail. Recky was too ill to make the trip. My mother would usually take me with her, and I visited Ella in the cell quite a few times. They never should have incarcerated her over a whole winter when she was pregnant. She was never going to hurt anybody."

The train trips to visit Ella in the Pictou jail were an adventure for the thirteen-year-old Bessie. "We always brought her goodies, like baking and magazines and clothes—she needed clothes. I remember she was really happy with the stuff we brought. And we always had lunch with her."

Finally, Ella learned that the spring sitting of the Nova Scotia Supreme Court for Pictou County would begin on May 12 with Mr. Justice W.L. Hall presiding. Besides Ella's capital case, eighteen-year-old Roy Haggart faced two murder charges in the killing of his uncle and aunt, Alexander and Agnes Haggart, in the small farming community of Laggan. Two others, George Mills of New Glasgow and Herbert Hugh Johnson of Balmoral Mills, were charged with vehicular manslaughter. The other serious charge was against Earl Willis Skidmore for "shooting with intent to murder" Ida Kilmer in New Glasgow. There were also seven non-jury civil cases and three divorce petitions on the docket. Ella's case would be heard last.

ON TUESDAY, MAY 13, THE DAY after the Supreme Court sessions began, Ella acquired a cellmate, a tall, thin black woman convicted that afternoon of common assault and remanded to jail to await sentencing at the end of the court's criminal session. Because Ella's case was not scheduled to be heard until the end of the month, the two would be together for two or three weeks.

Cora Mae Jackson was about fifty years old and a lot tougher than she looked. She had never thought much of the justice system, and particularly the way it treated blacks, and she wasn't shy about voicing her opinion. She wasn't complaining about her conviction, however, because she knew her circumstances could have been worse. Cora had faced a charge of "inflicting grievous bodily harm" on eighty-five-year-old William Pullman, who ran a small grocery store on Marsh Street in New Glasgow. After deliberating for an hour and twenty minutes, the jurors reported to Mr. Justice Hall that they were deadlocked. He sent them back, and they eventually returned with a guilty verdict on the lesser charge of common assault.

Cherry Paris, New Glasgow's first black teacher, who subsequently spent eighteen years with the Nova Scotia Human Rights Commission until her retirement in 1996, remembers Cora Jackson as "a very nice lady, but you just didn't bother her. She didn't like being discriminated against and she fought it all her life. Until recent years, Nova Scotia's treatment of its black citizens was abysmal and racism was extremely bad in Pictou County."

Paris remembers William Pullman from her school days. "He was an elderly man, and kids were afraid of him and his store," she said. "It looked more like a museum. There was a huge moose head inside and the place was always extremely dark, even in the daytime. It was scary, and when we were passing there, we used to hurry by. He didn't do any harm to anyone, but I think that the kids probably teased him."

The story Mr. Pullman told in court was that, just after 5:30 p.m., he was sitting alone in his store when "a small coloured boy" came in and asked him for apples. When he learned the boy had no money, he told him to go home and get some. Two other boys were outside the store at the time.

Pullman said the boy left, but about forty-five minutes later, Cora Jackson came into the store and demanded, "Why did you slap my grandson?" Before he could reply, Pullman testified, she picked up a chair and struck him over the head. Police were called and Constable Edward Joseph arrived to find Pullman slouched on a chair. The officer helped him to his home across the street, and Dr. H.A. Locke arrived and bandaged a cut on the top of his head.

Six-year-old Joe Jackson told the court that the other boys had sent him into the store to ask for apples and that Pullman had slapped him. His ten-year-old friend, who had been watching through the window, corroborated Joe's story. And Cora Jackson produced another witness who said she saw the old proprietor grab Cora and fall and strike his head on a box as he tried to push Cora out of the store.

The jury was faced with conflicting versions of the event. Pullman denied that he slapped the boy, and Cora denied that she hit Pullman over the head with a chair. Dr. Locke, the only independent witness, said the cut on the top of Pullman's head was consistent with being hit by a chair, as Pullman claimed.

CORA'S WITNESS, CLARA JACKSON, was described as a "friend" but was actually her sister-in-law—they were married to brothers. Amateur New Glasgow historian Fred MacPherson says Cora Jackson "was a character, who would fight just about any man." Cora's brother-in-law (Clara's husband) was the boxer Charlie Jackson, known as "Bearcat."

Bearcat became a folk hero to the black community when he took on and beat New Glasgow's deputy chief of police, George "Spinney" Wright, a boxer and former marathon runner who was also a racist. Ella's cousin, Harry Muir, says Spinney Wright "was bad on the black fellas. He used to whale the hell out of them anytime they came down the hill. He used to go up there too." And MacPherson says, "Spinney weighed about 240, and he was notorious for going up into the 'coloured section,' as it was called at the time. He was probably the only policeman who would go up there after dark, but he got to know quite a few of them and he used to fight with a lot of them."

It was probably Spinney Wright's taunting that led to the famous boxing match at the New Glasgow arena. "It would have been around 1946, shortly after the war," says Muir, who was at the fight. "I was about fifteen then. The rink was filled. They were hanging from the rafters and everywhere else—probably two thousand or more. Spinney didn't do much official fighting—not like Bearcat. They just got out in the middle of the ring, and the Bearcat whammed him with his right hand and down went Spinney. He was split wide open over the eye, but he got back up again. They let it go, and Bearcat hit him again and he went down, and so the referee stopped it." Doug Ince was also at the big match. "Spinney took a lot of ribbing after that. Whenever he was about to give somebody a ticket, they'd say, 'I'll get Bearcat after you if you do.'"

But Bearcat Jackson did what he had to do. With one punch, he became a local hero against a white cop who had been harassing his people.

AND CORA JACKSON DID WHAT *she* had to do. She always believed that she was as good and valuable as anyone else in society, regardless of race, and if you indicated otherwise, through words or actions, she wouldn't hesitate to come after you. As far back as early grade school, she had been fighting her own battles against discrimination. Even when her face was chalked by her classmates in an attempt to turn her white, "I knew I could beat them any day," she said. She remembered one boy approaching her with a shovel. "Just when he put the shovel down, I nabbed him...I beat the boy something desperate."[1]

In later years, when her husband, Hartley, who served in the First World War, was attacked in the street by a young white man, she again went into action. "This boy was fighting and struck my husband," she said. "So I just pulled the stake out and banged across his head. I did thirty days because he didn't hit me, you see."[2] Cora spoke out against the justice system at the time, saying it wasn't protecting blacks, forcing them to act on their own behalf.[3]

So there were many who would say that Cora Jackson was just as tough as Bearcat, and although Ella hadn't met her before, she was aware of her fearsome reputation. But she had no reason for concern. Despite the rampant racism on the outside, Ella and Cora were soon perfectly at ease in each other's company. "She was a lot older than me, and she knew I was close to having a baby," says Ella. "She was very good to me, and we talked and laughed a lot. I was by myself for a long time until they put Cora Jackson and another woman—a bootlegger—in there with me. It wasn't so boring anymore with three of us in there, and Cora was a very nice woman. I had heard a lot of stories about her, but she was very nice. And we had a good time playing cards."

JANE HURSHMAN FARED ABOUT as well as Ella had. Jane was worried when she was sentenced to six months after her second trial for killing Billy Stafford. She hoped she would get compatible cellmates. But when she first arrived to spend four days in a holding cell area, awaiting transfer to the general prison population, she was taking her turn in the shower when she heard a nasty voice.

"You Jane Stafford?"

Before Jane could answer, the voice continued, "I'd like to know who the fuck you know, or who the fuck you blew, to get only six months for what you did."

Jane was frightened. "I didn't know who was waiting for me behind that shower curtain. I didn't know what to say or how to react." Then she realized she would have to stand up for herself, "Or I would be used and abused the whole time I was inside." She took a deep breath and yanked the curtain back.

"And just who the fuck wants to know?" she shouted, surprised at the threatening tone in her own voice. She was expecting an amazon. Instead, she had to look down at a frail ninety-pounder with curly red hair. They stood staring at each other, and then the woman laughed. "I'm Pearl," she said. "I was just sentenced to ten years for shooting my old man. I was just wondering how you only got six months for the same thing."

"That was my one and only unfriendly encounter all the time I was in jail," said Jane.

ALTHOUGH ELLA ARMOUR WAS QUITE content with her cellmates, the judge who would preside over her capital murder trial was not. Two days before the trial, Mr. Justice Hall wondered aloud if Cora Jackson, awaiting sentence on a charge of common assault, and another woman serving time for a liquor offence were proper company for "a woman in her condition." He said he was aware that in the county jail there was no accommodation for the segregation of prisoners other than by sex. He suggested that, in her interest, she "shouldn't have this hanging over her head."

At the start of the session that morning, the Crown prosecutor read a letter from Nova Scotia's deputy attorney general stating that he considered it most undesirable to proceed with the trial of Mrs. Ella Ince "at this time" and that he would not oppose an application for bail if the case were traversed to the October sitting of the court.

But jail physician Dr. G.A. Dunn suggested that it would be detrimental to Ella's physical and mental health if she were not tried at the current session. "She is not a bit neurotic, but is perfectly calm," he told the court. "It would be better to try her now than admit her to bail. She at present is in a very small room with three cots in it."

"I am very strongly influenced by what the doctor has said," Mr. Justice Hall stated. The prosecutor said he was willing to go along with the doctor, and defence lawyer Charlie Manning said both Ella and her family requested that the trial go on. The judge agreed and ordered that it begin at 10 a.m. on Thursday, May 29.

On May 31, Cora Jackson was found guilty of common assault and sentenced to six months with hard labour.

10

Relative Justice

Natalie Novak, 20. Toronto. Natalie was stabbed to death in a house where she was living while she attended Ryerson University. Multiple calls were made to 911 and other students tried to intervene by forcing the door to her room, but it was too late to save her. Her ex-boyfriend, Arsooi Hindocca, was charged with second-degree murder. Police reported that he had also been convicted of assaulting Natalie the September before and was on probation with conditions to stay away from her. (May 2006)

A BARN THAT HOUSED A PIGSTY WAS REPORTEDLY THE VENUE for the first sitting of the Pictou branch of the Nova Scotia Supreme Court when the county was designated a separate district in 1790. In summer, jurors would retire to a nearby pasture to consider their verdicts. A proper courthouse wasn't built until 1813. Thanks to the county's growing economic prosperity, fuelled by the rich coalfields, that modest structure was replaced in 1856 by an ornate two-storey building whose exterior architectural flourishes were complemented by intricate wood moulding and carvings inside. The Supreme Court chamber soared the full two storeys, with a spectators' gallery and a stained glass window depicting the goddess of justice with her sword and scales. One government heritage report described it as "the most elaborately detailed courthouse constructed of wood in Nova Scotia."[1]

It was in this imposing building that Ella Ince's future would be decided.

ELLA NO DOUBT HEARD ENCOURAGING words from her lawyers and family, and from RCMP corporal George King on their drives between the Pictou County Jail and her parents' home in Westville. But the reality was that, even though she was pregnant, the authorities had not allowed her out on bail and, more sobering, the charge she faced was capital murder. "So many nights when I was alone in my cell, I lay there thinking, 'What if they should find me guilty?' If they did, they could hang me right there in the courtyard of the jail."

The chances of that were remote. Hanging was the only officially sanctioned method of execution in Canada, but since Confederation, only thirteen women had gone to the gallows. In fact, in January 1953, just seven months and ten days after Ella's trial, Marguerite Pitre became the last woman executed in Canada. Almost ten years after Pitre's execution, the death penalty was unofficially suspended in Canada and was finally abolished by statute in 1976. The country's last hangings were at Toronto's Don Jail on December 11, 1962, when Arthur Lucas and Robert Turpin went to the gallows for committing unrelated murders. Besides, Ella was pregnant, and hanging pregnant women was a practice shunned in most democratic countries.

It hadn't always been so. In his "Timeline of Capital Punishment in Britain,"[2] Richard Clark writes that killing your husband was considered such an affront to society that it was labelled "petty treason" instead of murder, and until 1793 it was punishable by burning at the stake. In that year, the punishment was changed to hanging. Nor had being pregnant always saved women. In Britain, it was legal to hang a pregnant woman until 1931.[3]

Nowadays, more than 140 countries have signed on to the International Covenant on Civil and Political Rights, which prohibits the execution of pregnant women. The U.S. agreed to it in 1976. But whether for sheer titillation or the fact that women were executed far less frequently than were men, the public's fascination with female executions never waned, and with the advent of newspapers, that interest was multiplied many times over. Boston College law professor Phyllis Goldfarb, in her review of Marlin Shipman's 2002 book, *The Penalty Is Death*, said that newspaper coverage of women's executions "underscored cultural expectations that white women were kindly, passive, virtuous caretakers and that violations of these expectations served to aggravate the crime of murder to the extent that execution seemed utterly appropriate."[4]

Shipman's book examines the shifts in press coverage of women's executions over the past 150 years in the U.S. Since the first execution of a woman in the colonies in 1632, about 560 women have faced the death penalty.[5] Of the fifty-one women currently on death row in the United States, fourteen of them—28 per cent—are there for killing their husbands or boyfriends. The average age of the women is thirty-seven and a half. Of the fourteen, one also killed her two children, and one other her twenty-six-year-old stepson.[6]

Goldfarb noted that it was easier for the public to endorse a woman's execution once the press, like the prosecution, had "defeminized" her. Coverage would often ignore evidence of abusive treatment by her husband, master, or employer and comment unfavourably on her size (describing her as "corpulent," for example), her attire (wearing "a gray artificial silk dress, loose and poorly fitting"), and her facial features ("her chin sharp and prominent, her lips thin, and her forehead retreating").

According to Goldfarb, a woman charged with murder and facing the death penalty became *newsworthy* because the act of killing was a violation of "feminine cultural norms." However, built-in "gender-based protections" would kick in if the woman was repentant enough and if the press played up her positive feminine attributes. But if those protections were withheld or withdrawn, she could be subjected to particularly harsh treatment and vilified by the press, making her imminently *deathworthy*.

Although some newspapers, including the *New York Times*, used gender stereotypes to *oppose* women's executions throughout the nineteenth and early twentieth centuries, others used those stereotypes to *justify* executions. In 1905, the *Burlington Daily Free Press* stated that when Mary Rogers killed her husband, she "unsexed" herself, and might have been spared "had there been one spark of womanliness in her."[7]

But gender worked as a "protection" in the real-life 1920s cases on which the play, Broadway musical, and hit movie *Chicago* were based. Belva Gaertner, described as "a married cabaret singer with a long history of dalliances," and Beulah Annan, a married bookkeeper, both shot their lovers (not their husbands) in separate incidents a month apart. The men they shot had announced they were leaving them. Both women were charged with first-degree murder and faced the death penalty. When another woman in the cells received the death penalty for killing her lover, Annan quickly announced that she was pregnant—although she never *did* give birth.

While Gaertner and Annan awaited trial on Chicago's "Murderess Row," reporter Maurine Watkins sensationalized their stories on the front pages of the *Chicago Tribune*.[8] Her reports, mostly sympathetic, were the talk of the city and apparently swayed the all-male juries to find the women not guilty. Watkins suggested that the juries were sensitive to the women's charms and that Annan "was given freedom by her beauty-proof jury."

THE CAPITAL MURDER TRIALS OF Ella Ince and Marguerite Pitre, just months apart, also illustrate the role of the press and the courts in defeminizing or unsexing one woman, thus rendering her "deathworthy," while providing special gender-based "protections" to the other.

Marguerite Pitre was involved in the bombing of a Canadian Pacific Airlines passenger plane carrying the wife of jeweller Joseph-Albert Guay on a flight from Quebec City to Baie-Comeau. Guay wanted his wife dead so he could marry his nineteen-year-old mistress and collect on the insurance policy he had purchased on the day of the bombing. Pitre was the sister of handicapped watchmaker Genereux Ruest, who worked for Guay. Pitre purchased the dynamite that her brother used to build the bomb. On September 9, 1949, she took a taxi to the airport and dropped off a package containing the bomb. It exploded in mid-flight, killing all twenty-three on board.

The prosecution used Pitre's testimony to assure a date with the hangman for her brother and Joseph-Albert Guay—then decided that Pitre should follow them to the gallows.

There was some opposition to executing her. But this was a horrific crime—the biggest mass murder in Canadian history—and the press weighed in with unflattering physical descriptions, including references to Pitre's considerable weight—"stocky"—and characterizations such as "sharp-spoken" and "hard-voiced." While Pitre was on the witness stand giving evidence against Guay—but before she was herself charged—Canadian Press described her as argumentative and duly reported the judge's charge to the jury in which he said, first, "You may have asked yourselves if she was an accomplice," and, second, that it was up to them to decide "how much faith should be placed in her stories."

Pitre eventually followed Guay and Ruest to the gallows in Montreal's Bordeaux Jail.

Ella's situation was a sharp contrast. She was young, attractive, quiet, and attentive in the courtroom, and very pregnant. Presiding judge Mr. Justice Hall had voiced concerns about her living conditions in the jail—sharing a cell with a convicted bootlegger and a coloured woman, Cora Jackson. He ordered that Ella have a doctor at her side in the courtroom. The press picked up on the theme. The first four paragraphs in New Glasgow's *Evening News* report on the first day of the trial were mostly about Ella and concern for her well-being.

"For five-and-a-half hours in a packed courtroom, a small dark-haired girl sat quietly in the prisoner's dock while 17 Crown witnesses recalled the events of a certain day in November," the report began, then described Ella as "the 19-year-old mother of two children, soon to become the mother of a third," and said that she "appeared to come through the day fairly well, although the closeness of the air in the courtroom seemed to bother her at times.

"Dressed in a dark blue silk dress, a light navy coat and a close-fitting gray hat, she looked older than her 19 years."

The report said Ella initially "seemed confused by the formality of the court procedure," but as the trial progressed, "she appeared to regain her composure in spite of such exhibits as the Winchester rifle and her husband's blood-soaked shirt and sweater." Then it provided the type of gender-based protections cited in Shipman's book: "The large number of women in court were relieved to know that Mrs. Ince had been provided with a cushion for her two sessions of two-and-a-half and three hours."[9]

MARLIN SHIPMAN'S BOOK CONCLUDES that by 1998 the attitude of both the press and society had changed dramatically, exemplified by a columnist from a Texas newspaper who wrote that convicted killer Karla Faye Tucker should not be spared the death penalty because she was a woman. In June of 1983, in a drug haze, Tucker and her boyfriend killed a biker and his girlfriend with multiple blows from a hammer and a pickaxe during an aborted robbery. Tucker was "born-again" in prison and was an ideal inmate for fourteen years on death row. Her case became an international *cause célèbre* for those seeking to abolish capital punishment. The Texas columnist, however, wrote that women can be just as violent and aggressive as men and the idea that women are defenceless and need men's protection "is probably the last vestige of institutionalized sexism that needs to be rubbed out."[10]

On February 3, 1998, Tucker was executed by lethal injection at the Huntsville State Prison in Texas, after then governor George W. Bush rejected worldwide appeals to commute her sentence to life in prison. She was the first woman executed in Texas since the Civil War and the first in the United States since 1984.

THE LONG-AWAITED CAPITAL MURDER trial of Ella Ince attracted a crowd that filled the old courtroom and overflowed from the building into the street.

There may have been good reason for the *Evening News* report that Ella "sat quietly" and "seemed confused" as her trial got underway in Pictou's historic courthouse. Dr. G.A. Dunn, assigned by the court to look after her throughout the Supreme Court sitting and her trial, had prescribed a steady supply of sedatives. "All through the trial, the doctor was giving me pills," said Ella. "He said it was so I wouldn't feel anything. He called them stress pills. Anything that the Crown prosecutor said did not affect me. He was only doing his job. Nothing he said bothered me, or any evidence he produced. These pills kept me in an I-don't-care mood and it was like they were talking about somebody else. But ever since the day it [Vernon's killing] happened, I felt that way and didn't really need any pills. The doctor spent the day with me in the courtroom, and he would come back to see me at night before he went to bed. The first thing in the morning, he was there again to check on me. He was a very caring man."

Drugs or no drugs, Ella may well have thought she was hallucinating when she looked up at the jury box and saw her dear uncle, Pearl's brother, Alex Muir, sitting as a member of the jury panel. In Canada at that time, a jury was all male. Women would be excluded from serving on juries for criminal trials for another twenty years—till 1972—while in some provinces they were not allowed on civil juries until the 1980s.[11]

Not only was Ella's uncle on the panel, but his fellow jurors had chosen him as foreman. Whether or not she thought that was unusual, Ella never said. There's nothing like having your uncle head the jury that will decide your fate. She contemplated her good fortune and remained silent as Crown Prosecutor E.M. MacDonald began calling his witnesses. She watched the evidence unfold.

The layout of the Maple Street house—with the store operated by Olive Fleming in the front, Doug and Susan Ince's two-room apartment on the ground floor, and Ella and Vernon's three-room apartment at the rear—was detailed in a plan drawn up by Sergeant Frank Robertson, from the RCMP's Criminal Investigation Branch in Halifax. He explained that the door from Ella's apartment to the store had been blocked off, but a hole remained where the lock had been and it was covered by a calendar. He said the door from the porch at the back of the house opened into the kitchen, providing a clear view into the living room, "As there was no door between the two rooms."

Robertson testified that when he arrived, he saw a large pool of blood at the front of the house about fifty feet from the back step of the apartment shared by Vernon and Ella and their two children.

New Glasgow photographer Orin Hanright identified pictures he had taken of the interior of the apartment, as well as photos of Vernon's body showing the entry and exit wounds to his chest and back.

The third witness in the morning session was Olive Fleming, who testified about the loud quarrelling she heard at intervals, through the hole in the door, over "money and a sleeping bag." She said the voices she heard were those of Vernon Ince and his wife, and occasionally of Ella's mother, Pearl Armour. Later she saw the Inces near their car in the driveway and heard a door slam. She was busy for a time in the store, then she clearly heard Ella's frantic voice saying, "Stay away from me. Leave me alone." She heard the sound of the door pushed open and heard Vernon say, "You haven't got guts enough to pull the trigger." Then there was a loud gunshot, and she quickly scooped up her store keys and headed for the door. As she was shutting it behind her, she saw Vernon stumbling around the corner of the house. He said, "Get a doctor," and Mrs. Fleming said she ran across the street to use the telephone at Mrs. Bain's house. When she returned, Vernon was lying face down on the sidewalk and Dr. J.B. MacDonald arrived at about the same time.

In cross-examination by Charlie Manning, Mrs. Fleming admitted she had heard the Inces arguing often over the two previous years and said Ella had complained to her that the children needed clothing but had not mentioned the sleeping bag. She said she had never noticed any scars or bruises on Ella and told

Manning that she operated the store as a tenant of Vernon's mother, Dorothy May Ince.

Susan Ince was called to the witness box after Mrs. Fleming. "Going to court wasn't very pleasant," says Susan. "It was the first time anything like that ever happened in my life. So I was very nervous, and I was very young. It wasn't a very big courthouse compared to what they have today, but it was packed and to me it seemed big at the time. They kept us [witnesses] in another room and then they called us in. I could see Ella in the prisoner's box, but I was so nervous I don't know what I was looking at. And they really didn't ask me very much. I don't know why I was called."

Susan testified that she was in her apartment on the morning of November 7 and through the window saw Vernon and his friend Malcolm Brown working on the car in the driveway. About 11 a.m. she saw Vernon and Ella walking toward Maple Street, and again later, but the second time Ella turned and ran back to the house with Vernon in pursuit. A few seconds later, Vernon ran past Susan's window, then she heard the car door slam and he ran back to the house.

After that there was a shot, and from her bedroom window Susan saw Vernon come around the house. She ran out. She met him at the front of the house, and when he fell to the sidewalk, she could see the hole in his back. She said he was covered in blood. A minute or so later, Ella and her mother came out of the house. Pearl Armour was holding two-year-old Estelle, whose face was covered with blood. Susan said she took the child into her apartment and washed the blood from her face.

When Manning's associate, Stellarton lawyer J.B. Baker, asked her to expand on what she heard in the adjoining apartment on the morning of the shooting, Susan said she heard "awfully loud talking" during the morning and before the shot there was a noise in the porch "like a scuffle."

The next witness, neighbour Janet Watters, told Charlie Manning, "It all happened very quickly," but she saw Ella standing by the car when Vernon, who had started to walk across the street, stopped and said something to her. "Then she turned and ran toward the back of the house, and he after her. A minute or so later, he came back and got something out of the car." Watters said Vernon ran back to the house, and shortly after that she heard a shot.

Pearl Armour, the last witness before the lunch break, testified she had come in from Westville at about 9:15 a.m. to help her daughter with the two children and the housework when she witnessed the quarrelling over the sleeping bag and money. She said Vernon left a couple of times, and then the two of them left together. When they returned, they were still arguing and Vernon was demanding Ella "go up the road" with him.

"I told him, 'Don't be like that, Vernon,'" Pearl said to the court. She said Vernon was in and out of the house with parcels from the car while Ella was starting the potatoes on the stove. "He came in cursing and swearing like a wild man and wanted her to go out with him," Pearl testified. "She was crying and very, very afraid of him. He hit her a couple of times. Then he pulled her to the door by the hair of the head and went out, and the door locked as it slammed."

She said he dragged Ella out to the porch and started "pounding her" and screamed at her, "Give me the money or I'll kill you." Pearl testified she called out to Olive Fleming to call the police, and when she attempted to get by him, Vernon released Ella and grabbed her, allowing Ella to escape into the house. She said he ran to his car for the keys, and "in just a second," he unlocked the door and opened it.

"I was in the porch," said Pearl. "He gave me quite a handling. When he opened the door, he stepped in. I was right behind him.

Ella said, 'Vernon, leave me alone.' He said, 'You haven't got the guts. I'll kill you.'"

Crown prosecutor MacDonald asked her what happened next. "I was standing right behind, dazed," she replied. "I didn't hear any gunshot. I didn't see the gun until after the accident, when it was in the dining room."

In the cross-examination, Pearl told Charlie Manning that Vernon got along with Ella "sometimes" and that her daughter had left him once but returned. She said Vernon had been employed in the mines and at the car works but had not worked for several months before his death.

Ella was crying and her face was bruised when she and Vernon came back to the house for the last time on November 7, Pearl told the court. When she asked her son-in-law what had happened, he said, "I did it and I'll knock her fucking head off."

THE COURT RECESSED FOR LUNCH at 12:30 p.m. Mr. Justice Hall would face an unprecedented dilemma upon his return.

During the noon recess, Alex Muir—perhaps surprised that no one had objected to the uncle of the accused serving as jury foreman, let alone being allowed on the jury in the first place—asked the county sheriff to inform Mr. Justice Hall of his relationship to Ella.

The practical problem for the court was that the jury pool called for the spring session had been discharged that morning once the jury was empanelled to hear Ella's case—the last on the criminal docket. Hall said it might mean summoning a new jury for a special session or traversing the case to the Supreme Court's October sitting. He said neither the prosecution nor the defence had challenged Muir's selection, "peremptorily or for cause," when they'd had the opportunity before the jury was sworn. He said he wasn't sure what action he should take, because he'd never been in a situation where an empanelled juror was related to the accused. If counsel for the Crown or the defence could cite authority for discharging the jury, he would do so, he said, but didn't believe there was such a precedent.

Ella's cousin, Fraser Muir, Alex Muir's son, wasn't at the trial. He had been overseas as a gunner with the RCAF and went back to school after the war. "I was twenty-eight or twenty-nine and I was at St. Francis Xavier University, in Antigonish," he said. "I just couldn't believe it when I heard that my father was appointed jury foreman. But I contend that he was such an honest man that nobody chose to oppose him. He made it known that he was Ella's uncle."

Manning said he did not have any contact with Muir and had not been aware of the relationship to his client. Both Manning and MacDonald said they were willing to proceed with the trial, and Mr Justice Hall agreed.

DR. J.B. MACDONALD, WHO ARRIVED at the crime scene just after 1 p.m. on November 7, was the first witness when court resumed in the afternoon. He testified that he found Vernon Ince "lying crosswise" face down on the sidewalk and that Vernon was dead on arrival at Aberdeen Hospital. He listed cause of death as massive hemorrhage and shock.

Later in the day, Dr. MacDonald said, he examined Pearl Armour, who had a puncture wound above the eye and several small metallic objects imbedded in the area. He also examined Ella, discovering the bump on the back of her head, the small patch of scalp denuded of hair, and the recent bruising on her thigh.

Under cross-examination, Dr. MacDonald told Manning that Ella seemed "quite rational, but excited" when he had examined her. He also said there were "old discolorations" on both of her shins.

The provincial pathologist from Halifax who'd performed the autopsy on Vernon, Dr. N.B.G. McLatchery, described him as "a powerfully built man of five feet, ten inches in height." He said there was no evidence of bruises or cuts "such as might have been received in a struggle," but there were some recent superficial bruises on his face. He described the damage done by the bullet to Vernon's ribs and lungs and said he found no alcohol in his system.

McLatchery told Baker in cross-examination that, from the angle the bullet travelled through the body, he believed it likely the shot was fired from some distance above Vernon, or that he was in a crouching position. And he said the light facial bruises he found had been caused by Vernon falling to the ground shortly before he died.

Arlene Kellock and her sister-in-law, Lois Kellock, confirmed that in October Ella ordered a $29.95 sleeping bag from the Eaton's mail-order office, but when it arrived, she asked that it be returned and was refunded the money. Then, on the morning of November 7, she returned to the office and asked that in the event Vernon showed up to please tell him that the sleeping bag would arrive in a few days. Lois said she'd told Ella she couldn't do that.

Arlene Kellock said she was working in the order office when the Inces returned together later that day, and when Ella asked her if the sleeping bag would be coming in on Saturday, she said no. She said it had been returned in October and the money refunded, as Ella had requested. Ella told her she didn't remember that. Kellock said Vernon Ince remained quiet during their conversation in the order office.

Malcolm Brown, Vernon's friend and hunting partner, testified that he had accompanied the Inces to the order office and waited in the car when they went inside. When they came out, Vernon said, "I knew you were lying. What did you do with the money?" And when Vernon threatened to kill Ella, she told him she had loaned it to Peter Keating.

Brown said that on the drive back to the Ince house, Vernon "made a couple of swipes" at Ella and that he raised his arm to ward them off.

Peter Keating testified that the Inces had approached him on the morning of November 7 and Ella asked, "Didn't I give you $30?" He said that when he told her, "No, you didn't, Ella," Vernon said, "Peter won't lie for you," and then they left. Questioned by Manning, Keating said Ella seemed scared or frightened and "worked up" over the $30.

Ambulance driver Hillman Payne told the court he removed a set of keys from Vernon's hand before placing him in the ambulance. He said he gave the keys to Vernon's uncle, Bedford Field. On the witness stand, Field confirmed receiving the keys and said he gave them to Corporal King of the RCMP.

King testified that he arrived from the New Glasgow detachment and learned that Vernon's body had already been removed, but he found a pool of fresh blood in front of the Maple Street store and bloodstains on the driveway and back steps of the Ince apartment. There was also a cap and a blood-stained dressing lying on the driveway. He said his men removed several metal (bullet) fragments from the porch and kitchen walls inside the apartment.

King said the .30-30 Winchester rifle was found in the baby carriage in the living room with one expended cartridge in the breech. In the pocket of the gun case found nearby were eight rounds of .30-30 ammunition. Ella and her mother, who "appeared injured about the face," were in the house when he arrived, King said.

King had taken a statement from Ella during that visit, but Manning didn't want it admitted as evidence because the officer had failed to take down what she'd told him about the long-time abuse she had suffered. King told the court he had written down what he considered "pertinent." Mr. Justice Hall ordered the jury to retire to the jury room while he heard arguments from Crown Prosecutor MacDonald and Manning before ruling on the admissibility of the statement.

THAT EXACT SCENARIO WAS REPLAYED in a quaint historical courtroom in Liverpool, Nova Scotia, thirty years later when Jane Hurshman's lawyer, Alan Ferrier, fought to exclude her first statement to the RCMP after she shot Billy Stafford. The young lawyer argued that the statement was taken after the police had kept her up all night and that it (like Ella's) didn't include the unremitting abuse she had suffered. The presiding judge ordered the jury out while the matter was debated.[12]

"The course of the evening was in fact designed to tire and frustrate a woman who was obviously very placid and quiet; who was under the influence of drugs [Valium]; and it was a design on their part to create an atmosphere of sympathy—to give her the impression that they understood her," said Ferrier. "She was almost constantly with one police officer or another for a period of nine hours from one o'clock in the morning until approximately 10. How would the average citizen react to that..." Crown Attorney Blaine Allaby countered that "at no time was there any threat, promise or inducement" given to Jane and that she was dealt with "in a reasonable, friendly, and...sympathetic manner." Ferrier said that to allow the statement into evidence would "bring the administration of justice into disrepute."

Mr. Justice D. Burchell said the conduct of the police "does raise some questions in my mind. It has not been explained, for example, why it was necessary to take the accused into custody in the middle of the night. The question is...whether the police deliberately set about to deprive the accused of sleep so as to make her compliant under interrogation." However, he eventually concluded that he was unable to determine if the police methods "affected the operating mind of the accused, nor am I able to say that of themselves they offend standards of decency or offend the integrity of the judicial process."

But he then turned to another of Ferrier's arguments—one also relevant in Ella's case. RCMP staff sergeant Peter Williamson, who took Jane's statement, had failed to include her account of Billy's battering and abuse against the two children. The officer testified that he excluded those incidents of abuse from the statement because he felt that they had occurred in the past and weren't relevant to the shooting.

"I take a serious view of the question of whether the statement that has been reduced to writing was a complete statement of the disclosures of the accused," stated Burchell. "If the prosecution decides to induce a confession, it must take the whole of it together and cannot select one part and leave another. On that ground, rather than on the issue of freeness and voluntariness, I conclude that the statement should not be admitted."

MR. JUSTICE HALL CAME TO THE SAME conclusion in Ella Ince's case. "A statement must be a complete statement or it is not a statement at all," he said. "As I understand it, she made quite a statement, and then later it was taken down. The first statement that was spontaneous is not here. It is not a complete record of what Mrs. Ince said. You only put down what you thought was relevant."

He ruled the statement was inadmissible, and the jury was returned. Corporal King resumed his testimony, telling the court he retrieved a hundred rounds of ammunition in the upstairs bedroom of the Ince apartment, as well as Vernon's bootleg stash, a large amount of beer and liquor, which he confiscated. When he first arrived at the residence, he said, Ella was crying but "became quite composed" after ten minutes or so, and neither she nor her mother was hysterical.

The last two witnesses for the prosecution were the RCMP officers who identified metal fragments they had removed from the wall in the porch of the Ince apartment and the blood-soaked shirt and sweater Vernon had been wearing when he was shot. The court adjourned just after 5 p.m.

When court resumed the next morning at 10 a.m., Ella Ince was the only witness called for the defence. With Dr. Dunn close by, Ella was apprehensive as she stepped into the witness box that Friday morning and was sworn in. Including Crown prosecutor MacDonald's cross-examination, she would be on the witness stand for just over an hour.

Under Charlie Manning's gentle prodding, she testified about her life with Vernon. She told Manning that when they were dating, Vernon had treated her very well, but it wasn't long after their marriage in May of 1949 that she "got a beating" from her husband for interfering over money matters. There were continual arguments over his using his money for gambling while she and the children went without at home, and every time they argued, she "got a licking."

Later in their relationship, she testified, Vernon began seeing other women and told her it was none of her business because he "didn't class himself as a married man." And in early June of 1951, after a serious argument, Vernon had beaten her and forced her out of the house [in her nightgown]. She said she and her son, Donald, had stayed with her mother in Westville, but Vernon's mother kept her daughter, Estelle. Vernon paid no support while they were separated and she returned to him in September, "partly to get her daughter back" from his mother. She said their relationship improved for a time, but soon there were confrontations when she discovered he was selling liquor for a living. She implored him to stop, "for the sake of the children." But he told her he was in a partnership [with his mother], refused to stop bootlegging, and beat her "for interfering in his business."

Ella testified that on the Saturday before Vernon died, she had paid a furniture bill at Eaton's with $30.40 of "liquor money" that she found in the house. When Vernon found out, she said he knocked her to the floor, kicked her, and pushed her down a flight of stairs, yelling that the money belonged to his mother.

Under questioning about the sleeping bag, she said Vernon told her to order it even though there were pressing needs at home and the hunting camp he was going to was well equipped with a stove and plenty of blankets. She felt the children needed winter clothing more than he needed a sleeping bag—which she believed he wanted only because Malcolm Brown had one.

Ella told the court her mother was at her house to help her on the morning of November 7 because she was still recovering from the injuries Vernon had inflicted on her the week before. She said that when Vernon caught her in the lie about the sleeping bag from Eaton's, she told him she had loaned the money to Peter Keating because she thought Keating was working and wouldn't return until after Vernon had left on his hunting trip.

When her husband tried to force her to go with him to Keating's home, she said, she was terrified and ran toward the house because Vernon told her that if Keating didn't have the money, she wouldn't be coming back.

"He told me I had to get the money before he left for camp or else I wouldn't be living long enough to get anybody any money," she testified.

Ella also told the court about escaping into the house when Vernon went after her mother, who was holding Estelle in her arms, and how the door slammed shut and automatically locked her in. She tried to escape through the living room window, but it wouldn't open wide enough. It was then that she'd picked up his hunting rifle and loaded one cartridge, hoping, she said, to scare him by firing it.

Everything happened quickly, said Ella, and the door suddenly burst open, and when she told him to leave her alone, Vernon came at her and said, "You fucking bitch, I'll kill you. You haven't got guts enough to pull the trigger." She testified she didn't know how she was holding the gun, but, "It exploded. He made a race at me, and I jumped back in the living room and the gun went off and Vernon said, 'Ella... Oh, Ella,' and ran out of the house." She said she didn't know where the bullet had gone and followed him out and saw him drop on the sidewalk. Leaning over him, she saw blood on his back and called out to him, but he didn't respond.

Convinced that all the other evidence they needed had been drawn from Crown witnesses during cross-examination, Charlie Manning rested the defence. Mr. Justice Hall called a fifteen-minute recess, and the trial resumed at 11:30 with Manning addressing the jurors. He spoke for half an hour, urging them to consider the extreme abuse Ella endured at the hands of her husband, culminating in the events of November 7.

"One thing about this case is the surprising maturity of this child, who stayed with her children and tried to do what she could for them," Manning said. "She was kicked out and went back, only to be beaten up again. I don't want to dwell on the aspects of the man's character, but it was one despicable thing after another until he wrote his own ticket to the grave."

Manning said that in the moments just prior to the shooting, "The door was closed and she was trapped, with no way to get away from this maniac. He hadn't been drinking—it was the normal behaviour of this man with his girl-wife. She was half-crazed, looking for some means of protection from this man, not more than six or seven feet from her, crouching over, ready for the spring.

"If ever there was a case where a person was justified in using force, this is it. I suggest she told you the accurate truth. The Crown did not prove the bullet came out of the rifle. Before she went on the stand, there was no evidence to say Ella pulled the trigger. She went on the stand and told you the precise facts, and I don't think there lives a human being who could possibly say this woman is guilty of murder, but a murder tag has been put on her— I say unjustly. She had been used worse than an animal, because if it had been an animal, the SPCA would have stepped in, but because she was a woman, no one lifted a hand. She has been in jail for six or seven months under conditions that are well known. The charge of murder was a mistake. I am not blaming the Mounted Police. I have always found Corporal King to be a gentleman, and I am not blaming him in the least."

Manning asked the jury to rule that Ella had acted in self-defence and urged a verdict of not guilty.

Crown Prosecutor MacDonald, whose final argument went on for twenty-five minutes, argued for a conviction on manslaughter. "With God's help, may you bring in the proper verdict," he said in closing.

The court recessed for lunch at 12:30 p.m., and when it resumed at 1:45, Mr. Justice Hall began his seventy-minute charge to the jury, reviewing the evidence, explaining the law, and outlining the three possible verdicts open to them: guilty of *murder* if Ella fired with the intent to kill; guilty of *manslaughter* if she shot to kill but under severe provocation; or *not guilty* if they were convinced she fired the shot in self-defence.

The judge said the case had attracted a lot of publicity and warned the jurors that anything they may have heard that had not been brought out in the trial should be "put out of your minds."

He told them to consider only the facts and testimony that had been brought forward in the preceding two days.

"If, on the evidence, you have no reasonable doubt, you must find her guilty," he said, "but equally so, if you have reasonable doubt as to her guilt, you must acquit her."

Quoting from the Criminal Code, Hall said, "Everyone unlawfully assaulted, not having provoked such an assault, is justified, though he causes death or grievous bodily harm, if he causes it under a reasonable apprehension of death or grievous bodily harm from the violence with which the assault was originally made and if he believes on reasonable grounds that he could not otherwise preserve himself from death or grievous bodily harm."

Hall said Ella "was not a husky woman. Her husband had beaten her, and there was evidence of hair freshly torn from an area one-inch in diameter, a bruise on her thigh showing fingerprints where she said he held her down. She was trying to avoid him and she went as quickly as she could." He said she was "frantic" to get out the window and, "There is every reason to believe the young girl shot her husband when he was in a position of attack. She was justified in her terror in shooting to protect herself. She had done nothing to provoke this attack upon her as he rushed at her with threats."

The final arguments by Manning, MacDonald, and Mr. Justice Hall were all a blur to Ella. "They had me sedated and I couldn't begin to tell you half of what they said. I was medicated to keep me calm and the doctor was sitting beside me, and I remember him taking my pulse and asking me if I was all right."

After Hall's charge to the jury, the jurors retired to the jury room just before 3 p.m.

"The place was full of people, and there were people outside in the halls when the jury went into deliberations," says Ella. "And the judge said I would return to my cell and they would come back

Five-year-old Ella (right) with her cousin Dorothy Muir (Watters).
(*Courtesy of Karen Gardiner and Bill Lyons*)

Ella with her parents Pearl and John (Recky) Armour.
(*Courtesy of Karen Gardiner and Bill Lyons*)

Ella in her teen years.
(*Courtesy of Karen Gardiner and Bill Lyons*)

Vernon Ince (left) boxing with friends.
(*Courtesy of Doug Ince*)

Vernon (right) with his mother Dorothy May Ince and a friend.
(*Courtesy of Doug Ince*)

Ella and Vernon's wedding. Doug Ince (left) best man at the wedding.
(Courtesy of Karen Gardiner and Bill Lyons)

Ella and Vernon.
(Courtesy of Doug Ince)

The house at "Asphalt Crossing" where Vernon Ince was shot. He died on the sidewalk in front. (*Brian Vallée*)

Doug Ince at Vernon's gravesite in 1951 . . . (*Courtesy of Doug Ince*)

and more than half a century later. (*Brian Vallée*)

A real Coal Miner's Daughter runs queen of country bars

CFHAMILTON - Bars (Drinking Establishments)

By DAVID WESLEY
Spectator Staff

THE GIRL IN the stetson took a long draw on her cigarette, leaned back and smiled. "If you can't feel relaxed at Elly's Place, mister, you never will."

During the day, Diane is a bank teller downtown. At night, she puts on her hat and heads for Elly's. Diane grew up with country and western music. Her parents, like so many other Hamiltonians, bought country records and made the yearly bus pilgrimage to Nashville.

If Texas has Gilley's, Hamilton has Elly's. Patrons come from as far away as Windsor and Ottawa, and a Toronto critic recently hailed it as the best country bar in the region.

On Wednesday, the deadest night downtown, it's almost full. On weekends there are lineups at the door.

As rock houses close right and left and disco does its last dive, country bars are popping up like prairie wheat. From the Golden Valley Inn in Dundas to Longhorn's and Rodney's on the Mountain, to the Leisure Place in the east end, more clubs in Hamilton with live

Now stars like Carroll Baker regularly drop in and sit in the audience with me."

Elly's used to be Duffy's Rock Pile, noted for brawls and bikers. Elly's is now full of smiling faces, known for its inexpensive roast beef, prime ribs and lobster tails, with Elly herself a certified chef.

THERE IS room for nearly 300 at Elly's. Long-haired construction workers chat with the likes of Paul Hanover and Mayor Jack MacDonald. Steelworkers and students rub shoulders with off-duty cops and

Hamilton Spectator

Elly with third husband, Harry Goodchild. (*Courtesy of Karen Gardiner and Bill Lyons*)

Miss Elly onstage with musicians at her Hamilton club, Elly's Place. (*Courtesy of Karen Gardiner and Bill Lyons*)

Elly's daughter Cynthia (Cindy).
(*Courtesy of Karen Gardiner and Bill Lyons*)

Elly's daughters Kathy (left) and Karen.
(*Brian Vallée*)

Miss Elly sings at a charity event with
singer-songwriter Ray Griff looking on.
(*Courtesy of Karen Gardiner and Bill Lyons*)

Elly with her common-
law husband Bill Lyons
who was with her for
the last 17 years of her
life. (*Courtesy of Karen
Gardiner and Bill Lyons*)

Canadian Country music singer Julian Austin with Miss Elly and Bill Lyons.
(*Courtesy of Karen Gardiner and Bill Lyons*)

Miss Elly's favourite "studio" photo.
(*Courtesy of Karen Gardiner and Bill Lyons*)

Mel MacLean, Elly's former boyfriend who still lives in Stellarton's "Asphalt" and speaks his mind.
(*Brian Vallée*)

Jane Hurshman.

Billy Stafford who
loved his guns.

Billy's decapitated body in the front seat of his truck, March 1982.
(*Photos from Brian Vallee's book* Life with Billy)

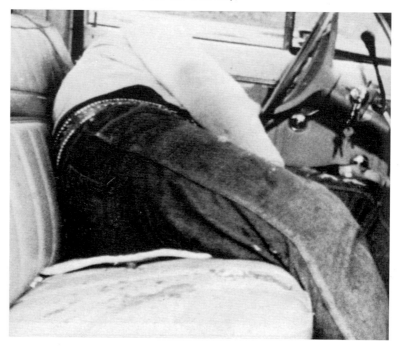

for me when the jury came in. I remember talking to my lawyers, and then I think I took only five or six steps out of the prisoner's box to leave when a buzzer rang or somebody came out—I can't remember exactly what happened—but all of a sudden the judge was back there, and he sat down and rapped his gavel and says the court is back in order."

Spectators, lawyers for both sides, and court officials were shocked when word came back from the jury room that a decision had been reached after just nine minutes.

"They were going to put me back in the prisoner's box," says Ella, "but the judge said, 'No, she does not go back in there,' and the doctor stood beside me and took my arm and I didn't even have to move—just stand there. The lawyers were sitting at the table. They weren't near me."

There wasn't a sound in the courtroom as proceedings resumed and the jury was quickly polled. "Gentlemen of the jury, have you agreed upon a verdict?" asked the court clerk. Ella's uncle, Alex Muir, was smiling broadly as he rose and said, "We find the prisoner not guilty."

The courtroom erupted in cheers and clapping as Mr. Justice Hall, who was also smiling, raised his hand for order. Ella's eyes filled with tears as she fought to control her emotions. "Well, the whole place went crazy," she says. "They were cheering and clapping, and the judge was trying to get everybody to stop and he's hitting the gavel, and people are coming over and they're pulling at my clothes and they're trying to touch me."

Order was somewhat restored, and Hall said he had to release the prisoner and discharge the jury. He quickly endorsed the jury's decision, saying as he discharged them for the final time, "I have no quarrel with your verdict and I think the evidence supports it." He then told Ella she was free to go and departed the bench to the safety of his chambers.

Ella was again swarmed by well-wishers and the news quickly spread to the large crowd waiting outside. "It was just like a movie," said Ella. "I couldn't believe I was free and it all happened so fast. I didn't know if they were for me or against me. It was total confusion. And they're trying to get me out of there to the door."

NOT EVEN IN HER MOST OPTIMISTIC moments could Jane Hurshman imagine for herself a Hollywood ending like Ella's. The trial in Pictou ended after just two days, but Jane's trial in Liverpool ran for eighteen. The courtroom was full every day and it was a gruelling, humiliating ordeal for Jane, who had to testify publicly about Billy Stafford's abuse against her and her son.

"I couldn't think," said Jane later. "And my sanity was wearing very thin. I just drifted from day to day, waiting and wondering when it would all end. There were times I was so frightened I didn't think I'd make it through the coming day."

As her day on the witness stand approached, Jane had nightmares and began losing weight. She couldn't sleep, and dark circles ringed her pale blue eyes. "I was terrified," she said. "I had two main fears. The main one was that they would show me pictures of Bill's body. I didn't know it until I read it in the newspaper that he was decapitated. The other fear was that I would get a mental block and just sit there and forget everything I had to say."[13]

On the first day of her testimony, she had been on the stand for two hours when the court adjourned. "I was not allowed to talk to anyone because I was still under oath. I felt awful— deserted. I had to go home and think all night about having to come back in the morning and take that stand again." Jane did go back to court and completed her testimony after another two and a half hours on the stand.

After an isolated existence in a small rural hamlet for several years, she was now forced to run a daily gauntlet of well-wishers and television and newspaper reporters scrambling for a quote. "Reporters were always waiting for me to arrive in the morning and again when I left at night," she said. "Thank God Alan [Ferrier] was there to reassure me. He told me just to say, 'No comment,' and that's what I did, day after day."[14]

The public and media attention were focused on the trial not only because there was widespread sympathy for Jane in a community aware of Billy Stafford's reputation, but also because the case seemed tailor-made to serve as a battleground for the women's movement in its struggle against male oppression and criminal domestic violence.

Nor was Jane as fortunate as Ella when it came to jury selection. While Ella's uncle was permitted to stay on as jury foreman, Doris Whynot was removed from Jane's jury when it was revealed that she knew the accused. The case proceeded with eleven jurors instead of twelve.[15]

In Alan Ferrier's final summation to the jury, it was evident that the best he was hoping for was a verdict of guilty to manslaughter, believing the judge would consider the abuse she had gone through and give Jane a light sentence. "The law is that the Crown must disprove provocation," he said. "It is not for the defence to prove it. The Crown must establish that this murder happened . . . without provocation. If you have any doubt whatsoever about provocation . . . it is an acquittal on the charge of murder, and a guilty finding on manslaughter. I urge that on you in the strongest way after hearing all of the evidence that you have heard."

Crown Attorney Blaine Allaby insisted in his closing "that first-degree murder is what this is. We may sympathize with Jane in her situation, but the law is the law, and what do we say to people out there? I would submit in this case we have to say we sympathize, but what you did was planned and deliberate, was not provoked, and was first-degree murder."[16]

Mr. Justice Burchell told the jury it could return one of four verdicts: guilty of first-degree murder, guilty of second-degree murder, guilty of manslaughter, or not guilty.[17] The jury began deliberations at 5:30 p.m., was sequestered in a local hotel overnight, and reached a verdict the next morning at 11:30 a.m.

The night before, Jane had packed a small suitcase to ready herself for prison, and in the morning, before arriving at the court, she said her goodbyes to her children and her family. Alan Ferrier had told her, "The longer the jury is out, the worse things look."

"They were out too long," said Jane. "I was sure I was going to prison for the rest of my life. I was mentally and physically exhausted...I sat there like a statue. But my heart was pounding so hard I thought that everyone else could hear it."

The jury filed in, but when the court clerk asked the foreman to hand him the indictment, he was told it had yet to be filled in. "We thought that was to be done here," said the foreman. "No, you must write it inside and bring it to me," said the clerk.

The jurors filed out of the courtroom to fill in the indictment. Alan Ferrier was out of his chair, pacing back and forth. Jane sat motionless. "I said a silent prayer," she said. "I couldn't take any more."

Jane stood up with Ferrier at her side as the jury returned a few minutes later. They announced that they had reached a verdict and passed the folded indictment to the clerk.

"Mr. Foreman, what was your verdict?" asked the clerk.

"Not guilty!"

The uproar that followed mirrored the outburst when Ella Ince was found not guilty. There were cheers, applause, tears of joy, and shouts of "Praise the Lord." Jane says that she was in shock. "I couldn't believe the verdict," she said. "Alan had prepared me for the worst. I didn't know how to accept the best. I'd never once allowed myself to think the verdict might be not guilty. Then everyone was hugging me, shaking hands. It was too much."[18] Alan Ferrier rescued Jane from the excited crowd pressing in on her, and in a quiet back room he warned her there would likely be an appeal. There was, and Jane was eventually found guilty of manslaughter and served two months of a six-month sentence.

Ferrier said many in the legal community thought it wasn't proper that Billy's character was on trial in the case. "But in some cases it's necessary," he said, "and in some cases it's obviously more important than the character of your client, because even if your client is charged with shooting...as Jane was in this case, her individual act of violence paled by comparison with the continuous acts of violence that this man perpetrated against her and her child."[19]

THE NOISE AND THE PRESSURE of the crowd were tumultuous when Ella made her way out of the courthouse. "I got the shock of my life when I walked outside," she says. "There were already a lot of people outside, and then all the ones from the court went out there too. I thought, how am I going to get out of here? I wanted to go back to the jail to get my things from the cell, but my lawyer said, 'No, there are too many people; you've got to get into the car.' They put me into their car and I left everything behind.

"We were ready to go, but the crowd wouldn't budge. They were still cheering. The police had a terrible time moving them aside so the car could get on its way. But a police car came up and led us through the crowd. It was a mad zoo."

Finally, Ella was on her way to Westville, to her parents' house, where her children waited. "I had a violent headache from the crowds and the stress and I felt sick to my stomach, but I was glad to be going home to peace and quiet," she said.

But it wasn't the homecoming Ella envisioned. As they turned onto Irving Street, "There were cars and people everywhere, and they were clapping and cheering as we passed by. And when we got to my parents' place, there was nowhere to park. The lawyers just stopped in the middle of the street and took me into the house. We entered through the back door—through a utility room that led directly to the kitchen. It was there that my parents had set up the big black old-fashioned rocking chair, and they put cushions on it for me and I sat down there.

"The place was jammed with people and I was so tired, I thought I was going to collapse. Then they started filing through the back door and out the front, shaking my hand or hugging and kissing me as they went by. It seemed to go on forever. I tried to be nice to everyone because they were happy for me. But I felt totally exhausted and the violent headache was making me very ill. Finally I said, "I'm sorry, I just have to lie down.'

"As I lay in bed, the realization that I was now free had set in, and I had nothing to be scared of for the first time in years. I just felt completely drained, and Cynthia was born a week later, on June 6. It was nice weather."

NOT EVERYBODY WAS HAPPY with the verdict. Doug Ince's uncle, Bedford Field, testified at the trial about Vernon's car keys and stayed on to listen to the witnesses who followed him and to the summations and verdict. "He was my mother's brother, and he was awfully mad when he came home because Ella's uncle was the foreman of the jury," says Doug. "He came over after and he was pretty upset. Jesus, he was some wild. He said it was all cut and dried before he even went there. Him [Alex Muir] being foreman of the jury tells you something right there."

But Alex Muir's son, Fraser, now in his eighties, says his father was known for his honesty and always "believed Ella would have got off no matter who was foreman." It would be difficult to argue against that logic, given Mr. Justice Hall's endorsement of the jury's verdict.

Doug says he didn't go to the preliminary or the trial, but his wife did. "Sue had to go because she saw it and she was a witness," he said. Does Doug think justice was done? "I wouldn't say that Vernon didn't hit her a few times, and he most likely pulled her hair," he says, "but I don't think it was as bad as she says. It's hard to say. I mean, we weren't there. I never heard them fighting, but we were just there a couple of months at that place.

"It should never have happened. I know Ella's father taught her to use guns, and I thought she might have fired a shot to scare him. But as time went on, I thought she never would want to shoot her mother, and her mother was standing behind him. So I figured she didn't mean to do it, but in a temper it just happened. When I look back, it was just one of those quick things and it happened."

The Asphalt's homespun philosopher, raconteur, and confirmed bachelor Mel MacLean, who is Doug's neighbour and longtime friend, knew Vernon and Ella. He is reticent to pass judgment but says Vernon "wasn't well thought of." There is one thing MacLean is certain about: he doesn't like men assaulting women. "But if it ever comes a day that I would hit a woman, then, by the Jesus, I could see me a terrible man if I did that. I don't say I don't get mad and argue, but I'd go out the door and go and cool off."

In the courtroom melee after the verdict, Ella says she caught a fleeting glance from the Crown prosecutor, who looked as if he was trying to make his way toward her. "There were just too many people crowded in there and he couldn't make it through," she said. "But he told one of my lawyers later that he agreed 100 per cent with the verdict, even though he lost the case. He said, 'The man just kept going and going until he dug his own grave.'

"I am not proud of what happened. And I feel no malice. I just feel sorry that it happened, and if I could undo it, I would. I was 95 pounds. He was 195 pounds. I'm five-foot-two and he was five-foot ten. So what chance did I have?"

11

Troubled Odyssey

Seema Badhan, 19. Toronto. Seema was thrown off the tenth-floor balcony of the building where she lived with her estranged husband. Neighbours heard screams and arguing but ignored it; then one heard a "huge, huge scream" and saw Seema lifeless on the ground below. Neighbours described the man as "peace-loving" and the couple as "so in love." Zohaib Shaukat was charged at the scene with first-degree murder. (May 2006)

C YNTHIA INCE WAS BORN ON THE EIGHTH ANNIVERSARY OF D-Day, exactly one week after her mother was acquitted of murdering her father. "It was a very difficult birth because I had very little exercise all the time I was in jail, and with all the tension and anxiety, I guess my muscles were all knotted up," said Ella. "But I got through it."

With just three weeks until her own birthday—she would be twenty on July 2, 1952—the young mother, with a baby and two toddlers, was free after seven months in jail and two and a half years in an abusive marriage. It was with considerable trepidation that she faced the future. She wondered if she could ever have the normal life she had envisioned when, as a confident sixteen-year-old, secure in her bed in her parents' home, she had daydreamed about her pending marriage to Vernon Ince. She knew she would need considerable material and emotional support from Pearl and Recky, the parents who had argued so passionately against her marrying Vernon.

Ella Ince had gone, under police escort, to Vernon's "viewing" at his aunt's house, where the coffin was set up in the living room. She remembered a rush of "mixed emotions," including guilt, and "it was a relief to leave there." But she hadn't attended Vernon's funeral and didn't know where he was buried.

Some weeks after her trial, she decided to visit his grave. "People told me where he was buried, and I used to ride a bicycle two miles to get there and two miles back," she said. "The first time I went, there was nothing there but a mound of dirt. It was an unmarked grave."[1] Over three or four visits, she "picked rocks out, levelled it off with a rake, and planted grass seed."

One day when Ella was tending the grave, the caretaker approached. "Are you crazy, after what that man did to you?" he asked.

"No matter what he did, he's still the children's father," she said.

Ella became emotional when she talked about why she *really* went to Vernon's grave. "I went in search of answers," she said. "I wanted to ask him things. I didn't understand why he did what he did. Almost from the day I said 'I do,' it started. It was terrible. And it never changed—it got worse. I wanted to ask him *why*. But how do you talk to a grave?" She paused, her jaw tightening and her eyes misting. "I can't talk about this," she said softly.

At first, Ella seldom ventured from the house. She continued to feel deep embarrassment, shame, and some guilt over Vernon's death.

IT ISN'T UNUSUAL FOR SEVERELY battered women who have killed their abusers to experience enduring guilt over the deaths, even though the women believe that they were unquestionably in an untenable *killed or be killed* situation.

While Jane Hurshman was in prison in the spring of 1984, Billy's father, Lamont Stafford, in a letter to the *Liverpool Advance,* said, "It is all very well to give statements to the court and to the newspaper when the one person who can deny them is dead...The many people who could have been called to testify on his behalf were never summoned by the Crown."[2]

A couple of days later, the newspaper requested an interview with Jane, but she turned them down. "I read Lamont's piece that was published this week and I wish no more hurt or bad feeling to him," she wrote the *Advance.* "He is a fine man and I respect him very much, but he has suffered dearly and I choose not to have any more printed, even if only for that reason. He is a man who has been good to me over the years, and I just want to let my past rest now."[3]

But years later, Jane was still plagued by guilt over Billy's death. Writing to a friend, she said, "He was a miserable SOB who deserved what he got, but it is extremely hard for me to deal with...because I cannot forgive myself. No matter what, Bill was a human being. I am not sorry that he is dead, but I am sorry it had to end the way it did—so violently."

Her guilt, combined with long-buried childhood trauma and Billy's abuse, led to serious problems with kleptomania. She shoplifted items she didn't need and could certainly afford. Arrests, court appearances, and embarrassing publicity followed. "There are times when I am angry over what he did, and all of its after-effects—I mean my shoplifting," wrote Jane. "By doing that, I shame and humiliate my kids and my family and hurt myself. It is my way of punishing myself for what I did—because of what he did to me." Even with counselling and psychiatric treatment, her compulsion persisted.

At one of her court appearances, where she was accused of stealing a child's jogging suit and two planter trays with a total value of $37.96, Jane, who by then was well known as a public speaker on behalf of battered women, said she wanted to stop shoplifting but couldn't help herself. The prosecutor asked her, "How much do you want to stop doing it?" Jane thought for a few seconds and said, "If I thought of the thing that I would *not* want to lose the most, it would probably be my eyesight—and I would trade that."[4]

Two weeks before that incident, she had started weekly visits to psychiatrist John Curtis, and she vowed to continue them until her problem was resolved. Dr. Curtis testified that "Jane has spent a lifetime of having things done to her—horrible things—and has never really expressed anger. Jane herself has no conscious intent or desire to steal. Her everyday self is in fact a very fine, caring, honourable, honest person who would never steal or do anything like that, but she does have ego states inside her that would do this— for very childlike and immature reasons."[5]

He said the reason Jane had a heightened urge to steal at that time "has to do with the fact that she's getting better. That may seem rather odd to you, but Billy, her husband, could not stand her doing well. Her father could not stand her doing well, and she was continually put down by these people. And this ego state [within her] is modelled after those people. So here you have an ego state that's going to get you in trouble if you do well."[6] Defence lawyer Linda Tippett said Jane was not insane. "However, she does have an illness that at the time of this incident rendered her incapable of forming the type of intent needed to sustain a conviction. A kleptomaniac she is—a thief she is not."

Provincial Court Judge Patrick Curran reserved his decision, saying he was not aware of a precedent for kleptomania "being recognized as a defence to a charge such as this. But I think there's a very important question raised here." In his decision of July 17, 1989, he found her guilty of shoplifting as charged but accepted her reduced responsibility as outlined by Dr. Curtis and commended her for seeking help. He placed her on probation and ordered her to continue her therapy. But he warned, "Notwithstanding some measure of reduced responsibility, the time is going to come sooner or later when the courts are going to conclude the only way to stop this kind of thing is to put you in jail for some period of time—which would be most unfortunate, especially since it seems in every other way that you live a praiseworthy kind of life."[7]

RCMP CORPORAL GEORGE BYRON KING, the officer who arrested Ella and then took a special interest in her welfare during her seven months in jail, became a more avid suitor once she was released. King was born in Nelson, British Columbia, joined the RCMP in 1935, and after training and service in Ontario was posted to H Division in Nova Scotia, eventually taking command of the New Glasgow detachment.[8] Ella appreciated his kindness in escorting her to visit her parents during her incarceration. After the visits, they would go out for dinner in Digby or Antigonish, where they wouldn't be recognized, but she wasn't interested in dating him.

The people who had once counselled Ella against marrying Vernon Ince were now urging her to marry King. Tina, Pearl's sister, had moved from Stellarton to Westville after the death of her husband. "We were just two doors away," says Tina's daughter, Bessie. "I was there and my mother was there and I certainly remember the discussions. They were encouraging Ella to marry him, saying basically it was a chance to change her life. She had three kids, and it was the answer to making a better life for herself.

He was a nice man and he would be good to her. There wouldn't be any more abuse."

Ella thought the arguments contradictory: they had told her *not* to marry Vernon because he was too old for her even though the age difference was only two and a half years, yet now they were saying she should marry George King, who, at forty-two, was twenty-two years older than she was. "All my family and friends said, 'Marry him, you'll have everything you want, he'll be good to you,'" said Ella. "I said no way—I didn't want to marry anyone." Her cousin Bessie said King "was a very good-looking man, and he did love her. And of course everybody wanted a better life for her because she had been through so much. But she felt he was too old for her."

Ella said it was more than the age difference. She simply wasn't in love with him, and her mind was still in turmoil from the past three years. "And don't forget—he was the arresting officer who charged me with murder," she said.

The RCMP eventually transferred King to another part of the province, but he continued to drive to her parents' place to take her out on his days off. "It was like a two-hour drive each way for him just to come and take me to dinner," said Ella. "He was a kind, thoughtful person, but I felt controlled again. He seemed obsessed with me, and he was upset when I refused to go out anymore. He gave me his phone number and told me to call him, but I never did. I didn't mean to hurt him, but I guess I did."[9]

George King wasn't the only visitor Ella wanted to avoid. Two or three weeks after Cynthia was born, Vernon's brother, Doug, arrived at her parents' house to arrange for his family, and his mother in particular, to see the children. "She *was* their grandmother," says Doug.

Ella met him at the door. "I wanted nothing to do with him or his family, so I told him no," she says. "He asked me to step outside. He said, 'If this is the way you want it, never enter the town where I live or you'll be killed.' To me, it was Vernon all over again, with threats. He said even if he didn't do it himself, he could have it arranged. I looked at him, and I was really angry—I felt I had been through enough. I didn't need any more death threats. I thought, 'When will this nightmare end?' He left then, and I went in and told my parents. I wasn't going to hide anything anymore. I was so upset."

Doug admits that he might have said something like that, but it had nothing to do with revenge over Vernon. It was because Ella was refusing access to the children. It was particularly hurtful to his mother, who had often looked after the children and had always been kind and generous to them. Doug says it's been more than fifty years and "too far back to remember" what was said between him and Ella, but anything he did say was "just words" in anger and he certainly would never have harmed her or anyone else. Those who know Doug agree. They say he is easygoing and it's not in his nature to be violent or hurtful.

It was her mother's persistent pestering that eventually ended Ella's self-imposed isolation. "Go out. You have lots of friends who will be glad to see you," Pearl would say.

"I wasn't hiding by staying home," says Ella. "I just didn't know who to talk to or not talk to, because people are funny when it comes to such a serious matter and I didn't know how they felt. I was also scared about crowds of people flocking around me like they did in the courtroom. I thought they might want to talk to me about what had happened, and I made a decision that I would not discuss it with anyone. They were either at the trial or had read about it in the newspapers and that was enough."

Ella decided that taking a bus ride would be a good way to test the reaction she would get if she started going out in public. "I took the bus just to see what people's reaction would be when they saw me," she said. "I made a point of sitting by myself so I wouldn't embarrass anyone and they wouldn't feel obligated to speak to me just because they knew me. So I sat by myself, and if they wanted to speak to me or sit with me, they could."

She was surprised when most people who knew her *did* sit and talk with her—and not one raised the subject of Vernon's death or her trial.

DURING HER SEPARATION FROM Vernon in the summer of 1951, when Ella lived with her parents, she had been out alone for an evening walk when she saw eighteen-year-old Mel MacLean with some of his male friends. She had met him once or twice through Vernon, but he wasn't aware that the couple had separated. She approached him, but Mel brushed her off.

It would be more than two years before Ella would see Mel again. Once she realized she wasn't being ostracized, about a year after her acquittal she began going out and was soon zipping around the ice on her beloved skates at the Stellarton Memorial Rink. There, in the fall of 1953, she again encountered Mel MacLean, then twenty, a year younger than she was. This time he didn't shy away, and the attraction was mutual. She didn't trust men, but he seemed charming. And innocent.

"I used to skate, and Ella loved skating too," says Mel. "She was skating that night, and that's how it all started." She accepted when Mel offered to drive her home after skating.

Melford J. MacLean—"The J stands for Johnson," he says. "There was a neighbour down there and his name was Melford Johnson, so they called me after him and put MacLean on the end of it"—had quit school in fourth grade, but he'd had a car since he was seventeen. "The first one cost only $50. My father bought it from a fella and it wasn't working right, so he spent his time getting it going for me. And then he says to me, 'Well, if you're going to drive a car, boy, you gotta learn how to fix them yourself'—so that's how I got into that game."

Mel was working as a grease monkey at a service station on Acadia Avenue near his home in the Asphalt at the time he met Ella at the Stellarton arena. Soon after, he started his first serious job, a seventeen-month stint at a warehouse for the Sobey's grocery chain that ended when he was sent home with the mumps and never rehired. "I used to drive there—until I got fired," he said. "Other people say laid off. They don't like to tell you they got fired. I tell it like it is." After that, he spent eight years delivering ice cream and butter for the Pictou County Dairy. "And I got fired there too—for shooting off my mouth."

Mel later spent eighteen years as a driver with Eastern Transport. "They hauled freight: stoves, fridges, furnaces—whatever anybody wanted delivered," he said. "I retired from a company called Polstar—another transport company. I was a truck driver there for nine years. I worked the day of my sixtieth birthday and then I said I'm not going to work any more."

He received a small company pension from Eastern Transport but couldn't collect on it until he was sixty-five. "I got interest on it, and I drew it out over five years. So now I just have my Canada Pension and Old Age Security." But he's not complaining. After his parents died, he tore down the old family home in the Asphalt and had a new one built on the same lot. "When my parents died, they had some money, and I had some money, and that's where I got the help to build this place. I always wanted to have a new house."

The automobiles Mel has owned are signposts along his life's journey. Mel says his first car, "The one I had when I took Ella home the first time, was a '39 Hudson. Then I had a '41 Ford. My brother gave it to me because it wasn't going. My father and I fixed it up. Then I didn't have a car for a while, so I used to drive my brother's. I had a '65 Ford, but I wasn't a Ford lover. My first new car was a '68 Bel Air Chev. Then in '74, I had an Impala four-door hardtop. I would say that was my best car. I guess I had six or seven new cars." He currently drives a 2006 Chevrolet Impala.

When Ella hopped into his '39 Hudson that night after skating, Mel says, his mind "was set on one thing only"—and she went right along with him.

"We're not going to do this every night, are we?" she asked afterwards.

"Oh no," said Mel, "not every night. Just tonight."

"I figured—get the start," he said, remembering that night. "You've got to get a start in everything. So that shows you what kind of mind I had."

It was apparently a fine "start," and they would see a lot of each other over the next three years. They enjoyed each other's company, but other than ice skating and riding around in Mel's car, they didn't have much of a social life.

"She was good to be with," says Mel. "She had a sense of humour and she had her good points. You couldn't beat it. Between me and her, it was six of one and half a dozen of the other. She was good to me."

Even today, Mel seems somewhat mystified that a woman would find him attractive or interesting. "I said before, and I say it again, why would anybody want to bother with me? Cause I don't do anything. I don't drink. I don't smoke. I don't dance. I can't swim. I don't fish. I don't go anywhere that much. All I do is drive around and that's it. That's why I say anybody that would go with me would have to be silly.

"Ella and I went skating a lot, and she liked dancing and stuff like that, but we never went to dances. She didn't drink at all back in my time with her, but I think she lived a little faster than me."

Mel says that he and Ella never once discussed Vernon's death. "His name never came up in all the time I went with her, I used to always think afterwards, does it ever bother her? I think it would bother me. But I shouldn't even be saying that, because you never know what others might be going through."

Mel once joked about it, but there was no response from Ella. "I was out to where she lived on Irving Street, and I said, 'Ella, now, when I knock, don't fire a shot through the door, because I'll be standing to one side and you'll miss, and then I gotcha.' This was when I was first going with her and we used to say a lot of crazy things. She never said, 'Don't be funny,' or anything. I think that's about the only time the subject came up. I was silly, but I'm not a bad fellow."

There was one other awkward incident—when Ella rose from the living room couch at her parents' place, lifted a corner of the linoleum, removed several photos, and without a word handed them to Mel. They were copies of autopsy pictures of Vernon's body taken at the H.C. MacQuarrie Funeral Home in Stellarton after the shooting. "I only remember the one," said Mel. "He was on the slab, lying on his back, and I could see where the bullet went in. By the size of that little hole, you wouldn't think he would die. But I didn't see the other side where it came out. A bullet doesn't do much going in, it does it coming out—it starts ripping, I guess. I'll remember her showing me that until the day I die."

DOUG INCE AND HIS FAMILY PERSISTED in their efforts to see the baby, whom Ella began calling Cindy, and the two other children, Estelle and Donny. Ella had denied them access, but she welcomed Vernon's father, Jimmy Ince, when he came for a visit. "We had dinner and talked over what had happened and we all cried," said Ella. About three years later, Jimmy was found dead along an isolated area of Old Foxbrook Road in Stellarton. "It was a drinking spot they used to go to up there," says Mel MacLean. Doug Ince says, "It was all woods at that time, and a fella coming into work in the morning found him. He was walking back to town and dropped dead. I think he had a heart attack and froze. He was a boozer at the end there. He drank every chance he got. The doctor always told him, 'Jimmy, you're going to die if you keep this up.' That's the way he wanted to go. He was fifty-seven."

Cindy was about eighteen months old when Ella finally relented and allowed the Ince family to visit the children. "When Doug and his mother came up to the house and parked in the yard, I never went out to talk to them," she said. "But my mother would take the kids out to see them. They had to get out of the car, because we were afraid they might take off with them if they got them into the car. Then they talked my mum and dad into letting them take the children to Vernon's mother's place for two hours once a week. I was afraid at first, but they always returned them and treated them like gold. Sometimes they even bought them clothes and things."

At one point, Doug and his wife, Susan, offered to adopt the three children, but Ella refused. "She wouldn't," says Doug. "That's one thing I'll give her credit for. She didn't give her kids up. We eventually adopted two boys and a girl of our own from Pictou County." And they now have two grandchildren.

To help her parents with expenses, Ella worked for a time as a maid for a couple of local doctors, but her life became considerably more complicated when, in October 1954, about a year after she began dating Mel MacLean, she discovered she was pregnant again. If she was distressed about it, he didn't notice. "She was pregnant, but we still went skating," he said. "She said I was the father, but how do you know? Knowing her, I didn't know what to think. She never settled herself to any one person, I don't think."

Ella didn't pressure Mel to get married and they continued their relationship as if all was normal. On July 10, 1955, she gave birth to her fourth child—a second son, christened John but known widely as Jackie. Mel was 450 miles away in Bangor, Maine, when little Jackie came into the world. "I never go anywhere, but this fellow who ran a grocery store was like a father to me," says Mel. "His brother was going to Bangor, and he asked me if I would go with him. I said sure. So I was up there at the time the kid was born."

Ella wasn't in the hospital before he left, and he had no idea she was about to give birth. He was away two days and went out to Ella's place as soon as he heard about the baby. "Jackie was the one born when I was going with her," says Mel. "She was on welfare or mother's allowance or something, and I had to sign a paper for supporting the kid so she could get that for one year or whatever."

Jean Muir, the wife of Ella's cousin Harry, says, "Jackie used to play with our kids when they were little. Ella and Mel were a couple for quite a long time, but they never ever married. I don't know that Mel ever really acknowledged that Jackie was his. I never asked him. But sometimes in the course of conversation you know that Mel knows definitely that Jackie is his son."

Mel's friend and neighbour, Doug Ince, says, "Mel is the father of John all right. You can't dispute it if you see the pictures. He and Ella never lived together. Mel still won't live with anybody."

"I'll tell you why I think I never married," says Mel. "I'm uneducated, and I didn't think I could be a good provider for a marriage. When I worked, I worked steady, but I never made any big money, because I wasn't smart enough to have a job making bigger money. I'm comfortable and I'm doing all right, but I never did much exciting in my life...I just go on from day to day. I figure I did all right for what education I had and what kind of work I did and the money I made—I did all right in later life."

Through the years, nothing much seems to have changed for Mel except that he and his women get older while his cars get newer. He is a contented man with simple tastes, and as he tells the boys at the mall, his only wish concerns his manner of death. "I said I want to die on the nest. I'd have a smile on my face and they'd never be able to wipe it off. So you know how crazy I am."

CINDY DEVELOPED MORE SLOWLY than Estelle and Donny had. Ella believed the beatings inflicted by Vernon while she was pregnant with Cindy were the reason. "She took a longer time to learn to walk and talk," she said. "She probably would have had a fairly normal life, though."

But Cindy would never have a chance at a normal life. On one of their visits to their paternal grandmother, the three children were across the street playing with neighbourhood children when Dorothy May called them for supper. There was no traffic, but Ella said, "When they were halfway across the street, a car came out of a side street very fast. The driver and his passenger were drunk and the car was full of beer and whisky. He missed Estelle, my oldest daughter, but hit Cindy and dragged her seventy-five yards under the car."

Ella was by then managing a restaurant between Stellarton and New Glasgow. "I think it was called the Homestead Restaurant," says her cousin, Bessie Flanders. "It was down near a trailer park by the East River. She was a wonderful cook and pie maker—and I don't know where that came from. She certainly wouldn't have done that at home."

Ella received a call at the restaurant informing her Cindy was seriously injured and they were taking her to the hospital. "They said I'd better get there right away," says Ella. She apologized to her customers and told them they would have to leave. "I said, 'I'm sorry, I have an emergency,' and I kicked them out, shut everything off, and locked the door. It was very fast. I think they were a little perturbed, but I didn't care. I jumped into the car. The hospital was a mile and a half from there and I put the pedal right to the floor. They didn't know if she would live or not. She was unconscious and the skin was all peeled off on one side of her body and her face. Her legs were broken in five places. She had a ruptured spleen, and they had to go in and take the pressure off her brain. The doctors said they did all they could do and it was up to the Lord above whether she would make it or not."

Ella stayed with her daughter for ten straight days and nights. "I slept in a recliner chair and my mother would bring me clean clothes," she said. "Both of Cindy's legs were in traction with sand bags. She started waking up on the eleventh day. But she didn't know me and she couldn't speak—only roll her eyes."

When she returned home almost two months after the accident, Cindy could neither walk nor talk. Gradually, she would learn to do both again, but the brain damage was permanent. She would never learn to read or write and would always need care. "Mentally, she's still like a little girl of six or seven," Ella said, half a century later.

A drunk driver careening down a quiet street was totally unpredictable—a tragic fluke—but Ella blamed herself for allowing the children limited visits with Vernon's family, and she blamed Dorothy May for not paying close enough attention to the children when they were in her care. "His family was never permitted to see the children again," she said. The drunken driver went to penitentiary. "I think he did ten years, but there was no insurance to help out."

ELLA HAD BEEN WORKING HARD to build up her self-confidence. Her bosses at the restaurant were impressed with her management and cooking skills, and despite the birth of a fourth child, she was beginning to feel good about herself for the first time in years. But with Cindy's critical injuries, doubts and self-recrimination resurfaced. She went back to work, but soon her "whole world was turned upside down again" when she received another urgent telephone call, "This time to come home immediately. No reason was given, only that it was an emergency. I thought something happened to Cindy. I told everyone to leave and I shut everything off, called the owners, and locked the doors and left.

"When I got home, Warren MacDonald, Dad's best friend, was there. My aunt and uncle and my mother—all of them were crying. They sat me down and told me my dad had a massive heart attack. He was eating when he suddenly grabbed the tablecloth and fell off the chair to the floor and everything came down on top of him. They said he was dead before he hit the floor." Recky was buried at the Heatherdale cemetery in nearby Sylvester.

The death of her father had a profound effect on Ella. Subconsciously, if not overtly, she blamed his death on the stress she had caused him, first by marrying against his wishes and then by saddling him and Pearl with her four children—stress exacerbated by Cindy's serious injuries. Ella's conduct over the months following Recky's death seemed erratic and frenzied to her family and friends.

THIS COMES AS NO SURPRISE TO Patricia Neilson, a clinical psychologist from British Columbia who has been called as an expert witness in a number of cases of battered women who have killed their spouses in self-defence. She believes the underlying cause of Ella's behaviour after her father's death was the horrific abuse she had suffered in her short marriage.

"Even without the abuse, a young person with four children at a young age as a single parent—that would be tough enough," she says. "But I think the abuse goes pretty deep. It would shake up her sense of who she is and what she's capable of. And can she really commit to a relationship? Does she trust herself as a mother? I mean, earlier on, she wouldn't even have been questioning that. She would have been pretty sure of who she was and how life was supposed to be. She had a strong sense that she was a good person. She had everything going for her and a perfect life. And after you've put all that investment into a relationship that becomes terrifying, horrific, and lethal, it really fundamentally shakes up your sense of who you are and what you can predict in your life—including your own faith in yourself."

Dr. Neilson says Ella did what most young women would do. She "internalized" it—as in *something is wrong with me.* "In other words, she asked herself, 'What's wrong with me that I should be treated this way, that I should be involved in an abusive relationship?' It was probably her first sexual relationship, definitely her first committed relationship. So what was at stake here just magnifies it, and then when it turns against her, it becomes incredibly hurtful, and most internalize that."

FOR ELLA, THAT INTERNALIZATION manifested itself in an almost manic need to be in new places around new people, searching for something she could never find. It was a search that would go on for most of her adult life. Dorothy Watters says the effect of Vernon's brutality on Ella was profound. "She never really got over that. It changed her completely. She lost her life, and her mother's life too, because Pearl was never the same either." Bessie Flanders agrees, saying Ella's time with Vernon "marred her for the rest of her life."

ELLA AND MEL MACLEAN WERE STILL dating when she told him she had found work at an army base in Petawawa, Ontario. He drove her to the train station. "She took off and the kids were with her mother," says Mel. "She called me all the time from up there. Time went by, and here the telephone company called me and said, 'Were you talking to an Ella'—I don't know if she went by Armour or Ince then, and I said, 'Yeah, I was talking to her.' 'Well,' they said, 'she skipped out and didn't pay her telephone bill,' and they wanted to know if I would pay. I said, 'I didn't make the calls. Why should I pay the bills—I'm finding it hard enough to pay my own bill.'"

Ella was soon back home again and they continued dating, but Mel suspected there were other men in her life, and one day, while working at the dairy, "My intuition aroused my suspicion. So I got in my car and I went out to her mother's place. This fella was in the living room playing with the kids and I went into the kitchen." There was no sign of Ella, but Pearl was at the sink.

"What the hell is going on around here?" asked Mel.

"Oh never mind, now, never mind," said Pearl. "Ella went out, but she'll be right back."

"Jesus Christ!" said Mel, who left quickly but saw Ella coming up the driveway as he closed the door.

"What the Jesus is going on?" he asked.

"Oh nothing, nothing," said Ella.

"So I jumped in the car and went home," says Mel. "Some fellas would probably want to start problems, but I'm not a problem maker and I'm not going to fight over a woman. So I took off."

He went home and was having lunch when Ella called and asked him to return to the house. He complied, but the "fella" was still at the house when Ella came out and got into Mel's car. "So we were coming down the road, and we were talking back and forth and I was complaining and growling, and she said, 'If you two could only be one, it would be the perfect man.'"

That did it for Mel. "I don't give a fuck what you say, girl, I don't want no part of that fellow and I know he don't want no part of me," he said.

He pulled his car to the side of the road. What he didn't know was that the "fella" had called a taxi and was following them a short distance behind.

"I stopped the '39 Hudson right there and I said, 'Get out, Ella. Get the fuck out.' So she got out of the car and got right into the taxi, and away they went. So that was the beginning of the end. Christ, she was like Hank Snow—she's been everywhere. I think she had all kinds of friends—me and many more. We went out a lot, but you can always find the time. I said the hell with it. But believe me, I was no better than she was. I had other girlfriends too."

They made up, but Mel says it was never the same after that and Ella was soon gone again. "My mother sent me to Montreal to my cousin's place," said Ella.

"My goodness, Aunt Pearl had an awful time with her," says Bessie Flanders. "It was just terrible, and Aunt Pearl looked after the kids. I remember my mother made coats and hats for them and bought them little white boots with white fur on the top and sewed for them to help out. And when Estelle was three or four, I took over all the toys I had for her to play with."

Montreal didn't work out, and Ella returned when she found a job as head chef at the Heather Hotel in Stellarton. And when she rented "half a house" on MacKay Street in Stellarton and moved the children in with her, it took the pressure off her besieged mother.

Jean Muir says Ella was "quite a go-getter and an excellent cook. And we used to go down to her house and play cards. She loved to do that. She was something else. We played poker, but we didn't play for money. Sometimes we'd play to one or two in the morning. And after we were all done playing cards and whatnot, she'd go down to the Heather and make up a great big plate of sandwiches for us. She was full of the devil all the time."

Mel MacLean says, "When she was head chef at the Heather, we might have been out only one time. I must have been dating somebody else by the time she came back to work there. When she left, the bad just got to worse. And I wasn't planning to make it a career with her. I never thought of settling down with her."

Nor was Ella ready to settle down. No one seems to know whether it was restlessness or a problem at work, but she decided to head back to Montreal once again, this time convincing her mother to sell her house and follow her.

Mel MacLean was surprised. "Jesus Christ, she packed up four young kids in the car and headed off. I think it was a lime green '51 Chev. I don't know where she was headed. For somebody to just pack up and take off like that, she must have had a lot of nerve. She had something on the ball, but it seems she never stayed with one thing. When she took off again, that kind of wound it up for us. She was more experienced in that kind of life than I was—but I wasn't a stupid boy."

No one knows whether Ella was looking for a better job in Montreal or she had a plan to open her own business. Whatever the strategy, it failed, and her cousin Bessie says that after a few months they couldn't pay their rent and were literally "put out in the street. They came back because they didn't have anywhere to live in Montreal."

Pearl was now impoverished and returned to Westville with the four children in tow. Ella stayed in Montreal for a time and then moved on to Halifax. Pearl moved into the Muir family home, by then owned by her sister Tina. "When Aunt Pearl went to Montreal, she left her sewing machine and a few things with my mother and they were there for her when she came back, and my mother and Aunt Margaret Hale found her some furniture and stuff," says Tina's daughter, Bessie.

Pearl was now essentially raising her daughter's children. If Ella had any reserve of self-esteem, it was now used up. She was broke and felt she was not only a failure as a mother but had forced her own mother, now without a home, into poverty.

"I always heard she was in a desperate state in Montreal," says Bessie. "And I know one time she just took off from the apartment in Westville—Mother said something like in the middle of the night, without notifying her. I think she owed Mum a lot of money for rent and things. She went to the Halifax-Dartmouth area, but I don't know what she was doing there. Ella hid a lot. But she was just a kid, when I think about it now."

Ella's troubled odyssey took her next to Moncton, New Brunswick, about a two-and-a-half-hour drive from Stellarton, where she was soon involved in a whirlwind romance with Edward Melanson, a bartender almost four years her junior. They decided they were in love and set a wedding date for January 17, 1957. His sister would later say that Eddie's mother was concerned when she learned her son was "taking on a widow with a child. Then all of a sudden it wasn't one kid but two, and then three, and by the time they got married it was up to four." Despite the mother's protests, the wedding went ahead in Dieppe, New Brunswick, a month before Eddie's twenty-first birthday. Ella was twenty-four, and her children were still in Westville.

Marriage didn't slow Ella down, or curb her nomadic proclivities. She convinced her new husband to move with her to Montreal and try to make a go of it in the hotel and restaurant business. He would manage, and she would run the kitchen. Eddie was on a runaway train with no known destination, but it would be ten years before he realized he would have to jump off for his own survival. In Montreal—their first stop—their first child,

James, was born on March 11, 1959. The next stop was Truro, Nova Scotia, where a daughter, Pearl, was born on September 30, 1961. In Thompson, Manitoba, their second daughter, Karen, was born on February 7, 1963.

Now Karen Gardiner, married, with her own children and living in Winnipeg, that daughter says Ella would "get paranoid and move every couple of years. Even if she stayed in a city for a while, she'd move from one side to the other. She just constantly moved. It became a big issue with my father. She would just up and be gone. She was always looking over her shoulder."

Meanwhile, back in Westville, Ella missed the wedding of her cousin Bessie while Pearl Armour continued to raise her first four children. The eldest, Estelle, then fourteen, was Bessie's maid of honour. "The kids were there, but Ella wasn't," says Bessie.

But another tragic accident brought Ella back to Westville in 1964. This time, it involved her mother, who on July 18 was a front-seat passenger in a car driven by a local man she was considering marrying. Also in the car was Pearl's niece Tina, the daughter of her sister Florence. It was a pleasant summer day and they were headed to the beach when they were struck by a car travelling at high speed as they pulled out onto the main highway.

Ella was living in Thompson, Manitoba. "I got a call from my Aunt Jean, and she told me they didn't expect my mother to live," she said. "I got there as fast as I could. All the driver got was a cut ear. Cousin Tina was hurt bad, but not as bad as my mother. She went through the side window and her leg was ripped very badly and she was unconscious." Pearl got the worst of it, and doctors said she would spend months in the hospital recuperating.

Bessie Flanders, who by then had been married two years and was a registered nurse, offered to take the children, "But she said no. We felt terrible, because we were concerned about their care. But she was the mother, so there was nothing more we could do."

With her mother beginning her seemingly long recovery, Ella decided to return to Manitoba with her four children. Jackie—the son she said was Mel MacLean's—was nine then. Now married and living in Winnipeg, Jackie remembers Ella coming for them, and later arriving in Thompson. "We lived there for a while," he says. "She was working in a restaurant. She and Eddie were always wheeling and dealing around restaurants and hotels. They could walk into a place with no money and walk out with a pile. That's how good a talker she was."

However successful they were in Thompson, it wasn't good enough for Ella and soon their expanded family was headed back to Montreal. It was there that on January 24, 1965, in the final weeks of yet another pregnancy, she got word that her mother had died in hospital at age fifty-eight.

"I was in the room at the hospital when Pearl died," says Bessie Flanders. "Her last words were, 'Ella. Ella…'"

Two days later, Pearl's newspaper obituary stated that "Except for one week, Mrs. Armour had been a patient in hospital since July 18 of last year following injuries received in a car accident." But Bessie says that while she was being treated for her injuries, doctors discovered Pearl was suffering from terminal cancer and that it was the actual cause of her death. "I went up to see her as soon as she had the accident" she says. "I really didn't think she would live, but she did. She died of cancer, but it could have been both."

"My heart was broken when my mother died," said Ella. "She had helped me and my children and so many people. The day of the funeral, it was snowing and windy. She was buried from the United Church. They had a snowplow ahead of the funeral procession from the house to the church and from the church to the cemetery, where a tent was set up for the service.

"The neighbours came in and washed and waxed floors and polished everything. Everything was spotless. I think it was their way of saying goodbye. At the service at the church, I was so hurt that Mom was dead and I thought to myself, 'If there is a God, please show me a sign that Mom is happy and with you.' And then a ray of sunshine came through the stained glass window right on my mother's casket. It was only for a few seconds, and when we went outside after the service, there was a blizzard. So I knew she was happy."

In Montreal, three weeks after Pearl's funeral, Ella gave birth to Kathy, her fifth daughter and eighth child. It was February 1965 and Ella was thirty-three years old. Kathy would be her last child, but Ella certainly wasn't done moving. It was time to head west.

12

And Then There Was One

Cindy MacDonald, 29. London, Ontario. Cindy was found in her backyard with a knife through her chest. Her boyfriend, Melvin Flores, was charged with second-degree murder. Flores was out on bail with a no contact condition that had been ordered in April after a charge of uttering a death threat against Cindy. (June 2006)

CONSIDERING THEIR STARKLY DIFFERENT CHILDHOODS, THERE were surprising similarities in the lives of Ella and Jane from their mid-teens onward.

Ella Armour's youth, if not perfect, was free of trouble and happy. She was a loving and much-loved, carefree child who grew up surrounded by friends and doting relatives. She was a dancer, a speed skater, a singer, and the only girl in an all-male pipe band. She brimmed with self-confidence.

Jane Hurshman was a good student and athletic enough that her basketball and volleyball teams won first- and second-place ribbons. And when her father was posted to Germany, she beat a hundred competitors to win a second-place medal in a seven-mile cross-country race at a track and field meet for schools from Canadian army bases. That she accomplished anything, however, was an incredible tribute to her inner strength, considering her disastrous home life—including an abusive, hard-drinking father and the trauma of being sexually assaulted by someone close to the family.

For both girls, childhood ended at age sixteen when they became pregnant and entered bleak and disastrous marriages. Living dirt poor with an unfaithful alcoholic, Jane may have initially felt that she was slightly better off than her mother because she herself wasn't being physically abused. And she had the gumption to do something about her situation. When her first son was old enough to go to school, she went back to school herself and completed Grade 10 with straight As. The next summer, she enrolled in a typing course. By then, her husband was no longer working. The family was living on unemployment insurance and the $50 a week Jane received from Canada Manpower for enrolling in the course.[1]

Soon after starting her course, Jane discovered she was pregnant again. She thought about an abortion but dismissed the possibility. After the birth of her second son in October 1972, Jane was despondent about her marriage but resigned to her fate. She tried to make a go of it for the sake of the children. But within three years, she could take no more. A few days after New Year's in 1976, her husband came home after drinking all day. He set a forty-ounce bottle of rum on the table. Jane eyed him and the bottle.

"It's either me and the kids or that bottle," she said.

With a smirk, he picked up the bottle and kissed it. "I guess you lose," he said.

Jane went into the bedroom and threw some clothes for herself and the kids into a garbage bag. She woke the boys and bundled them into the family's beat-up twelve-year-old Ford. The Canadian army had transferred her father yet again, this time to Cornwallis, Nova Scotia, about a hundred miles away. Jane planned to go there for a few days until she figured out what to do.

Jane did not return to her husband, but within a year she had moved in with Billy Stafford, her "knight in shining armour," beginning an unimaginable five-year nightmare that ended with Billy dead, a humiliating trial, a surprising acquittal, a lost appeal, a guilty plea to manslaughter, and two months in jail.

Jane suffered more sustained abuse over a longer period than Ella did, but Jane was in her twenties by then, and as a child she had been conditioned by witnessing her father batter her mother. Ella's abuse started when she was seventeen, but in her life experience there was no context for the violence wreaked upon her by Vernon Ince.

While both became mothers as young teenagers, Jane did not have her second child for another seven years, while Ella had two children, a miscarriage, and was pregnant with a third within a two-and-a-half-year span. And although Jane's life with an alcoholic husband was miserable, there was no physical abuse, while young Ella, barely out of childhood herself, was under sustained physical and emotional abuse while trying to cope with two children and a third on the way.

However, the violence and sustained threat of violence against Jane was all-consuming, extended to her child, and lasted two years longer than the abuse to which Ella was subjected. If Ella, during her brief separation from Vernon, had somehow managed to regain custody of Estelle and had *not* returned to him, it may have ended differently. Would he have stayed away and let her live her life, or would he have come after her, as many batterers do, with vengeance on his mind?

Both women were charged with the most serious form of murder in their day—capital in Ella's case and first-degree in Jane's.

Ella's violent action against Vernon was a clear case of self-defence, yet she served seven months in jail before her trial. In Jane's case, Billy was asleep and there was no "imminent" threat against her, which under the law at the time ruled out self-defence. Yet she was allowed out on bail and eventually served only two months on a reduced charge of manslaughter after the jury had ruled that it *was* self-defence and acquitted her.

Some people might think that, with their abusers dead, victims of battering like Jane and Ella would then be free to get on with their lives and live happily—or at least *normally*—ever after. Others might say that they got away with murder. The reality is that they *got away* with nothing and faced uncertain futures fraught with demons spawned by the years of abuse.

For Jane, compelled to help other battered women, it was continuous flashbacks of her life with Billy whenever she listened to their tragic stories and offered counsel and support. And it was the curse of kleptomania, which held her so tightly in its grip that she saw suicide as the only way out.

For Ella, living at a time before the advent of counselling and support services for battered women, it had become an instinctual but frenetic and fruitless search for the road back to the life she knew before Vernon—now magnified in her mind as utopian and a true Shangri-La. So far, it was all a myth and her dreams had turned to dust.

PSYCHOLOGIST PATRICIA NEILSON SAYS it's short-sighted to think that if you just get rid of the bad guy, life will be good. "Simply getting rid of one abusive man doesn't change their life story. In Elly's case, it doesn't change the psychological impact it would have had on her."[2] And in a thirteen-page self-analysis three years after Billy Stafford's death, Jane wrote: "When I was told that Bill was dead,

I was in my own world. I heard no noise—the world was sound-
less. I felt like I was floating...I kept going, fighting to hold on to
the rational me—trying to let everything sink in. Bill was really
dead. Maybe now there would be peace. I couldn't cry. I don't
know if I wanted to, but I couldn't.

"When Bill died, I thought it would be over. It wasn't over. It's
still not over. It keeps coming back at me. It was very rough and
still is."[3]

A task force studying the health effects of woman abuse for the
Middlesex-London [Ontario] Health Unit released a report in
September 2000 that included a list of long-term psychological and
psychiatric effects of battering. Here are some of those that apply
directly to Jane and Ella:

Both Jane and Ella	Jane Only	Ella Only

• Depression
• Post-traumatic
  stress disorder
  (PTSD)
• Low self-esteem
• Self-abusive
  behaviour
• Hypervigilance
• Chronic stress
• Insomnia, sleep
  disturbances,
  nightmares
• Flashbacks
	• Suicidal thoughts
	• Acute anxiety
	• Dissociation
		• Dysfunctional
		  parenting
		• Arrested develop
		  ment (immature
		  behaviour)
		• Evasiveness

As a concept, post-traumatic stress disorder (PTSD) has been
around officially since 1980, when it appeared in the third edition
of the *Diagnostic and Statistical Manual of Mental Disorders*—

considered the bible for psychiatrists and other mental health prac-
titioners. First widely used to describe the emotional disruption of
many U.S. soldiers who returned from combat in Vietnam, PTSD
had different names in earlier wars—"soldier's heart" in the U.S.
Civil War, "shell shock" in World War I, and "battle fatigue" or
"combat fatigue" in World War II.

But recent studies show it also affects large numbers of battered women. In January 2000, San Diego State University
researchers released a report monitoring the results of forty-two
previous studies on PTSD and domestic violence, and concluded
that "symptoms exhibited by battered women are consistent with
the major indicators of PTSD."[4] According to this report, a nation-
wide U.S. sample of adult women reveals that those suffering
partner abuse "experienced more lifetime and current episodes of
depression, post-traumatic depression, and substance abuse. PTSD
is a normal reaction to abnormal events. The diagnosis occurs most
commonly as a stressful reaction to a catastrophic event involving
actual or threatened death or injury." Symptoms include persistent
reliving of the trauma, trouble sleeping, trouble concentrating, fear,
avoidance, hypervigilance, irritability, and psychic numbing,
including dissociation. "There is no support for the belief that violence toward women that is perpetrated by their husbands is less
traumatizing than violence by others," the report states.[5] And factors such as early-age onset of violence and its duration and
severity exacerbate the symptoms.

Domestic violence scholar Cathy Humphreys, who teaches at
the University of Warwick in Coventry, England, said in 2003 that
post-traumatic stress disorder, initially defined as a "stressful, life-
threatening event," recognized a specific group of symptoms
"which consistently developed for people exposed to incidents of
trauma, whether they were rape victims or soldiers returning from
war, and could persist with frightening and destructive effects for

years."[6] According to Humphreys, its symptoms can include flashbacks; reliving the trauma as though it is happening again; avoiding thoughts, feelings, people, or incidents that might remind those afflicted with PTSD of the trauma; a sense of impending doom and not expecting to live a long life; inability to feel love for others; hypervigilance; irritability; inability to concentrate; extreme watchfulness; inability to get to sleep or stay asleep; jumpiness; or a hair-trigger startle response.[7] Dr. Humphreys said an overview of eleven U.S. studies reporting the disorder in women exposed to domestic violence "shows very high rates of PTSD varying from 31% to 84%. More general studies of PTSD have highlighted the link to rape and sexual violence." A 1998 U.S. study, for example, found that 40 to 45 per cent of women who experience domestic violence had suffered sexual violence. "It is not surprising, with these levels of sexual assault within intimate relations, that the link between domestic violence and PTSD is high."[8]

The devastating physical and emotional fallout from intimate-partner criminal violence found in study after study demonstrates the depth of the crisis in North America and around the world. The San Diego State University report concludes, "Domestic violence, if considered a disease, would be declared a national epidemic based on the magnitude of its incidence. In the United States each year, intimate partners batter between two [million] and four million women of all ages, races and classes."[9]

HOW DOES THIS RELATE TO Jane Hurshman and Ella Armour? There is evidence that many women suffering depression, PTSD, and other battering-related psychological and psychiatric trauma are able to recover their mental health once the violence—the source of the stress—ceases. Ella Armour did recover—partially. Jane Hurshman did not.

CONSIDERING WHAT JANE WENT through, it's a wonder she survived as long as she did. As Dr. Humphreys states, "Having multiple victimization experiences [childhood and adult sexual abuse] increases the likelihood of PTSD and many other types of psychiatric disorders," including an inherent risk of suicide.[10]

Some of Jane's "disorders" were detailed before a full courthouse. Halifax clinical psychologist Rosemary Sampson, who interviewed Jane before her trial, testified she found her deeply depressed, "with many defences. In other words, she has ways of keeping herself pretty well encased, as it were." She said Jane saw herself as a victim and had "extremely low self-concept. She's an extremely anxious person, very guilt-ridden. I think she's an emotionally immature woman whose life history reflects poor interpersonal... relationships. She presents a pattern of anger which has continually been internalized, which eats away at the person."[11] Dr. Sampson said, "That type of a person would very often think of suicide, but she had a moral strength in her that would not act upon that, unless really pushed to the extreme."

Dr. Carol Abbott, a Halifax doctor specializing in psychiatry, described the five years of Jane's life with Billy as "one of overwhelming stress, both physical and mental. I think it affected her in terms of her passivity... to the alleged abuse. She could never predict when he was going to react the way he was, and I think it's this unpredictability that made it difficult for her to feel that she could do anything to control the situation." Dr. Abbott said Jane was outwardly compliant and could never express her feelings to Billy, "because of the risk of provoking him, and I think this was constantly there. Even when he was away... there was a fear that it [anything she said] would get back to him. So that although she repressed or denied her feelings, these were the defence mechanisms with which she dealt with the stress at the time."[12]

Jane's lawyer, Alan Ferrier, asked Dr. Abbott if Jane had suicidal tendencies.

"Yes, she told me she had considered suicide at times... but she never carried out anything because of the fear of leaving her young son to suffer further abuse."

Dr. Abbott said Jane suffered "a tremendous loss of self-esteem—loss of any kind of personal integrity... any sense of one's own effectiveness in that situation."

"Would there be a similarity in the sense of being psychologically imprisoned?" asked Ferrier.

"I think that's a very good way of putting it—of feeling *encased*—shut in without seeing any way of escape."[13]

Of the bestiality aspect of the sexual abuse Jane was subjected to, Ottawa psychiatrist Dr. John Dimock said, "The use of a dog I've seen on occasion, but I think when that kind of behaviour is involved, then one is really involved in a very serious sadistic type of a relationship."

Ann Keith was executive director of Services for Sexual Assault Victims in Halifax when she began counselling Jane in early 1985. "When she started talking about things that really bothered her, I'll never forget her eyes—they were humongous. She would almost dissociate herself. I remember thinking to myself, it was like looking into the pits of hell. What she was carrying around was incredible." Keith said there were times "when I felt like I couldn't really help her, that it was getting over my head." But she and Jane became good friends and the counselling continued for five years, until Keith referred her to psychiatrist John Curtis for more advanced help.

Keith believes that when a woman is abused, it's akin to a life-long prison sentence. "People who have not experienced violence don't understand the long-term psychological effect. Flashbacks of the abuse can be triggered by something very minor—a smell, a touch...anything."[14] That's why Keith is convinced that every time Jane spoke out on behalf of battered women, it brought back memories of Billy's abuse. "If you heard her, especially in her later speeches, you might not get that impression," says Keith. "But I'm sure that's how she felt, and she did express that. If you've been abused, you put on masks. You can be three or four people. You can be hurting and have the biggest smile on your face. You could be tearing up inside, but you are not going to let anybody know, because you have been conditioned that way all your life."

Jane began speaking out publicly to help others and heal herself, but despite years of counselling and psychiatric treatment, and intimate knowledge of the dynamics of spousal battering, her demons won out. In February 1992, she was found dead of a self-inflicted gunshot wound in her car in a parking lot on the Halifax waterfront.

ELLA ARMOUR'S SHORT AND violent time with Vernon Ince left her vulnerable to a host of long-term problems that would haunt her for the rest of her life. The fact that intimate-partner criminal violence was never talked about in her era, and that there were no shelters, counselling, or treatment available to her, compounded the difficulty she would have in her largely futile search for a life even remotely resembling her early years with Pearl and Recky Armour.

Of what Ella went through with Vernon at such a young age, Dr. Patricia Neilson says, "Most women would describe it as messing up their sense of trust—trust in all the things she committed herself to," and this would profoundly affect her relationship with her children. "When something horrific happens after you've put all that investment in a relationship that becomes terrifying and lethal, it really fundamentally shakes up your sense of who you are and what you can predict in your life, including your own faith in yourself. You know, can you be a good mother?

"When the one relationship in your life that you're supposed to absolutely trust becomes lethal, how does that change your psyche? I know cases of abused women who have kept themselves at a distance from their children, because they just didn't trust their sense of love and they were almost fearful of hurting their children by becoming too attached to them. It gets totally messed up. What they had counted on was supposed to be loving, safe, and secure, and then it's not. And then they don't trust other relationships, including the one you would expect them to have—their mothering relationship. So they just don't trust that they can even be a safe parent."

Dr. Neilson says Ella, "in general, would have a lot of confusion there—wanting to be a good mum and do the right thing, while at the same time not trusting that she was capable of doing that—and sometimes people run from that." She says Ella would blame herself for "showing such bad judgment in her own life—so how could she trust that she could be a good mother or keep her children safe?"

If treatment and counselling had been available to Ella in the weeks and months after she was released from prison, her relationships with men and with her children might have been vastly different. The hugely positive factor that allowed her to survive at all was her early upbringing in a loving home environment.

Dr. Neilson says it's difficult "for people to understand why abuse could have such an impact on a woman like Ella, who had such a secure background." She says that because Ella doesn't fit the mould, her case encourages the "blame the victim" mentality. "It would be easier for us to think abuse only happens to women [like Jane] who grew up in traumatic circumstances. That's so easy to make sense of, but it's also easier to blame the victim.

"I think it shows that the entrapment and the impact are the same no matter what kind of environment you come from—although, fortunately, Ella developed some other resources."

But, she says, the lack of protection and the obstacles facing them as a result of the abuse were the same for Ella and Jane. And both were entrapped by the expectation that they should be able to manage the fallout from the abuse and their feelings of shame. "That entrapment is the same," says Dr. Neilson. "So you have to continue to look at the genesis of this and where is it coming from. Looking too much at qualities of the victim or her background gets away from the point. Why are we looking at, what is it in a woman's personality or background that makes this [battering] happen—instead of looking at the guy and saying, why does he batter?"

Although Ella's marriage to Vernon was half a century before the San Diego State University report in 2000, every part of this statement can be applied to her circumstance: "The empirical evidence does suggest that [abused] younger unemployed women, with a relatively large number of children, with low income, and low levels of social support, are more at risk to experiencing PTSD symptoms and other mental health problems than women without those characteristics."[15]

And studies show that domestic violence can severely impair the women's ability "to nurture the development of their children...They may be emotionally withdrawn or numb, irritable, or have feelings of hopelessness. The result can be a parent who is less emotionally available to their children or unable to care for their basic needs."[16]

Ella was certainly a dysfunctional parent, leaving the first four with their grandmother through their early years, and then giving birth to four others while moving from city to city and province to province.

After fathering four of Ella's children and moving so many times he lost count, Eddie Melanson had had enough. He was thirty-one years old and had four children—of his own—under the age of six.

In the spring of 1967, the same year as Expo, they had left Montreal and were back in Manitoba, this time in Winnipeg. Ella's eldest daughter, Estelle, would turn eighteen that year and was out on her own. Cindy, almost fifteen, was no longer living with the family.

"There was an issue with Cindy in her teenage years," says Ella's daughter Karen. "She was very hard to handle, and she used to have temper fits and throw things—knives or whatever was handy. You couldn't control her. Mum tried to get drug therapy, but nothing seemed to work. She was a danger to herself. She wouldn't listen to anybody. My brothers, Don and John [Jackie], had to sit on her and hold her because she was ten times stronger when she was angry."

Cindy presented a real danger to the younger children, and her unpredictability led to considerable tension between Eddie and Ella, who was loathe to place her daughter in a home or institution. Eventually, however, she had no choice. There was a large staircase in their house, and in one of her fits of anger, Cindy grabbed one of the infants, held her by one foot, and dangled her over the railing. "And the next thing I know, Cindy was gone," says Karen. Where Cindy was gone was the Manitoba School for Retardates in Portage la Prairie, fifty miles west of Winnipeg.

Cindy's situation poisoned an already tenuous relationship, and when Ella hinted about relocating yet again, Eddie decided on his own move. "I guess they had been fighting a lot before and my dad said, 'This has got to stop—that's it,'" says Karen. "The issue with Cindy arose just before my parents split. I'm sure he told my mother he was going to go. So my dad packed everything up, and when he left, he took the four youngest children, which were his own. Estelle was already gone, and by then Donny was spending a lot of time with his girlfriend and was pretty much on his own. And my dad hadn't adopted John, so he had no legal right to take him. John was at school when we left. I was just three and a half. We took the train to Moncton, New Brunswick, and it took three days. I was sick the whole way."

Karen says twelve-year-old John came home from school and saw that "a bunch of things were gone, so he went over to one of his friends for a while." Ella, meanwhile, returned home from the restaurant where she was working to find no one there. "There was no note or anything," says Karen. "So she just packed her clothes, locked the place up, and left."

When John returned to the house, he tried the front and back doors but couldn't get in. "The door was always open, but now it was locked," he says. "So I looked in the window and everything was gone out of there, even the curtains. I didn't know what happened. I sat on the stairs and cried."

It was spring and still cold at night, so John kicked open the back door and stayed a few days until the heat ran out. "Nobody came around for the rent or anything," he says. "Then I drifted for a while and did whatever I wanted to do." Sometimes he stayed with friends. "But you can't stay there all the time. I never told them that I was on my own. You always had friends, but sometimes you didn't eat for three or four days." He did a little panhandling, and as the weather warmed, he slept in parks. He would stay on the streets until he was seventeen. "I was living homeless," says John, "but I wasn't a runaway. I just had no home to go to because they just up and disappeared."

When he was fifteen, John heard that his mother was in Portage la Prairie working as a chef in a hotel restaurant. "She was on her own," he says. "Cindy was there in a home, and that's probably why she went there. I hitchhiked down there, and her reaction was like nothing ever happened. She told me she came home and nobody was there. She said she thought I was with Eddie. Eddie and the others didn't know where she was. Nobody ever knew where she was. I was only there for the day. She was living in the hotel where she was working as a chef. She asked me to come and live there, but I went back to Winnipeg because I had commitments there. You know what young kids did back then—parties and things. They were in the same predicament that I was in, and you basically hang around and everybody becomes family. But I'm not friends with any of them anymore."

John says he did drugs while living a "hippie life" on the street, and "I got busted shoplifting a loaf of bread at Safeway. I was hungry. They phoned the cops and I was held overnight. They let me go the next day." He worked at odd jobs in Winnipeg until he found work at a garage on Main Street, "changing oil and pumping gas." It's an interesting coincidence that John's early years—including the lack of formal education and a job at a service station—exactly paralleled that of Mel MacLean, the man Ella named as his father. And he would later drive trucks for many years, as had MacLean.

IT BOTHERED ELLA THAT HER daughter was in an institution, and in 1970 she took Cindy back to Winnipeg. This mother of eight was now, in effect, a single mother living on her own with just one child—Cindy.

It's not clear whether she had a job offer when she left Portage la Prairie, but Karen says her mother always found work "in a restaurant, a bar, or a hotel." Ella did well-enough that she was a regular visitor to Winnipeg's Assiniboia Downs Racetrack, and it was there that she met Harry Goodchild, who owned a thoroughbred that raced there. "He had short, dark, slicked-back hair," says Karen. "All the men Mom ever dated were dark-haired. My mother and Cindy eventually moved in with him, and they bought a second horse together."

John was still living in Winnipeg. "And when she met Harry, they moved into a townhouse," he says. "She introduced me to him at the bar at the McLean Hotel. She said 'Oh, we're just friends,' and I said, 'Yeah, right.' I was sixteen or seventeen and she allowed me to drink. I did whatever I wanted to do. I had adapted to street life and was still living on my own. But I ended up staying with them a few nights."

Ella found a job as head chef in a large Winnipeg hotel with several banquet rooms. "It was a busy place and a lot of people worked for me—full-time and part-time," she said. "I laid out all the menus. There were several kitchens and the food was brought up from the main kitchen, which I supervised." But she also knew how to operate the equipment. "I could take a side of beef and put it on the band saw and cut it up," she said. "One night, I had a banquet for seventy in one of the rooms and they wanted steaks. So I took the side of beef down and cut out the T-bone and the porterhouse steaks and some sirloins. And I used what they call the salamander. It's like a big grill that cooks with gas, and you slide the steaks in and out on a rack. It's open on the front, and we barbecue in there.

"I used the service elevator to take the steaks and vegetables up in stainless steel pans on two carts. The door opened, and as I pushed the cart forward, the elevator dropped about a foot and everything slid back towards me. Maggie, the banquet manager, came out and tried to lift the front of the cart while I'm trying to lift the rear. And one of the pans slid back and ten or twelve steaks flew off and went right down the elevator shaft. If there were any rats at the bottom, they would have had a feast."

The women successfully wrestled the wagons out of the elevator, but Maggie was in a panic over the lost steaks. "Don't worry about it. I'll be on time," promised Ella. "You just put all this stuff on the steam table and I'll handle the rest. Leave the bar open another ten minutes. They won't know what's going on."

Ella put the unsafe elevator out of service and took another one down to the main kitchen and grabbed a large frozen prime rib. "I said the hell with it, I'm not going to take out another whole side of beef. So I put the prime rib on the band saw, cut a dozen steaks, and shoved them into the salamander. It took exactly twelve minutes and I took them right up there. And Maggie said, 'Holy shit, I'd hate to see you if you were in a hurry.'"

As satisfying as she found her job, Ella soon decided once again that it was time to move on. She and Harry were married in April 1971—although her children have never found divorce papers for her and Eddie Melanson. The next year, Ella and Harry moved to Hamilton, Ontario, with Cindy. "Suddenly they packed up and took off," says John. "They didn't say anything and I didn't know where they went. But she called up people I knew and left messages for me to call her collect."

"Where the hell are you now?" John asked.

"I'm in Hamilton," said Ella.

"What are you doing there?"

"Oh, I'm a caretaker of an apartment block. Why don't you come down? We'll give you a ticket and you can have a room here."

John paused a moment. "I'll think about it," he said.

He had been doing well at the garage, but when his boss increased his responsibilities, "There was more paperwork and I couldn't do it, so I got let go." Besides leaving school early, John had a learning disability and couldn't read or write. He decided to take up his mother's offer to move to Hamilton. "So I went down there to this big high-rise," he says. "She and Harry were the caretakers and I got in with them. They had a two-bedroom suite, and I had one bedroom."

John says it took a bit of time, but he was largely able to bury the pain and anger over his childhood abandonment and get along fairly well with his mother. "I had my guard up because you never knew what was happening with her, but I could come and go as I pleased and she had no control over me. Even if she did tell me what to do, I didn't listen to her."

When John first arrived, Ella helped him find work as a security guard for a friend who owned a hotel- and restaurant-supply company. John soon discovered that the company made its own deliveries, and "I've always messed around with vehicles, so it didn't take me long to jump onto a truck." Soon he was behind the wheel of a three-ton truck, delivering hotel and restaurant supplies all over Ontario.

Meanwhile, Ella was becoming bored with high-rise caretaking and decided to follow up on one of the many ideas percolating in her mind. "I went and talked to a hotel manager and his wife who were friends of mine, and I asked them if they had an empty office," she said. "They had one coming up, and they gave it to me for six months rent-free. That started it. I opened a brokerage company servicing nursing homes, and I ran it for several years."

The company was called Complete Nursing Home Services Ltd. and she was named president under the name Elly Goodchild. From then on, she became Elly, at least to the public. The vice-president was her partner in the venture, Cathy Szela.

The company would eventually be endorsed by the Ontario Nursing Home Association (now the Ontario Long Term Care Association) as a principal supplier of goods and equipment to nursing homes across Ontario. "As a broker, I represented three hundred manufacturers, and because I did so much volume, I could get the homes prices they couldn't get anywhere else," she said. "I had to study the markets inside out to get the right manufacturers and proper pricing. And I worked through the Ministry of Health. I would supply beds and bedding and whole kitchens—all stainless steel—for health care facilities. I supplied everything, even all the food. For instance, a jug of milk might cost $3 in a store, but they would deliver it to the homes on my service list for half that price. Everybody had to sign a contract with me. I represented the manufacturer who made the products or provided the services I needed. Then they would send me an invoice and I would pay them, and then I billed the government."

The success of her company and the extent of her marketing skills were evident in June 1978. When Dundas Manor opened in North Dundas, just south of Ottawa, Ella took out a full-page ad in the local newspaper to congratulate the owner and to plug her own operation.

"I started with one guy that had sixteen health care facilities, and I serviced every one of them," she said. "Then, as the word got out, I signed up more and more of them."

One of her best customers was Helmuth Buxbaum, a multimillionaire who lived near London, Ontario, and owned eleven nursing homes. "I sold him everything that went through the door except drugs," said Ella. "All the equipment, all the food—everything. Even all his linens. I dealt with Dominion Textiles, which manufactured the linen. I didn't deal with the side guy. I went right to the source." Ella said she was in Buxbaum's home, and "It was beautiful."

This was the same Helmuth Buxbaum who would later hire a hit man to kill his wife, Hanna. In July of 1984, Helmuth pulled his car over onto the shoulder of a main highway to make it look like a random daylight robbery and murder in which his wife was shot in the head but he survived. Police soon discovered, however, that the churchgoing father of five, with more cash pouring in than he ever dreamed of, had developed an insatiable appetite for cocaine and young prostitutes. And after a sensational four-month trial,[17] he was found guilty of first-degree murder in October 1985 and sentenced to life in prison.

"I thought he was a very nice man," Ella says, "but I get the shivers when I think about what he did to his wife."

WHILE ELLA'S BUSINESS WAS thriving in Hamilton, her four youngest children were being raised by her ex-husband, Eddie Melanson, in his hometown of Moncton, New Brunswick, where he had many relatives. "At first there was Kathy, Pearl, James, and me with our dad," says Ella's daughter Karen. "But eventually he remarried and we had a stepmother, Debbie, and then Terry, our half-sister, was born when I was seven. I think dad was in the hotel business, and then he ended up managing a small motel."

Karen says her birth mother was never talked about in all the years she spent in Moncton. "I knew that Debbie was my step-mum, so I just assumed my mum was dead. Never once did I know she existed, and I found out later all the pictures had been destroyed. So I was never ever told about my mum. She and my dad split when I was three and a half. This is awful, but I have my dad in my earliest memories, but not my mother at all—I didn't even know she existed."

But everything changed when Eddie Melanson was diagnosed with cancer of the stomach and the esophagus. "He had surgery when I was twelve," says Karen. "And they took out his esophagus and replaced it with a plastic one. He had been given a certain amount of time to live, but he didn't tell us that he was dying of cancer. Then all of a sudden we abruptly up and moved to Hamilton. He sat us down beforehand and said, 'There is something I haven't told you about.' Then he explained about our mother and how he felt we were now old enough to know the truth and that it was time we got to know her. That was the first time I heard about her."

Eddie told them he and Ella had separated because she was a workaholic and they felt the children would have a more stable upbringing if they moved to New Brunswick.

"We didn't really want to go to Hamilton," says Karen. "We thought, if she didn't want to see us all that time, why should we see her now? He insisted, so we went to Hamilton in 1975. But we didn't know about the cancer then."

Eddie was on medication and receiving a disability pension when he and his wife, Debbie, arrived in their new city. With them were James, Karen, Kathy, and their half-sister, Terry. The other daughter, Pearl, had opted to stay in Moncton.

Ella had arranged a rental townhouse for the family. She and Harry lived in a rented house about twenty minutes away. Ella's son John was living in his own place by this time. "When she opened that medical supply business, they moved into a house and I had my own little shack by then—for $150 a month," he says. "Eddie and the kids were living in one place and Elly and Harry in another. But she somehow managed to get Eddie and Harry to become so-called friends. I think she was still in cahoots with Eddie, you know. I can't prove it, but I think they were still lovers when the other ones weren't around."

Karen says that this scenario is possible, because her mother told her that she and Eddie had stayed in contact during the years the children lived in New Brunswick, "And she swore that all through my childhood she sent birthday cards with money in them."

"Mum, I never ever got a birthday card from you," Karen told her. "I'd remember something like that."

"That's because your stepmother would destroy them," said Ella. "She'd get the mail first, and she'd destroy them."

"But she's not a vengeful person. I can't see her doing that."

Karen says Ella told her about sending people around "to secretly check up on us to see that we were okay. I really don't know what to believe. Part of me thinks they were in touch, but why would she and my father hide the fact that she was still alive?"

Karen would soon learn that there was a lot she didn't know about her mother.

MISS ELLY

13

Elly's Place

Angela Harkley, 33. Shrewsbury, Ontario. Angela's body was found in a shallow grave in a marshy area close to a home she shared with her boyfriend. After standing off the police for several hours, her boyfriend was taken from a car when he was overcome by fume from a propane tank he had with him. Bradley Thomas Warwick was charged with first-degree murder. (September 2006)

WITH A NEW HUSBAND, A SUCCESSFUL BUSINESS, AND FIVE OF her eight children now living in Hamilton, Ontario, Ella saw an opportunity to exorcise some of the guilt she felt over her failures at motherhood.

Daughter Karen Melanson, who would eventually fully reconcile with her mother, believes that Ella's strongest maternal bond was with Estelle, "her first-born, who went through everything with her. I think theirs was the closest to a normal mother-daughter relationship." In fact, if there was a strong bond between Estelle and her mother, much of the credit would have to go to Pearl Armour, who ensured that her granddaughter was raised in a

loving environment and did her best to explain away Ella's continued absences.

By the time Ella moved to Hamilton, Estelle was married to a
U.S. serviceman and living in Iowa. "She was a very pretty girl,"
said Ella, "and she met this U.S. soldier in uniform when he was on
leave. He was very polite and they went out a lot. When he left,
they wrote back and forth, and then he asked her to marry him. She
called him at his base in the States and said yes. She was so happy.
They were married in a Catholic church in Iowa. I went there and
I met his family. They were very nice people and they had a beautiful home. They raised cattle and grew wheat and corn as far as
the eye could see."

That was the romantic picture that Ella would paint. She left
out the fact that Estelle, in a scenario remarkably similar to her
own, was pregnant, and a teenager not much older than Ella had
been when she married Vernon. Both women believed they were
wildly in love and both were teen mothers. Ella was seventeen and
Estelle was eighteen at the time each gave birth to her first-born.

Estelle's husband was slightly older but still a teenager himself
when they started their life together in a trailer park in a small
town about an hour and a half from Des Moines. Ella believed her
daughter had found happiness and became a proud grandmother
when Estelle's son was born in August 1968. When her husband
shipped off to Vietnam, Estelle and son Brad went to live with her
in-laws on the family farm. "I was born in August 1968, before
my father left for Vietnam," says Brad, "but he had to leave before
my first birthday. He probably returned sometime in early 1970.
I know that my mother and I were flown to Hawaii to visit him on
his leave. I have no memory of it, but I heard the stories and have
photos from that trip."

When his father returned from Vietnam, the family moved back
to the trailer park and Estelle had two more children, a girl and a

boy. "As far as I can remember, we were a poor family," says Brad. "We lived in a trailer house, and my father was just starting a business then. He bought the land out there where the trailer park was."

But the man who returned from Vietnam was different from the teenager Estelle had married. Brad says his father never talked about the war, "But I know it played a big part in changing him. Even my grandmother on his side told me that." Ella said that after the army, he started a successful business involving grain elevators and also started drinking heavily.

When Estelle discovered her husband was also seeing other women, the marriage disintegrated and he moved out of the trailer. She found a job managing a bar and also began buying and renting out mobile homes, eventually becoming manager of a large trailer park. "I would say that it would have been a joint venture between my mother and my dad," says Brad. "When they separated or divorced, she stayed in the trailer park and my dad left. He's a very successful businessman today—a multimillionaire."

When Ella married Eddie Melanson, he didn't legally adopt her first four children but she gave them his name, and when Eddie and Ella arrived in Iowa for a visit with Estelle and her children, young Brad thought he was meeting his grandfather Melanson. No one told him about Vernon Ince. Later, after Ella remarried and moved to Hamilton, she showed up in Iowa with Harry Goodchild, and Brad remembers also referring to him as his grandfather.

NOTWITHSTANDING ELLA'S APPARENT neglect of some of her own children, throughout her life she showed unusual compassion for those in trouble or in need—particularly children and animals. Even early on, while her first four children were with Pearl and she was working in other parts of the Maritimes, Ella was taking in other people's children.

"My friend Jeanette and her husband, Gilbert, had five young children," said Ella. "She was a good mother, but he was never at home. He provided for them well, but he had affairs on the side and was always away. She confided in me. She had to take the children wherever she went and she was always totally exhausted. She would get her children to bed early, and then she was always alone. I was working and had my own things to do, but I called her every other day."

Jeanette was hospitalized for depression, and Ella looked after the children until her friend returned home. Jeanette later committed suicide, and Ella again took the children, this time for several months. "They were Catholic and I wasn't," she said. "The welfare department and the church wanted to keep them together. Social Services appeared one day and picked them up. They wouldn't say where they were going, only that it was a good home. I never saw them again and I often wondered about them."

Ella's son John says his mother "seems to have helped a lot of people through the years. She always had a boarder or people in there. And it didn't matter who you were or what you were."

During his stay in Hamilton, John became a full-fledged long-haul trucker. He also got into a bad marriage and had three children. "John kept the kids when they got divorced," says his sister Karen. "I think they were one, three, and five. He later married Chris, who adopted the kids. But before that, Ella ended up looking after them for about a year and a half because he was a long-hauler and you can't take kids on the road when you're doing that. So Mum was there for him when the kids were little."

Ella had the same attitude toward animals as she did toward people. "She was always taking in strays," Karen says. "There were always two or three cats and three or four dogs. One dog, Scruff, died of old age. It was beaten and starving when she took it in. She rescued another dog, Muffin, in a back lane where kids were throwing rocks at it."

Karen says that one time in Hamilton, Ella and Harry were out driving, "And she saw something move along the side of the highway and made Harry stop the car. It was a newborn kitten that somebody had dumped. It still had afterbirth on it. She kept it and called it Gypsy."

ELLA'S HELPING AND REACHING OUT to others was the equivalent of Jane Hurshman's formally speaking out on behalf of battered women at every opportunity while helping countless others on a one-to-one basis. "I know that by my reaching out and trying to help other victims, I am also helping myself heal," said Jane.[1] "My emotional scars are very deep. Eventually, with time, my feelings of fear and anger and powerlessness have lessened and a sense of purpose has replaced them."

Jane, like Ella, also had a love and empathy for animals. In an emotional audio message left for her family—essentially an electronic suicide note—she spoke calmly and clearly about her feelings and listed what she wanted done after her death. Only once did her voice break—when she talked about the possibility of her dogs having to be "put to sleep."[2]

WITH A DIAGNOSIS OF TERMINAL cancer hanging over him, Eddie Melanson had largely achieved his goal of reuniting Ella with their children. One daughter, Pearl, stayed behind in New Brunswick, but James, Karen, and Kathy all made the move to Hamilton. Karen says James "was always a wanderer," and after a year or so, he left Hamilton "and buggered off on his own."

Karen says her mother "did establish a relationship with some of us, but it was difficult to get close to her because there was a wall around her. I think it was because of the abuse she suffered years before. Most of us found she was always all business. She loved her kids in her own way, but she came across as a very cold person. She was afraid to put her emotions out there. But it would get better in later years."

When Eddie Melanson's cancer worsened, he decided to return to New Brunswick. He and his wife, Debbie, and their young daughter, Terry, left Hamilton in the fall of 1978. "My sister Kathy went with them," says Karen, "but I stayed in Hamilton and went to live with really good friends of my dad [Eddie Melanson], because I wanted to finish school."

Karen saw her mother from time to time. But Ella always seemed busy with her brokerage business, and her marriage to Harry Goodchild wasn't working out. "I never really cared much for him," says Karen. "He was a gambler and an alcoholic. He would go to AA and not drink for a while, and then he would go on a binge that could last for two or three weeks." Karen said that when Ella discovered that Harry had physically abused Cindy, her mentally challenged daughter, she kicked him out.

Meanwhile, in the spring of 1979, Eddie Melanson, by now frail and weak with cancer, was at home in Moncton preparing for the marriage of his daughter Pearl that April. "Mother decided that she and I and Cindy would drive to New Brunswick for the wedding," says Karen. "We were about eight hours away when we stopped at a motel overnight. Mother phoned to tell them we would be there the next day around suppertime. The wedding would be the day after that."

But in that phone call, Ella was told that Eddie Melanson had died in the hospital that very day. "Ella was quite upset when she learned he was dead," says Karen. "And she was the one who had to tell me. I was very, very close to my dad and I didn't believe her. We were very angry, because no one had told us that he was that sick or that he was even in the hospital. Mom said we wouldn't have taken the time to drive down—we would have flown there in time to see him before he died."

The wedding was postponed until after Eddie's funeral. "I was just fifteen and I took it very hard," says Karen. "There was two days of viewing. My dad knew a lot people and that church was packed for his funeral. It was a Catholic church."

Estelle's son Brad said he remembers his mother leaving their trailer home in Iowa to attend the funeral. "As far as I knew then, my mother's real dad was Ed Melanson."

One of the "real" children not to make it to the funeral was James Melanson. "He was backpacking across California when our dad died and he didn't find out about it until four months later," says Karen. "He also missed his sister's wedding. We buried my dad one weekend, and the following weekend Pearl was married. I was the maid of honour. It was a very small wedding. I was really upset after the funeral, but we had to leave because I was already missing school. It was very quiet driving back."

With Harry more or less out of the picture, Ella had rented a more upscale home in a Hamilton suburb, and Karen and Cindy lived there with her. "It was a nice ranch-style house with an in-ground swimming pool," says Karen. "Ella also had two poodles, a German shepherd, and two cats when we moved in with her." After Eddie's death, Kathy decided to return to Hamilton and moved in with them. Ella also rented a seasonal cabin right on Lake Ontario where they spent a few summers.

At their father's funeral, Karen and Kathy spent time with their half-sister Estelle. They got along well, and Ella decided to send the girls to Iowa for the month of August to stay with Estelle and her children. "I give my mother a lot of credit for that," says Karen. "We had a month at the cabin and then spent August with Estelle. Kathy had a blast. It was the first time she ever flew and she was really scared. Ella paid for everything. It was a nice thing for her to do after our dad had just died. Estelle and her kids were fantastic. We stayed with them in their large trailer home. I was fifteen and it was a wonderful summer. She was divorced or separated and seeing a very nice man who owned a bar. He was her boyfriend."

Two months later, in October 1979, with Karen and Kathy safely back in Hamilton, Estelle was killed instantly in a one-car accident at midnight on a country road in Iowa. The local newspaper reported the next morning that "the car was southbound on the blacktop, left the roadway, hit a bridge and overturned several times in a farm field." The driver was Estelle's boyfriend, who owned the bar where she sometimes worked as manager. He survived the crash.

Ella said she found out about Estelle's death in a 4 a.m. telephone call. "I was in shock." There was no answer when she called Estelle at home, and Ella frantically tried to contact the police. "I didn't know what county it was in. The operator was very nice, and she kept getting the state police in each county. She stayed on the line with me until she hit the right one and they confirmed Estelle was dead."

Estelle had enjoyed Karen and Kathy's visit so much she'd called Ella a few days before the accident to say she was planning to drive to Hamilton with her children for a return visit. "She drove to Mason City with her boss from the bar to buy a new car for her trip home," said Ella. "Her boss left his car in Mason City and they were driving back in her new car. He decided to take a shortcut and he came upon a wooden bridge just a few miles from her home. The car had to be going fast, but he denied it. He said he was swerving from side to side on the bridge to avoid chunks of mud, which must have fallen from a truck or something. He lost control and the car rolled. Estelle was thrown out. She hit a light pole and broke her neck."

Estelle was buried from the Catholic church where she had been married. The events of the weeks following Estelle's death have blurred with time, but it is certain that Ella wanted to take Estelle's children. "My memory is that she called me," says Brad. "It was very shortly after my mother's funeral and I was a young kid—eleven years old. She did come over, and I know that she wanted us to go with her, and me being a little kid, I was afraid of everything and I didn't know what to do. I don't know exactly what happened, but I know my dad found out she was in town and got ticked off about it."

Ella said she drove down to Iowa and stopped in the bar where Estelle had worked. "I wanted to see if there was a motel around," she said. "I had Canadian licence plates, and all of a sudden two policemen in uniform came in and asked for me. I got up, and they said I was under arrest for attempted kidnapping. I walked back to the table and told Estelle's friends what had happened. They gave me the sheriff's number and I told the policemen I had to make a phone call. I called the sheriff at home and told him what was happening and he said, 'Let me speak to them.' I told the officers they were wanted on the phone and one of them took it. All I heard him say was, 'Yes, sir. Yes, sir.' When they hung up, they apologized and said they were sorry for the problem."

Brad says that he never heard from his mother's family again. "That was the last contact I ever had—when she stopped by the house shortly after my mother's death."

In 1991, twelve years after Estelle's death, her younger son, Bruce, was killed in Iowa in a similar rollover. He was seventeen. His sister was upset when they heard nothing from Ella or other members of Estelle's family. "These people had nothing to do with us for years," she says. "Even when our little brother died, we heard nothing."

But Ella's daughter Karen said they didn't know Bruce had died, nor did they know where Estelle's children were. "I know in later years Mum found out Estelle's daughter was in the army, but that's all we ever heard. I tried to contact them several times, but we could never find them. I think the last time was when I wanted to invite them to my wedding in 1994.

"It was all such a tragedy. I was fifteen when she died. My birthday is November 2, and she died right at the end of October 1979. So it wasn't a sweet sixteen for me."

NOW FORTY-SEVEN, WITH eight children fathered by three different men, depressed over the death of her daughter, and bored with her brokerage business, Ella decided it was time for a drastic change.

In the three decades since her first marriage, she had gained considerable weight, transforming her figure from waifish to heavy-set. Along the line, she had adopted a signature beehive hairdo that would defy changing styles for the rest of her life. "She said it made her feel taller," says Karen. She had always loved music, country in particular, and she had spent a lot of time working in bars and restaurants. She liked the lights, the smoky atmosphere—the escape. She decided to get out of the brokerage business and open a country music bar.

Just before Christmas 1979, about two months after Estelle's death, Ella opened Elly's Place in a leased King Street East venue, once the home of Duffy's Rock Pile, which had been frequented by bikers and known for its brawls. "You'd never recognize it as the same place with its bright, friendly atmosphere and the rich lively country sounds coming from the stage," wrote Doreen Pitkeathly in her *Hamilton Spectator* column, "At the Clubs," in March 1980. "Hamilton has always had a lot of country music fans. And now a country-loving lady named Elly has given them a place to come and hear their fill. Ever since Elly opened the doors, the club's been packed every night with country music lovers and some of the top names in Canadian country entertainment."[3] To the patrons and musicians, Ella would forever after be known as Miss Elly, and she told Pitkeathly that opening the country music club had been "a lifelong dream of mine."

"With hard work and plenty of support, Elly has turned her club into a showcase for country music and it is quickly gaining a reputation as one of the best around," wrote Pitkeathly. "Last week the radio show *Opry North* did two tapings at the club and every week Elly gets another act to rival the last." The week her column was written, one of Canada's top country groups, Johnny Burke and Eastwind, was performing. "Elly's a fine lady," Burke told Pitkeathly between sets. "This is a great thing for the city and for us. There's never been any big country club in this city and people were crying for it."

There was more good publicity for Elly's Place three months later when the *Spectator* ran a major article with a three-column headline and bookended by photos, including one of Elly feeding the club's juke box between sets. "If Texas has Gilley's, Hamilton has Elly's," wrote staff writer David Wesley "Patrons come as far away as Windsor and Ottawa, and a Toronto critic recently hailed it as the best country bar in the region. On Wednesday, the deadest night downtown, it's almost full. On weekends, there are lineups at the door.

"As rock houses close right and left and disco does its last dive, country bars are popping up like prairie wheat…and queen of them all is Elly's Place. In operation since last December, it has already featured the likes of Carroll Baker and Gene Watson. Lined up for future dates are no less than Loretta Lynn, Hank Snow and Faron Young. Overseeing her realm is Elly herself, Hamilton's own Coal Miner's Daughter."

"My daddy was a coal miner in Nova Scotia for 27 years," Ella told Wesley. "I was always a country fan and this is my dream come true. I saved for years [along with husband Harry, who was involved in the startup] for this club. Now stars like Carroll Baker regularly drop in and sit in the audience with me."

Elly's Place had a capacity of almost three hundred, and besides the music, Wesley wrote, it was also known for its "inexpensive roast beef, prime ribs and lobster tails, with Elly herself a certified chef."

Wesley observed that at Elly's Place "long-haired construction workers chat with the likes of Mayor Jack MacDonald. Steelworkers and students rub shoulders with off-duty cops and their wives. They also mix with country's top stars. Even if they aren't playing Elly's, they'll stop in after their own shows. In the past two months, Charley Pride and John Prine have stopped off after performing elsewhere in town, sung a few songs, talked to Elly and had a few beers."

Karen says she remembers when Charlie Pride came into the club. "That was cool to me, and I'll never forget the waitress. She was such a fan of his, she was just shaking. And I remember Stompin' Tom Connors up on the stage. He had quite a few drinks because they kept bringing them to him, and his foot was going like crazy. He is such a nice man. He was funny and I liked him a lot."

The *Spectator* article quoted Ella saying, "My daddy told me years ago that if you look after the working man, the working man will look after you. That's my code in here." And Wesley concluded his article, "As Elly's puts Hamilton in the forefront of country music across the province, the working man is looking after Elly very well indeed."[4]

Apparently, however, not well enough. Ella's string of misfortunes continued when the club was hit with serious flooding and she learned the building's plumbing was in bad shape, with sewer backup pipes so decayed they could be punctured with the slightest pressure. "It was devastating for her," says Karen. "She had fire and theft insurance on the place, but she didn't have flood or sewer backup insurance." Elly's robust income was soon being poured into plumbing repairs—repairs she couldn't keep up with as other bills went unpaid.

The first public hint of trouble appeared in the *Spectator* in early November 1980 in a short article with the two-column headline "Customers Go Dry as Barmen Strike."

"The staff at Elly's Place on King Street East refused to serve customers at about 8 p.m., claiming wages were up to six weeks overdue. About 80 customers waited patiently with empty glasses as the staff sat resolutely at a table by themselves.

"Tavern owner Elly Goodchild arrived shortly before 9 p.m. and strongly denied she owed her workers for more than the most recent two-week pay period."

Ella told the reporter someone was spreading false rumours. The workers were called into her office individually and paid in cash. But a spokesman for the waitresses, doormen, and bartenders claimed pay was a constant and continuing problem. "We can't tolerate any more of this," he said.

But most of the customers didn't leave when the drinks stopped, and a former employee told the *Spectator* he wasn't surprised. "It's a pretty loyal crowd," he said. "They were really supporting the staff because many of them have kids and mortgages and they have to be paid. The bands are good here and there's been good crowds."[5]

Less than a year after she opened her club, Ella was forced to close it. In a letter to the Liquor Control Board of Ontario dated January 19, 1981, she wrote:

I wish to inform the board that I cancel my liquor licence…The plumbing is a disaster. Floods all the time. Also the sewer's backup pipes you can put your fingers thru [sic] by just touching.

Plumbing firms figure it would all have to be redone as it's all breaking down and plugging the drains.

Sincerely yours,
Elly Goodchild

About three weeks later, Ella started work as a promoter at a tavern in nearby Winona, Ontario. "Elly's really gone country at the famous El Morocco Tavern," stated a flyer advertising her latest venture. The owner said Elly wasn't employed by him or renting his premise but was strictly into promotion. "She approached me because she had some good bands going to her place, but now she had no place to go," he said. "She said, 'I'm going to promote, and if you do good, you give me a commission.'"

The next day, February 9, 1981, the *Hamilton Spectator* ran an investigative article with a five-column headline—"Promoter Elly Back in Business"—that ruined whatever was left of her reputation and swiftly ended her new career as a promoter.

Gone were the kind words of earlier stories. "A country and western music promoter is back in business just two months after closing her tavern and leaving debts totalling more than $100,000," stated the lead sentence, setting the tone for the piece.

It said Elly was forced to close her doors in December 1980, "after more than $95,000 in judgments had been issued against her and the sheriff had seized her liquor supply as partial payment. During its year in business, Elly's Place was one of the most popular country and western spots in the area. Mrs. Goodchild put a sign on the door explaining she was closed for plumbing repairs and has been out of business ever since. Although her business apparently has no assets, she has not dissolved the company, nor has she declared bankruptcy."

The judgments against Elly, her husband Harry, and/or Elly's Place included about $35,000 for a defaulted mortgage—likely on the house they had lived in when they first moved to Hamilton or a property they'd invested in when the bar was booming—and about $28,000 owed in provincial and federal taxes. Money was also owed to the Royal Connaught Hotel for entertainers' accommodation and to singer Carroll Baker for a performance. About $3,000 was owed to former employees for back pay and wages.

Leo Barnett, who owned the building, said Elly owed him "a large amount" but he wouldn't try to collect because "it would be a lost cause. I was very generous with her and perhaps unwisely so...I certainly wasn't going to make her walk the plank. I'd rather lose the money than send the bailiff in."

Perhaps most devastating to Ella's personal image, the *Spectator* reported that after a benefit concert organized by her for the Ontario Society for Crippled Children (now the Easter Seal Society, Ontario), she issued the charity a $1,600 cheque that bounced and was not made good.

When the *Spectator* contacted Elly for comments, she said she didn't want to talk about the money she owed. "I don't think that's any of your business. If you want to speak to somebody, speak to my lawyer." When the reporter asked her for the name of her lawyer, she said, "Find out on your own," and hung up.[6]

The week before the article appeared, Ella was slated to appear in provincial court to face charges against Elly's Place under the Income Tax Act. She failed to appear, and the club was tried in absentia for failing to remit $425.80 in federal taxes deducted from employees. The judge entered a plea of not guilty, but after hearing the evidence found the company guilty and fined it $200.

The article included a report about Elly's promotion venture with the El Morocco. But she was let go eight days later, after a spokesman said the tavern received "a tremendous number of telephone calls from people saying they wouldn't patronize the place, and musicians who said they wouldn't play, if Elly Goodchild was here."[7]

ELLY COULD SEE NO FUTURE IN Hamilton, and when Harry Goodchild called to say his mother had died and asked her to return to Winnipeg to live with him and his elderly father, she quickly accepted. "Harry's dad was a real gentleman," said Elly. "He was around eighty but very agile. He belonged to a club that met twice a week, and they'd have jam sessions, and he'd go there for the music and get up and dance."

Karen says Elly felt sorry for Harry when his mother passed away. "Kathy and Cindy moved with her to Winnipeg," she says. "They moved into Grandpa Goodchild's place. Everybody called him that. He was a nice old man. I didn't go with them because I was tired of Mother telling me how to live my life."

Karen says that from the time she moved to Hamilton from New Brunswick, Elly was "really picky about how I should dress and if my nails weren't done right or my makeup wasn't the way she liked it. And as I got a little older, she started bugging me about not having a boyfriend. For nine years, she wasn't in my life and I didn't even know she existed, and now she's at me all the time. Then she introduced me to Frank, who happened to work at Elly's Place. So we dated, and then we got engaged. Everything was fine, and when I was eighteen, we moved in together. And then suddenly Mother decided he wasn't good enough for me and he drank too much."

Karen's relationship with Frank ended when she walked in unexpectedly one day and found him with a prostitute. It would be some time before she learned that Elly had played a role in that incident.

Once settled in Winnipeg, Elly was soon running the kitchens in two different restaurants. No one seems to know whether she ever paid the debts left behind in Hamilton. In later years, she spoke of the successes at Elly's Place and could rhyme off a long list of country recording stars who played for her. She spoke of the plumbing problems that led to the demise of the club, but made no mention of debts or other problems.

Karen says that in Winnipeg, Elly was still having problems with Harry over his drinking and gambling and his treatment of Cindy. "I was visiting her once, and we were going out. She and Harry had been fighting, and as we were leaving, she said, 'Don't you dare lay a hand on Cindy.' And he said, 'Don't worry, I won't touch her again.' Apparently, sometimes when he was drunk or drinking, he'd get mad at Cindy and hit her and lock her in her room."

As Karen entered her twenties, her relationship with her mother improved considerably. "I had left and I moved out to Calgary for two years," says Karen. "I came back to Winnipeg, and for probably a year, everything was fine. And then we were at a party and she let it slip that she had paid for the prostitute I caught with my boyfriend Frank in Hamilton. We ended up in a huge fight."

"I was just thinking of you," pleaded Elly. "He was no good for you."

"You were never a part of my life when I was young, so who the hell are you to run my life now?" said Karen.

It is difficult to defend such reprehensible conduct, but Elly's motives for hiring a hooker to lure Frank away from her daughter must be looked at in the context of her own life and of Estelle's marriage and recent death. Elly may have felt guilty for harping at her daughter for not having a boyfriend, thereby coercing her into the relationship. And if Frank did in fact have a drinking problem, Karen would thus avoid the drink-related problems that Elly was experiencing with Harry. Sending a prostitute to entice Frank may have also been a test of his fidelity to Karen—a test that he flunked.

Whatever Elly's rationale, Karen wasn't impressed. "All that criticism I took from her had just built up," says Karen. "She'd have a fit over how I lived, how I dressed, how I wore my hair—it was just too much controlling, and I lost it. I told her, 'I'm an adult, so fuck off,' and I didn't talk to her again for ten years. That was from the time I was twenty-one."

Although Elly wasn't moving around as much as she had, the personal rifts and professional failures were taking a physical and mental toll. The decade she spent in Hamilton was the longest she had been in one place since her childhood years in Westville, and by 1986 she'd been settled in Winnipeg with Harry Goodchild for five years. But she worked hard, was overweight, never slept properly, frequented bars and clubs with Harry, developed a taste for cold beer, and chain-smoked cigarettes, all the time swearing she never inhaled. "She always smoked," says her son John. "She was like a walking stovepipe. Christ, she used to go through two or three packs a day. She puts one out and reaches over and grabs another and keeps going."

That, plus working two jobs, left many wondering where Elly—Miss Elly to many patrons at the track or in the clubs—got her energy. Being constantly on the go, working and playing until she was exhausted, was a way to ward off the demons and keep her from replaying over and over in her mind the personal tragedies that dotted her life. And she always feared that the next trauma was just around the corner.

In late 1986, her fears were realized when she returned to her home on Plessis Road to find Harry's father on the couch in the living room. "He was crying and I could hear my daughter screaming. I ran upstairs, and Harry had his belt off and Cindy was on the bed trapped against the wall. The belt had a big country buckle and he was beating her with that. He didn't hear me, and I grabbed him and threw him out of the room and down the stairs. Cindy's body was full of red welts where the blood had surfaced when he hit her with the buckle. I thought Grandpa Goodchild was going to have a heart attack. He was so upset."

Harry was banished from the house, and soon after that incident, his aged father became seriously ill. Elly was with him the night he died. "I was sitting with him when Harry showed up," said Elly. "Grandpa was lying on his left side and he put his hand out to me between the bars on the bed rail. He said nothing to his son, and I was holding his hand when he died. I was very upset, because we were always close."

Harry didn't know it at the time, but he had cancer that would later be diagnosed as terminal. "He called me a few months after his father died and asked if he could move back to the house," said Elly. "He was diagnosed in March [1987] and said he had a short time to live. I gave him a room. I couldn't just throw him out on the street. And I was doing it out of respect for his father. I took him to the hospital three times a week for radiation and other treatment.

"He got religious and he used to go to the Salvation Army. And when he went into the hospital near the end, they would come to see him. They would stay all night, and that's the only way I could get a break. I'd get maybe two or three nights of sleep through the week. Then they put him on liquid morphine every three hours and he wasn't even in this world."

Harry Goodchild died in palliative care on September 7, 1987. He was cremated four days later.

A few months after the funeral, Elly asked Cindy if she remembered Harry.

"Yeah. He died," Cindy said.

"I know he died," said Elly. "Did you like him?"

"Nope."

"Why not?"

"He beat me up."

"When did he beat you up?"

"I don't know. But he hurt me with his belt."

"I just wanted to see if you remembered."

"Well, he can't hit me no more."

After she buried Harry, Elly decided once again that she needed a change of scenery. If Hamilton had done one thing for her, it had reaffirmed the love of country music so rooted in her past. Now she decided the next best place to "down home" was Calgary, Alberta, 825 miles to the east. Miss Elly was going to Cowtown.

14

Cowtown

Brenda Demoor, 39. Brockville, Ontario. Brenda was found dead in her apartment. No cause of death was given, but authorities indicated there was trauma to her body. Neighbours said the apartment had been the site of a few disturbances in recent months. Donald Hutchinson, who lived with Brenda, was charged with second-degree murder. (October 2006)

WHEN ELLY ARMOUR MOVED TO CALGARY IN NOVEMBER 1987, she was fifty-five, and she decided it was time to slow down, perhaps even retire. But the pull of country music brought her to a bar called Shorty's, where "as a favour" she began managing the place and booking performers. And not just local musicians and singers.

Since the mid-1970s, Elly had been travelling to Nashville, making business contacts with singers, writers, producers, and recording studio managers. One of the singers she befriended was country singing star Del Reeves, who had joined the Grand Ole Opry in 1966 and would perform there off and on for the next thirty-five years. Miss Elly persuaded Reeves[1] to travel north to Canada and perform at Shorty's, thus putting Shorty's—and herself—on Calgary's country music map.

Jan Patterson-Levi, a Calgary writer with Canada's *Country Music News*, remembers the first time she saw Elly. "We walked into Shorty's one day and I saw this lady who I'll never forget. She just seemed to be the only person in the room—her presence was so overwhelming." Patterson-Levi asked who she was. "Miss Elly," was the response. "Wow," said Patterson-Levi, "she's a cross between Dolly Parton and Shirley Temple. She has Dolly's boobs and Shirley's curls." The two were introduced and became fast friends.

Elly didn't retire. She stayed at Shorty's for fourteen months, then went on the move again when the opportunity arose for a partnership in a truck stop on the Trans-Canada Highway near the village of Paynton, Saskatchewan, between Saskatoon and Edmonton. The deal was made, and Elly moved Cindy there and rented a house nearby.

Bill Lyons was working and living in Paynton when Elly and her partners bought the place. "It was called the Big 3 when they bought it, but they changed it to the Fireside. It had gas pumps, a restaurant, a motel, and a truck stop with a big yard for the rigs. I was a grader operator for the municipality and I was also working two part-time jobs."

The truck stop was at the intersection of the highway and a gravel road about four miles from the centre of town—population about 150. In early 1990, Elly telephoned the municipal office and asked if she could get her parking lot graded to make it presentable to the truckers.

"It was probably in May, just after the spring breakup, and I went in and did the job," says Bill. "She seemed like a nice lady, and she said come back and visit—have a coffee or whatever. She was very busy and Cindy worked there with her. She was in a partnership with another man and a woman, so she never did get to do everything she wanted, but she put in a stage and brought music into the place."

Elly said Bill "was just a customer, but when I decided to renovate, he helped the carpenter with all the walls, woodworking, putting in the stage, and laying the carpet. It was a lot of work, and he wouldn't take any money for anything."

Bill says Elly "brought in musicians from Calgary to play. It was always country music on Fridays and Saturdays. Local farmers and others came out and it was always crowded."

Bill was forty and Elly was just days away from her fifty-eighth birthday when they met, but there was a strong mutual attraction and he soon became a fixture at the Fireside. The place was licensed, and once again Elly called on her friend Del Reeves to play for her. "He played there for six days," says Bill, and she had me watching the door and taking pictures of Del with customers for autographs, and I was actually his bodyguard so nobody would bother him."

Bill, a hard worker and solidly built, stood more than a full head taller than the five-foot-two Elly. Despite the age difference, they began living together in October 1990. "We both had houses," he says. "She was renting and I kind of moved in with her. Then she decided she didn't want to rent anymore. I owned a house, so she and Cindy moved in with me. On August 25, I put an engagement ring on her finger."

Bill was divorced and his children, a boy and a girl, were living with their mother nearby. He and Elly spent some time with them. "I've got pictures of my kids where she put on a birthday party for them," he says. "But then my ex-wife remarried and they moved with the kids to Edmonton."

ONE DAY, ELLY RECEIVED A TELEPHONE call from an acquaintance in Calgary who knew of Elly's reputation for helping people in trouble and who claimed that her children were being abused by her common-law husband. Paynton was nearly four hundred miles away, but Elly promised to do what she could. "We drove to Calgary," says Bill, "and Elly went to the trailer where the woman was living and she talked to her."

Elly quickly assessed the situation. The woman—who had once worked for her as a waitress, but who had also been an accomplished accountant with a good income—had a drug problem, and her common-law husband was an abusive drunk. He was not the father of her two children, ten-year-old David[2] and his eight-year-old sister. David told Elly that the man had physically and sexually abused him and his little sister and that he would drink beer and cook and eat in front of them but never allow them to eat. Elly sent Bill out to pick up two large pizzas, which she later said the children "gobbled down, because they were half-starved."

The woman asked Elly if she would take David. Elly agreed immediately, and she also arranged to have his sister sent to live with her maternal grandmother. Then she went directly to the Calgary police station and a warrant was issued for the common-law husband. He was from Newfoundland, and when he learned the police were looking for him, he reportedly headed back to the Maritimes. "He used to work in lumbering, and they were looking for him in the woods of Newfoundland," said Elly. "I don't know if they ever caught him."

Elly raised David until he completed high school, and he continued to live with her off and on until he was twenty-one. He worked for a time in waste management with the Saskatchewan government and later moved to Toronto, where his sister also lived. "He was very smart and a computer whiz," said Elly. "I got him a computer for his room, and when he was younger, he loved the [Anaheim] Mighty Ducks so much he made wallpaper with their emblem on it and covered his room with it. He did all that on his computer."

IT'S NOT CLEAR EXACTLY WHAT went wrong, but by the spring of 1991, the Fireside was in trouble. There was considerable acrimony between Elly and her partners, and the business closed. "It went down the tube and we moved to Calgary," says Bill.

"I missed Calgary," said Elly. "I was tired of being *countrified.*"

Bill says they lived in a mobile home in a trailer park, and it was there that, a few months later, a series of incidents concerning his children—then living in Edmonton with their mother, stepfather, and older stepbrother—led to a catastrophic emotional breakdown.[3] Bill went into a severe depression. Elly said Bill "had turned white" when he learned what had happened to his children in Edmonton. "He sat with his head down and said nothing. It took its toll on him."

A day or two later, with Easter coming up, Elly "walked to the store to pick up a few things. When I came home, Bill had moved from the kitchen to the bedroom. I called out to him, but there was no answer." She saw a note from him on the table saying, "Have a Happy Easter and please explain to the kids."

"Explain what?" she thought.

She went to the bedroom. "The door was open, and he was sitting on the edge of the bed with his rifle between his knees and the barrel in his mouth," said Elly. "He was just staring—like he was in a trance. My heart was racing. He had long arms and his thumbs were on the trigger."

She had known Bill had a hunting rifle, but he had always kept it concealed. It was a .30-30—the same type as the one Vernon Ince had used for hunting, and the one that had killed him.

"I was thinking, "Oh no, not a gun in my life again,'" said Elly. "I tried not to panic." She called his name softly, but there was no response. "He was still staring into space and I kept talking to him, telling him I was going to walk slowly to the bed and sit beside him. I was terrified the whole time that he would pull the trigger and blow his head off."

Bill didn't respond as she moved closer, one slow step at a time. "I was in a real state," he says. "I don't remember any of it."

Elly gingerly sat down beside him on the bed. "Think about your children," she said. "They are going to really need you. You have to be around for them." Finally, he unhooked his thumbs from the trigger and removed the barrel from his mouth. "I think talking about his children must have got through to him," said Elly, "but that's only my guess. I grabbed the rifle, ran into the living room, and threw it under the sofa. He never moved. I called a friend and then the doctor and read him the note. He told me to get him to the hospital immediately. I drove and my friend sat with Bill. He never said a single word. The doctor had called ahead and they were waiting for him in emergency. Doctors and nurses tried to talk to him, but he said nothing."

Bill was eventually transferred from the emergency department to the hospital's psychiatric ward.

"It was a lock-up, and he wasn't allowed to leave," said Elly. "I went home and I cried. I was so upset. I had never seen anything like this before or since. I was terrified."

Bill says Elly stood by him through his ordeal. At one point, his depression apparently deepened and doctors feared he might go into a catatonic state and not come out of it. "I called his mother and had to tell her over the phone," said Elly. "She came down with his brother and they stayed with me. I warned them both to expect strange things. Bill was talking at that point, but he made no sense. It was like he was with kids playing in a sandbox."

The hospital telephoned Elly at two in the morning and told her that Bill was in crisis. The alternatives were electric shock treatment or a powerful experimental drug. "She had to make a life-and-death decision for me," says Bill. "She didn't want them to do the shock treatment, so she told them to go ahead with the drugs."

The fear was that the drug would cause his heart to stop or adversely affect other vital organs. Elly says Bill was administered a pill every hour or so. "I don't know how many pills they gave me," says Bill, "but it shut my kidneys down for part of one day, and then they gave me something else to get them going again. The doctor had warned Elly it would be dangerous. She made the right choice, or I wouldn't be here today."

In time, Bill made a full recovery and was out of the hospital in three months. Elly didn't want him to return to the surroundings where the gun incident had occurred, so they rented a four-bedroom house on Pinewood Close in a quiet neighbourhood in Calgary's northeast.

Bill is not ashamed of the breakdown, nor reticent to talk about it. "I've slipped a bit once in a while," he says, "but through the counselling I've had, I recognize the symptoms and can deal with it before it becomes a problem. It's just depression. You start thinking about something and it can overwhelm you. You just have to get your mind off it and move on."

Bill also makes himself available to help others on an informal basis. "My friends know what I went through, and if they hear of someone who needs help, they put them in touch with me. I do that for people who are feeling down. It's just conversation between friends. I open up to them, and then they open up to me because we're both on the same page—we've got something in common."

BILL WAS SOON RUNNING A warehouse for a construction company providing cement products to Calgary's booming home-building industry. In his spare time, he helped Elly, who had taken over a downtown bar called Buckaroos. "She was managing it for a guy, and he was about to lose it, so he sold it to her for $1," says Bill. "So he walked out and she took over. They chased *him* for his debt and we ran the place."

But they wouldn't run it for long. Elly took over in late 1993, but by March her bad luck had caught up with her yet again. "The band was playing one night, and they were complaining and everybody was saying their eyes were burning. I didn't know it, but we had carbon monoxide escaping through the furnace," said Elly. "A few days later, I noticed I was tired all the time and my legs started to swell up, and I couldn't figure out why. I thought maybe I was just working too much. The next day, I put out a cigarette just as we pulled up at Buckaroos. Seven staff were waiting for us, including morning cooks, waitresses, and bartenders."

Bill Lyons was a fully trained volunteer fireman, and as soon as he opened the door, he was hit with the smell of raw gas. He screamed at everyone to get away from the building and to call the fire department. "The building is going to go up!" he shouted.

"I'm just lucky I put my cigarette out before I tried to go in there," said Elly. "Bill said the blast would have taken out a whole city block and we would have all been dead."

Bill covered his head with his jacket and entered the building. He went to the basement and shut off the furnace and the gas supply. The fire department arrived and opened all the doors. There were no windows in the upstairs bar, and if the furnace had blown when the place was full, there would have been considerable loss of life. Necessary repairs to the building would have been hugely expensive and would have taken weeks, if not months.

"The furnace crapped out, and Elly didn't have insurance to cover for loss of income, so the landlord locked the door," says Bill. "The furnace guys came in and found out where the raw gas was coming through and the leaks that were causing release of carbon monoxide.

"That was when Elly ended up with a major heart attack."

Bill says Elly and her daughter Kathy, who was staying with them at the time, were playing cards at the kitchen table when "Elly got short of breath and went into the living room and sat in a chair. Her chest was heaving and she'd had a massive heart attack. Kathy and I got her to the car and rushed her to the Calgary General Hospital up on Memorial Drive. She had two blood clots in her heart, and they gave her blood thinners to dissolve them, but it didn't work. They couldn't operate on her, but she was in the hospital for about two weeks. She ended up in a wheelchair for a year and a half."

Karen Melanson hadn't seen her mother in ten years, other than the time Elly came to see her in the hospital after the birth of her son Ryan. "That was it until 1994, when I decided to get married after living common-law for several years," says Karen. "I agonized about it for about six months before the wedding, and then I thought the kids should at least meet her, so I invited her."

Elly did her own agonizing. Karen says Bill told her, "She didn't want to come because I had had nothing to do with her for so long. He convinced her to come. The worst part was she had just had a massive heart attack. But she came down in her wheelchair anyway."

The reunion at the wedding was a watershed moment for mother and daughter, who on that day became Karen Gardiner. "From that time on, we had a lot of long talks and I told her, 'You can't rule my life," says Karen. "She didn't like my husband, and I

said, 'You have no right to criticize—you don't even know him.' I
was quite nasty and laid everything on the line, because she didn't
want to let up. She got the message. And then she relaxed and we
became best friends. It was like a big soap opera."

THANKS TO BILL LYONS, being in a wheelchair didn't curtail Elly's
lifestyle. "They told her many times to quit smoking. But she kept
saying she didn't inhale and she was going to have her cigarettes
and beer because that was her pleasure in life. I drove her everywhere. She wanted to go out to the clubs and bars, so I would take
her in the wheelchair. And if I couldn't get her upstairs by myself,
the musicians would come out and help me lift her and the chair.
And when she got tired, we would take her out."

A year after her heart attack, Elly had angioplasty to open a
clogged artery at the front of her heart. "She felt better, but she was
still in the wheelchair," says Bill. "I had no strength in my legs, and
I was depressed lying in bed," said Elly. "And I am not a person to
be depressed."

Bill encouraged her, suggesting she could formalize her practice
of helping singers and musicians get a start by arranging recording
sessions, setting up meetings with established musicians, or lining
up venues that would allow them to perform. "I told her she could
do a lot of that over the phone," says Bill. "She had all kinds of
contacts here and in Nashville."

Elly saw the logic in his suggestion and quickly formed a new
company called Canada's Rocky Mountain Productions and Talent
Agency Inc., which became known as Rocky Mountain
Productions, with Elly as president. She appointed Bill Lyons vice-
president and daughter Karen in Winnipeg as entertainment
chairman. And one of her Nashville friends, Dotty Wilson, would
run a satellite office of the company out of her home.

"Dotty offered to be her liaison down in Nashville for channelling performers to the U.S." says Karen. "And in Winnipeg, I filled in once in a while, lining up bookings in Saskatchewan, Manitoba, and Northern Ontario for performers and musicians. Mother did most of it on the phone herself. She would also send out demo CDs, and if a club or bar or casino liked it, they would call with a booking. If she booked them, she would get a cut."

Describing her company, Elly said, "I promote talent, record them, and put them on the market. The pull for me is, there's lots of talent out there, but a lot of them don't have the money or the knowledge to get exposure, so I help them with that. I record some people for free if I think they are good enough. I've done that and put them on the market, and some of them get picked up and make it and some don't—but at least they get a chance. My only rule is that they have to work at it. It takes a lot of hard work to make it."

Elly was enjoying her growing new business venture but hated being confined to a wheelchair. She decided a year and a half was long enough and it was time to help herself. "She knew that her heart wasn't going to get any better," says Bill. "They couldn't operate because of blood thinners, which she had to stay on. Because she smoked, her heart functioned at 75 percent before her heart attack. After that, it was down to 30 percent, and that's where it stayed."

"I made up my mind to beat it and start walking," said Elly. "I had Cindy set the chairs up in the kitchen, and I would hold on to them and take two steps and then sit down, and she'd move another chair over and I would start again. We just kept moving the chairs around, and that's how I started. I did a little more every day until I could finally walk without holding the chairs, and then I got rid of the wheelchair."

Throughout all of Elly's health problems, Bill was at her side, just as she had been for him. They cared deeply for each other, but he was chagrined that, after an engagement now in its fifth year, Elly wouldn't agree to marriage.

Elly confided her concerns on the phone to her daughter. "Karen, if I marry him, he will die," said Elly, "because every time I get married, they die. I haven't done too well. The last two husbands I picked died of cancer. What if I marry him? He's just going to turn around and die of cancer."

"Mom, that's dumb thinking," said Karen.

"Yeah, but I can't get it out of my head."

"Is it really necessary to get married?"

"No."

"Then don't worry about it. As long as you're happy, that's what counts."

BILL LYONS HAD TO ACCEPT Elly's penchant for helping others, even if it meant inviting them to live in their home. He was used to her daughter Cindy and young David, who had become part of their family, and he was aware that many others had come and gone in Elly's life before him, including a mentally challenged male adult she looked after for about a year until she found his family and convinced him to go home.

"Then John moved in about 1995," says Bill.

John was an elderly married pensioner who had had his life savings extorted and been reduced to eating on credit at Zellers, where he had breakfast and coffee once a day and paid his bill each month when his pension cheque came in. "They let him do that because he'd been a regular there for years," said Elly, who met him there when a friend told her about him. "He started stuttering because he was so upset. This gang would pick him up and drive him to the bank and order him to go in and withdraw his money. It would be $5,000 here, $7,000 there. They threatened him with a gun and he was scared to death. They went through $65,000 and then they went to his three-bedroom mobile home and cleaned out everything. The only thing that was left was a washer and dryer, and not even a glass for a drink of water. They stripped everything—his coin collection, stamp collection, radio, even his father's watch and jewellery. All of his keepsakes were gone."

John was given his own room and settled in as part of Elly's expanded family. He would live there for more than eleven years, until dementia forced him into a nursing home.

Besides young David and old John, both of whom stayed long-term, many others came for short-term stays. At one point Elly actually hired a nurse's assistant because the woman could barely support her family. When the woman confided she was having trouble with her fifteen-year-old daughter, who was "on the street," Elly took the daughter in too. "She was with us for about four months," says Bill. "Elly talked to her a lot, and then she went home, and hopefully not back to the streets.

"There were others who stayed periodically—a week or two here, or a week or two there. She would have them at the house to get them straightened out and on their feet. And there was one musician who stayed for ten months. He was on crack, and she got him straightened out and sent him on his way. And he's living on his own now and working a day job and playing music at night."

Asked why, Elly said, "I take people in and make them feel secure. I've taken in twenty-three over the years, mostly children, and I brought some of them up and I'm very proud of that. I'm not a foster parent. I just took them in, and I never asked for any money from anybody." She said the exception was old John, who used some of his pension "to help with room and board."

But what was Bill Lyons' reaction to so many people traipsing through his life?

"It was fairly easy once I got to understand her," he says. "It was all trust and honesty. She did her thing and I let her do it. It was easier just to go along. But sometimes I would argue and explain what I felt if I disagreed with her. I admit I was a little testy when she first brought people in, but then I understood that it was something she had always done. It was part of who she was and I was fine with that. She was a good person."

JIM FISHER RETIRED FROM the Calgary Police Service in 2004 after a twenty-five-year career, mostly as an undercover officer. "Elly had a big heart and she would go out of her way to help others," he says. "She was definitely a character, and I had a lot of respect for her in a lot of different ways."

At the time they met, Fisher was a senior officer in the department's organized crime sector, "running a deep undercover unit targeting high-priority criminals. We did insertions, putting my guys in positions where they would have long-term—months or half a year at a time—interactions with the bad guys to generate information that would lead to charges."

Fisher was at work one day when he received a tip from a friend at the ICPB (Insurance Crime Prevention Bureau) who said he had "this lady" who had information about a sophisticated theft ring.

"Elly was in his office when I went over," says Fisher. "It kind of baffled me. We're into organized crime, and this elderly lady with the big hair is going to provide us some information? It was kind of humorous. After talking to her for an hour or two, it became apparent that she really had her faculties and she knew what she was doing and she was really helpful.

"She had lots of stuff, and I dug into her background to determine if she would be a reliable informant. I had to establish that. We had her registered as an informant for a period of time when we were first operating that case. Over the years, she did provide an awful lot of information to different investigators."

In that first case, Fisher says, Elly had met a husband-and-wife team who were selling jewellery at a flea market. "She had a feeling they were selling stolen property," he says, "so she just talked to them a little bit. And she was pretty adept at picking things out. She was pretty certain this is what they were doing, and she was willing to work with me on it."

Elly was upset that the two were using about twenty young people to steal vehicles and to break into businesses to steal high-end computers.

"It was just a small-town organization," says Fisher, "but they had hundreds of thousands of dollars in computer equipment that they moved regularly and it was a coordinated effort. They would have these young people steal the computers and store them in a warehouse they had and then ship them out to Kelowna, British Columbia. And in Penticton they had an actual pawn shop. They would change all the guts in the computer towers so you couldn't really determine which was stolen and which wasn't. They totally interchanged them and sold them in B.C.

"She had conversations and meetings with these people, and she was able to identify all that stuff. I think fifteen or twenty stolen vehicles were recovered and about $400,000 in stolen computer equipment. I think we brought in ten or twelve suspects, besides the ringleaders. We videotaped everything she told us because we were worried about her condition and that she might pass on before she went to court. She was a protective informant, but she was prepared to testify if necessary. In the end, she didn't have to because they pleaded guilty. The perps never did know about her.

"Elly was a very cooperative informant, and we were almost going to agentize her and do a letter of agreement and provide her with X amount of money for service, but given her age and her heart condition, we kind of thought that's not a good idea. I just ended up using all her information and made arrangements so that she actually received money from the ICPB, because ultimately she provided us with the information that led to the convictions."

Fisher says he enjoyed working with Elly and they became good friends. "I think in the ten years or so I knew her, a month didn't go by without us speaking. She was in the hospital when my daughter was first born and she held her before I did. So she became a cherished friend."

Elly laughed whenever she remembered Cindy's reaction to Fisher when he once visited their home in full uniform. "He was at a police funeral, and they were always in full uniform for that," she said. "I made him a sandwich and he was having a coffee at the kitchen table when Cindy came upstairs from her room and stopped dead in her tracks."

"Are you really a cop?" asked Cindy.

"Yes, I am," said Fisher.

Cindy became very nervous. "And you've got those things you put on people's wrists?" she asked.

Fisher showed her his handcuffs.

"And you have a gun?"

Fisher removed his service revolver from its holster.

"Is that real?"

He laid the gun on the table. "It's unloaded, if you want to hold it," he said.

Cindy was now wide-eyed. "Are you going to arrest me?" she asked, and then ran away before Fisher could answer.

Cindy had probably watched too much television with her mother, who preferred police documentaries and dramas. "Her favourite television show was *Quincy, M.E.*," says her daughter, Karen Gardiner. "She liked any detective shows and any crime-fighting shows. *Law and Order,* CSI, *Unsolved Mysteries*—she loved them all, and that's all she ever watched. And she liked to read murder mysteries and crime."

Elly hadn't liked the idea that the couple she helped convict had tried to sell stolen jewellery to her. "You have to do things right and I don't let people take advantage of me," she said.

Fisher says Elly "just couldn't let somebody else have one over on her. Like these particular people we charged, I mean she was *mad* that they were doing something—taking advantage of people. I liked that, admired that in her quite a bit."

He initially treated Elly like any other informant. "But she really wanted to get involved with it. She had a lot of information and she was always around the flea markets and the Crossroads Hotel, which had a country bar that she frequented fairly often. So she really had good insight into what was going on. She was totally fearless, and that established our relationship."

15

All That Glitters

Thayalini Subramaniam, 31. Markham, Ontario. Mother of three. Thayalini was found dead in her garage by her seven-year-old daughter. Cause of death, according to police, was "homicidal hanging with blunt force trauma injuries to the head." Her husband, Sugirthanraj Kailayapillai, was charged with second-degree murder. (November 2006)

ELLY WAS DELIGHTED WHEN SHE HEARD FROM HER FIRST cousin and childhood playmate, Dorothy Watters, after so many years. Dorothy and her husband, Tin, dropped in to Calgary on their way to Michigan to visit their son. Tin Watters also had a first cousin in Calgary—Earl Joudrie. "He moved west when I was just a baby," he says. "And Earl eventually became a big oil tycoon."

Earl and his wife, Dorothy, a former high school English teacher, had four grown children and were part of the social elite in Calgary. But by January 1995, they had been informally separated for five years and he was living with another woman in Toronto. When Earl showed up with divorce papers—outlining a settlement that would give Dorothy $1.9 million, plus $2,000 a month for two years—she lured him into the garage, where she had hidden a .25-calibre Beretta under the driver's seat of her Jaguar. She fired six shots into Earl's back and was charged with attempted murder.

They nicknamed her "Six-Shot Dot." The jury found Dorothy *not* criminally responsible of attempted murder by reason of temporary insanity. She was held in custody at Edmonton's Alberta Hospital for five months, then granted an absolute discharge in 1998.[1] Earl Joudrie recovered from his wounds and resumed his business career, with four bullets still lodged in his body.[2]

"She pumped a few into him all right," says Tin Watters. "So when I'm talking about Vernon and Elly—my wife's cousin—I can't help but think about my cousin too. Small world, isn't it?"

Small indeed. But the Joudrie shooting—involving a country club couple with all the trappings of the rich—could be seen as a metaphor for what was happening to Calgary itself. Dubbed Canada's new "golden city," oil money was pouring in and construction cranes dotted the skyline. But behind the new glass and steel facades lurked serious social problems that would affect more and more women.

POPULAR CANADIAN COUNTRY music singer Julian Austin is known within the Canadian forces as "GI Jules." He has performed on bases around the world, including Bosnia, Alert (in the Arctic), and Afghanistan, which he visited several times. "I love playing for the troops," says Austin, who wrote and recorded the song "The Red and White," described by the *Toronto Sun* as "a raw and moving tribute to Canadian soldiers who have fallen in war. "

Austin also loved Miss Elly. And the feeling was mutual. But it was the music that sold Elly on the tattooed, straight-talking singer with the earrings, the trademark cowboy hat, and the powerful stage presence.

Austin moved to Calgary in 1998, and the two met at the Country Roads bar at the Crossroads Hotel (now the Radisson). "Back then, there were bands playing Tuesday night to Saturday night," says Austin. "So everybody and their dog was there. The musicians would go there to see other bands. I used to get up and jam with all of them."

The first thing he noticed about Elly was her hair—dyed blonde and piled high on top with long cascading curls down the sides and back. "The big hair," he laughs. "A lot of wigs could be made out of that. It was always perfect. I swear to God it was custom-made and she could take it off, set it down, and put it back on like a hat. It was like it had snaps or something. She took great pride in how she looked. She was a total lady."

Karen Gardiner says her mother went to the same hairdresser "for years and years. She would do it just the way Elly wanted it. She loved her beehive, poofy hair. The weird part was, it was all her own, and yet when it was down, there wasn't much to it. It was just all teasing. It's amazing what a hairdresser can do."

Once, during a four-hour trip to the hairdresser, Karen asked her mother why she wore her hair that way. "It makes me feel taller," said Elly. "It makes me feel like a lady. And it makes me feel pretty. That's why I have it done like this."

Julian Austin says, "Everybody in country music in Alberta knew of Miss Elly. She was a well-known and well-liked lady, and she loved to be around musicians. You'd see her at Sam Buca's, you'd see her at Crossroads, at Town and Country, at Ranchman's—she went to all of them. She always supported us, and I couldn't believe the people she knew. She introduced my wife, Angela, and me to Stu and Helen Hart, and we got to see them on occasion."

Stu Hart had been an outstanding centre for the Edmonton Eskimos before becoming the patriarch of an internationally famous wrestling clan. Stu and Helen had twelve children, including eight sons, and Hart was respected around the world for developing and training young wrestlers, including two of his sons, long-time champion Bret "The Hitman" Hart, and Owen, who was killed at the age of thirty-four in an accident in the ring in 1999. Stu retired after selling Stampede Wrestling to Vince McMahon in 1984, was named a Member of the Order of Canada in 2001, and died two years later at the age of eighty-eight.

Another wrestler who trained with Hart and his sons was Montreal-born Christopher Benoit, whose ring name was the "Canadian Crippler." Benoit won the wwe world heavyweight championship in 2004. "He learned submission wrestling from my dad, and right away you knew he was a natural," says another son, Ross Hart.[3]

The entire wrestling world was shocked in late June 2007 when the news broke that Benoit had strangled his wife, Nancy, on a Friday night in their million-dollar home near Atlanta and the next day suffocated their son, seven-year-old son Daniel, then hanged himself with a weight-machine pulley in his exercise room.

In 2003, after three years of marriage, Nancy Benoit had filed for divorce, citing "cruel treatment," but later retracted. She also dropped a request for a restraining order against her husband that stated he had threatened her and broken furniture in their home. The couple reconciled and built their dream home in the Atlanta suburb of Fayetteville.

Nowhere in the world was the shock and grief over Christopher Benoit more profound than it was in Calgary.

JULIAN AUSTIN SAID HE DIDN'T know anything about Elly's past or that she had killed her first husband, Vernon Ince. Elly once said, "I don't think 99 per cent of people even know my name. Everybody just calls me Miss Elly."

"Miss Elly certainly did love us misfits, and she was truly a great ambassador for country music," says Austin. "She helped a lot of young musicians get a start, and some older ones too. She was pro-Canadian, that's for sure, and her heart was bigger than Canada. But she also knew so many people down in Nashville too. She introduced to me to Ray Griff [now based in Calgary] and a whole bunch of great people and respected people that knew Miss Elly. It was like, WOW." Elly considered Canadian-born Griff, who spent thirty years in Nashville as a successful singer-songwriter, a dear friend. Griff wrote more than two thousand songs for a wide range of country music artists including Jerry Lee Lewis, Dolly Parton, Hank Snow, Chet Atkins, and George Jones.

Austin played several fund-raisers that Elly promoted. "She would call me for help with a charity event," he says. "She helped abused kids and others. I'm going to have to do more, because Miss Elly made me an 'ambassador' for her organization.

Elly sponsored eleven charities. "I did shows for them," she said, "and all the bands played for me. I did one for kids with cancer, and another when three singers asked me to arrange a fund-raiser in Calgary for a woman dying of cancer in Newfoundland. We had a capacity crowd in a two-hundred-seat bar. We raised $3,200, and it helped pay for her funeral and lighten the financial strain on her family."

"There were people like Miss Elly who were good for the music industry," says Austin. "They were underdogs—and some times you realize it's too bad they're not around running things."

Elly worked hard to gain the respect of the musicians and singers—the people in the industry who meant the most to her. "Hard work keeps me going," she said. "It keeps me happy. I'm very well respected here and nobody knows my background." (She was talking about her violent marriage, not her failed business ventures.)

Elly was often on stage introducing performers, but from time to time she could be convinced to perform herself. "Remember, I used to sing with a band when I was young and I sang in a church choir and I did solos," she said. "I'm used to using a microphone. The last time, I sang the song 'Pass Me By (If You're Only Passing Through).'"4

Elly did a bit of songwriting herself, including one called "Toolbox," about a mother who liked "to party" and who left her husband and her little boy "for the bright lights" while the boy cried for her every night. "I didn't have the voice to record it," said Elly. "It's a nice song, but a sad song."

It's also clearly autobiographical, probably born out of her guilt over the separation from her children and abandoning John at a young age. In the song, the boy prays to God to "send my mommy home...I love you mommy, I forgive you mommy, please come back home." The chorus explains the title: "Don't cry, daddy, mommy left us all alone...I'll go and get the toolbox so you can fix our broken home."

WHEN KAREN GARDINER travelled from Winnipeg to visit her mother, it usually meant a night out at the Legion or one of the country bars to listen to music. "On one of my visits, a band was playing that she knew really well," says Karen. "One of the guitarists with the group made a pass at me. I told him no thanks, I was married. He said he had split from his wife and he gave me his card and he said if anything ever happens to please think of him and give him a call. I said yeah, sure, okay."

Two weeks later, Elly called Karen in Winnipeg.

"Do you remember that guy who was hitting on you?" she asked.

"Yeah."

"Well, he killed his wife," said Elly. "He beat her and stabbed her to death."

That murder affected Elly, who was already distressed over the seemingly endless newspaper and television accounts of women and children being killed or brutalized. "It seems like it's happening all the time," she said. "The other day there was a girl, seventeen, who was killed. She was three months pregnant, and her boyfriend got mad about something and he stabbed her to death— in the stomach, everywhere. He stabbed her, and stabbed her, and stabbed her. I can't stand it."

IN FACT, THE BOOMING CITY and province in which Elly was then living is one of the least safe places in the country for women. In December 2006, *Toronto Star* writer David Olive reported that after "recent years of soaring prices for oil and gas, Alberta lives in the imagination of many Canadians outside the province as a nirvana of exceptional prosperity."⁵ And a seven-page *Maclean's* magazine article by Anne Kingston described Calgary as "Canada's new power nexus" and "a city on steroids."⁶

Kingston said the city—whose population passed the one-million mark in 2006—"is in turbo-drive, fuelled by an oil price jump from US$10 a barrel to more than US$60 now."⁷ That was in March 2006. Five months later, the price had risen to more than US$70 a barrel. "With no sales tax and a flat provincial tax, Alberta, with zero debt and a budget surplus of more than $10 billion, has become a wealth magnet," Kingston wrote. One local businessman told her that if the province "could lose the federal tax, we'd be the Grand Caymans of Canada."

Kingston said Calgary's "redneck reputation is a tourist conceit, rooted in the yahoo-cowboy legacy of the Calgary Stampede… but Cowtown is in fact a corporate, white-collar centre."

The source of Calgary's wealth is Alberta's vast oil sands, second only to Saudi Arabia's oil reserves in size and being developed at a furious pace, 460 miles to the north near Fort McMurray, by companies and suppliers headquartered in Calgary.

Both Olive and Kingston touched on some of the negatives— besides the high cost of new and rental housing and the minuscule vacancy rates—that have surfaced in Calgary along with the oil boom. Olive wrote about the widening gap between the rich and the poor, and cited a report by the Pembina Institute, a Calgary-based think-tank, which stated that increasing stress levels due to work demands and financial challenges were resulting in increased rates of obesity, problem gambling, and suicide.

Even the June 2007 interim report of the Alberta government's Crime Reduction and Safe Communities Task Force stated, "Some people are thriving while others are struggling to keep up." The report said that homelessness and a lack of affordable housing were serious issues affecting safety and security, particularly in the two major cities of Calgary and Edmonton, and that the high level of disposable income was a source of crime. What the report described as a "work hard, play hard attitude" encouraged increased drug and alcohol use.

"Steroidal growth doesn't come without side effects," said the *Maclean's* article. "Major strains on the system are evident. Tradespeople are in short supply. It can take more than two and a half years to get a house built. A record low three-per-cent unemployment rate has resulted in a paucity of minimum-wage workers...Vacancy rates hovering near zero mean shortage of choice. Crime is on the rise."[8]

Neither the *Maclean's* nor the *Toronto Star* article mentioned that the Calgary Police Service averages more than 11,000 "domestic-violence-related" calls every year and that women's shelters in the province received more than 100,000 crisis calls in the fiscal year ending March 31, 2007.[9] But the task force did report that in 2004, "Alberta had the highest rate of spousal assault against women," and that from 1975 to 2004, the province "has generally had the third highest spousal homicide rate" in Canada.[10]

The interim report of the task force, released after two months of consultations across the province, states that "Alberta has one of the highest rates of violent victimization among the provinces (160 per 1,000 people). To put that in perspective: in one year, adults in Alberta were victims of 54,000 sexual assaults, 42,000 robberies, and 315,000 assaults."

The report continued, "In many communities, we heard about domestic abuse and family violence and the impact it has on families and children. Sexual assaults were raised as an issue...along with a concern that we're not hearing the full story because so many sexual assaults are not reported."

Jan Reimer, former mayor of Edmonton, knows the statistics and is blunt in her assessment of what they mean. "Alberta is in fact the most dangerous province in which to be a woman. We lead the provinces in the number of women who report being stalked, who report being assaulted by their partners, and have one of the highest rates of murder-suicide. We also have one of the highest rates of homicides related to domestic violence."[11]

Since 2002, Reimer has been the provincial coordinator of the Alberta Council of Women's Shelters (ACWS),[12] which represents forty-one agencies involved in emergency, second-stage, and senior's shelters. In its report covering the fiscal year ending March 31, 2007, the council reported that the more than 100,000 crisis calls received by Alberta's shelters was a 15 per cent increase over the previous year.[13] In addition, the report found that

- 37 per cent of women admitted to emergency shelters requested and received police assistance

- 78 per cent of women resident in shelters are at high or serious risk of danger in their intimate-partner relationship, while 96 per cent of those in second-stage shelters are at high or serious risk of assault or homicide
- 21 per cent of emergency shelter bed capacity and 81 per cent of second-stage shelters remain *unfunded* by the provincial government
- 13,000 women and children were resident in Alberta's shelters, but nearly 15,000 women and children were turned away *because they were full*. The turn-away number was up by over 1,500 from the previous fiscal year

Carolyn Goard, director of integrated services for the Calgary YWCA, says, "We are more often than not faced with providing women support in the community as they wait for space to free up in a shelter. We never turn women away, even when we are full. Women and children stay temporarily in the YWCA Mary Dover House, our transitional shelter. We also work closely with the other four women's emergency shelters in the Calgary area to refer women when we are full." And if a woman is at high risk in the city, Goard says, her organization will make arrangements to move her to a shelter elsewhere in Alberta, or even to another province, to keep her safe.

"Affordable housing in Calgary is virtually nonexistent," says Goard. "We have very few second-stage transitional safe housing apartments in Calgary, compared with the estimated 2,700 women and children accessing our emergency shelters in Calgary every year, many of whom need the added security provided by a second-stage shelter. We at the YWCA do our utmost to support women finding housing and are constantly frustrated with our lack of success."

ELLY ARMOUR WASN'T LOOKING AT numbers and statistics. She was distressed over the deaths of "real people" like Mary Kay Schmidt, a fifty-two-year-old grandmother who was killed in her home by her common-law husband and long-time abuser, forty-nine-year-old Michael Steven Mitchell, on September 25, 2005. Like Elly, Schmidt was a cat lover, and several of them "scurried around the yellow police tape cordoning off the home" after police found her dead.[14] Mary Anne Sanderson, executive director of the Calgary Women's Emergency Shelter, said at the time that, with three months still to go, 2005 had turned into the deadliest year in Alberta's family violence history, with fourteen deaths. Mitchell was charged with second-degree murder.[15]

Then there was Brenda Moreside, stabbed to death by her common-law husband, Stanley Willier, at her home in High Prairie, Alberta. The night she was killed, she called 911 and the RCMP for help, complaining that Willier, who had a long and violent criminal history, was intoxicated and trying to break into the house. No one came. She was told that he could not be arrested because he was damaging his own property. Twelve days later, her decomposing body was discovered in her home and Willier was charged with second-degree murder.[16]

Cases involving children were particularly upsetting to Elly. Three-year-old Alex Fekete and his mother, Betty, were murdered by her estranged husband, Josif, in Red Deer, Alberta, in September 2003. Two days before, the boy had told an aid worker his father would murder him. "Daddy's going to kill me," he told Joanne,[17] a worker at the Central Alberta Women's Emergency Shelter who testified at an inquiry into the murders a year and a half later. The inquiry also heard that when the couple first separated in 2002, "Alex cried and clung to his mother and seemed very afraid of his father" at a custody hearing in Calgary. On the stand, a Red Deer shelter worker named Janice berated the child welfare office for failing to help Alex and his mother in those final days. She said Betty Fekete tried to tell them it was a protection issue but was informed that it was a matter of custody. "The job of the child welfare office was to protect Alex and they didn't," said Janice.[18]

Josif Fekete had returned Alex to his mother at 6:30 on a Sunday evening after a court-ordered visit. When Betty Fekete came down from her third-floor apartment to pick up the boy, her husband pulled out a sawed-off shotgun and killed both of them and himself.

The inquiry found that police had failed to act on the woman's repeated complaints that her husband had threatened to kill her and that he had guns. No charges were ever filed against him, and he kept his weapons. In 2002, Betty had been forced to flee from a women's shelter when her husband threatened her, and the shelter had reported to police that Josif Fekete had firearms. Provincial Court Judge David Plosz, who headed the inquiry, recommended that all police forces in Alberta get specialized training in handling domestic violence and that officers not treat chronic complaints as a nuisance. He also said that police should seriously consider applying for an order prohibiting firearms in such cases.[19]

In a scathing article after the inquiry, Jan Reimer and ACWS researcher Kate Woodman attacked police and others for failing miserably in the Fekete case. "Those with authority did not believe Betty and Alex—or their neighbors and family, who all spoke with one voice—that Josif had deadly intent," they wrote. "When women and children seek help and protection from domestic violence, they are frequently dismissed, with their needs placed second to the rights of the perpetrator. Abused women are too often advised by authorities to keep silent about the threats against them, because speaking up might jeopardize child custody.

"While the mother and child were believed by local shelter staff, the authorities refused to trust and act upon the recommendations of these front-line family violence experts. The police responded to Josif's complaints that Betty was transporting Alex without a car seat (in taxis and buses). But the police, knowing guns are the weapon of choice in family violence, did not investigate Betty's assertion that Josif kept several in his home and threatened to kill them with one. These unregistered guns were quickly found after the murders. And there it is, the cold fact brought to light through this inquiry."

Reimer and Woodman said that instead of reacting to Betty's cry for help, the courts increased Josif's custody rights to Alex. They said the inquiry proved Betty and Alex were telling the truth. "He had the gun; they had the death threats. Josif Fekete was going to kill them; and he did. We cannot send women and children to their death because we do not believe them. Canada's death penalty for women and children must end."

Elly was "angry and sickened" when she heard about another case. "I don't know how people can do these things to women and innocent children," she said.

She was talking about Liana White, who, four months pregnant in July 2005, was stabbed to death in a violent struggle and left for a week to decompose in a ditch. Her three-year-old daughter was left motherless.

Liana's husband, Michael White, twenty-eight, was arrested just hours after a search party he organized found her body on the outskirts of Edmonton. White, a heavy-duty mechanic and ex-soldier, was initially granted bail, but public outcry and a petition led to the court's revoking it. In October 2005, he was back in jail.[20]

Before he was arrested, but clearly in his own defence, Michael White said he was no Scott Peterson (who killed his wife, Laci, and their unborn child in an infamous case in the United States). In fact, both men were initially part of the search teams looking for their missing pregnant wives, and both were eventually arrested and found guilty.

The similarities end there. Scott Peterson was charged with first-degree murder in the death of his wife and second-degree murder in the death of his unborn child. Michael White was charged with *second-degree* murder in the death of his wife and was *not charged* in the death of his unborn child. Peterson is on death row awaiting execution. White will likely serve no more than fifteen years.

Many front-line shelter workers are upset that so many men who kill women are charged with second-degree murder or manslaughter, even when there is a history of abuse.

READING NEWSPAPER ACCOUNTS of women or children being killed or abused induced flashbacks for Elly, as listening to other women's stories of abuse did for Jane Hurshman. Both women were also hypervigilant, one of the symptoms of post-traumatic stress disorder.

When Karen Gardiner made overnight visits, she noticed her mother "didn't sleep much, and any little noise and she was up. If I came upstairs to go to the bathroom—and I'm fairly quiet—before I even got there, she would say, 'Who is it?' and I'd say, 'Just me going to pee.' And if I happened to wake up at four or five in the morning, I'd often hear her roaming around upstairs."

Bill Lyons says all the time he knew Elly, "She was always up and down in the night. At three o'clock in the morning, she would be in the kitchen doing paperwork because she couldn't sleep. And lots of times, she wanted to be by herself, so that was her breathing time—her quiet time. She didn't sleep a lot, but she still had the energy to keep going."

Anything that reminded Elly of her time with Vernon Ince would trigger extreme distress. Bill Lyons came home one day with a pair of safety boots and she screamed at him to get them out of the house. "She was just freaking," Lyons says, "as soon as I said 'steel toes,' she just cringed. She was paranoid and shaking, and she just wouldn't let me bring them in the house." Elly was reliving the painful kicks from Vernon's workboots that she'd endured through most of their relationship.

She had a similar reaction when Doug Ince telephoned to say he was in town for a visit.

Elly had earlier received a letter from Vernon's brother seeking word on his niece and nephew, Cynthia and Donny. The letter was friendly and there was no mention of Vernon or the shooting. In a second letter, addressed to "Dear Ella and Family," Doug thanked her for sending "the very nice picture of Cynthia. Good-looking girl, thanks very much. I will frame it and tell everyone who she is...Donny sent me a nice picture and I have it sitting here in a frame beside me." Doug also reported on the death of his mother's second husband, Big Ray, and talked about his own problems with his heart. He signed the letter, "Love, Doug Ince."

But when Doug called Elly five or six years later to tell her he was in Calgary and wanted to visit, "She just freaked," according to her daughter Karen, who was visiting when the telephone rang. "When she hung up, she was just staring wide-eyed. Then she started puffing like crazy on her cigarette."

"That was Doug, my ex-brother-in-law, and he wants to come and see me and Cindy because she's all grown up now."

"What did you tell him?"

"I said I'd pick him up at the corner at 52nd and Memorial at noon tomorrow."

Elly had a flashback of Doug threatening to kill her, and she was reliving the terror she had felt then. Karen says her mother started "really shaking."

"What's wrong?" she asked.

"He threatened to kill me," she said.

"When?"

"After I shot Vernon."

"But that was fifty years ago," said Karen. "He's an old man now."

"But what if he tries something?"

Such thoughts are not unusual for a battered woman who had never resolved the traumatic incidents of half a century ago, but Doug Ince had long ago put the death of his brother behind him. He and a friend were on a long-anticipated four-month cross-continent journey in a Toyota RAV4 wagon. They had travelled through the U.S. to the Prairies and, after stopping to visit Elly in Calgary, would continue to Vancouver, through B.C. to Inuvik, then on to Alaska.

In fact, Elly picked Doug up at the designated intersection the next day and drove him to her home, where Karen and Cindy were waiting. "He seemed pretty laid-back and stayed at the house for about three or four hours," says Karen. "We sat in the kitchen the whole time. We had coffee. He didn't smoke, but mom smoked half a pack of cigarettes. Everything was very casual and he bragged about his adopted children and grandchildren.

"You can call me Uncle Doug," he told Karen.

"But you're not my uncle."

"That's okay."

"So now I call him Uncle Doug," says Karen. "He was a jolly guy, with grey hair, glasses, and a big belly. We didn't bring up anything from the past. Mom introduced him to Cindy as Uncle Doug and it went very well with her. He told her how pretty she looked and talked with her for a little while, and she showed him her colouring and her bowling trophies and other little things."

Elly said Doug went to Saskatchewan to visit her son Donny, who was working there at the time. "Donny said he was very pleasant and very mellow and seemed like a nice guy," she said.

Elly's initial reaction to Doug's visit might seem extreme or odd to an outsider, but author Lori Haskell says women like Elly who have experienced abuse or serious trauma "should not be stigmatized. Instead, it is important to recognize that the effects and symptoms of abuse-related trauma are themselves normal responses. They are ways of coping with the harm inflicted by the abuse."[21] In a handbook she wrote for front-line workers, Haskell—a psychologist, researcher, and educator on issues of violence against women and children—says, "In many cases women don't recognize the effects of abuse-related trauma in themselves yet they struggle in their daily lives to cope with their distress in its hidden forms."

Karen Gardiner has come to understand that many of her mother's "faults" and her sometimes offensive conduct toward her children "reverts right back to the abuse. Even though [Vernon] was dead and gone, she was always looking over her shoulder. She was very secretive and she never trusted anyone. I don't think she truly trusted me, even at the end. She was very closed.

"When you think about it, it's understandable. I never once saw her in shorts. And she never ever wore dresses, other than long ones to the ankle. You could still see the scar marks and indentations in the back of her legs from where he kicked her. I asked the doctor about it, and he said somebody would have had to kick her hard repeatedly to leave marks like that all those years later.

"I also gathered from her that he was very domineering and really degraded her—telling her she was worthless. I think that's why she was constantly seeking reassurance and asking me what I thought of her. It was like she was saying, 'I'm not stupid.'"

LATE IN 2005, ELLY BEGAN thinking seriously about her own mortality and about what kind of future her mentally challenged daughter, then in her mid-fifties, would have without her. And with the incessant newspaper and television accounts of women and children abused and dying, she thought it might be time to tell her story.

"The way I look at it is, I'm here for a reason," she said. "And if I don't think things are right, I would tell you, and I wouldn't care who you are. And it's not right what's going on in the world today. I'm sick of the violence and sexual molestation in families and the children getting hurt, and getting raped and getting killed. And men killing women or ruining them for life with beatings. That's why I want to tell my story. It's not current, but I lived it, and if I can help anybody by telling my story, that's what I want to do.

"I said to myself, do you have the guts to do this? Well, something gave me the urge, and I did it. It was hard, because I had to relive everything and in my mind I could picture every part of that house [in the Asphalt with Vernon] and I could even tell you where the coal bucket was."[22]

LIKE COMBAT VETERANS WHO are often most at ease with those who shared their battlefield experience, Jane Hurshman said she was always most comfortable speaking to other battered women, and her favourite venues were the shelters that offered them refuge. "It is therapeutic for me to be with others who have suffered what I suffered," she said.[23] "When I'm with them, I don't feel like a freak anymore. We don't shock each other. We don't get embarrassed. We don't feel set apart. We feel safe enough to share, to cry, to laugh. We don't just sit around airing our grief. We also reaffirm life. We say that we are ready to live again and what we want is to find out how.

"By relating my feelings, I hope to help other battered women realize they are victims and they are not alone and they don't have

to blame themselves." She said it was a long time after Billy
Stafford's death before she realized she was a victim, "and even
longer to understand that I was not to blame, nor did I have to
carry the guilt for his actions. I knew nothing of transition houses
or support groups. I felt totally isolated and trusted no one.

"Battering isn't the taboo—talking about it is. And it can only
continue if we keep silent."

ELLY'S HEALTH BEGAN TO DETERIORATE in 2005, but it barely
slowed her down. She was still active with Rocky Mountain
Productions, out listening to her favourite country singers and
auditioning hopefuls, young and old, who wanted into the business. Beyond that, Elly had a "big plan" she'd been working on for
several years—a huge casino for Calgary, with an adjoining hotel
and a fully realized "old west town" built at the back of the prop
erty as a major tourist attraction. The complex would also house a
grand theatre and stage, primarily for country performers, and the
Canadian Country Music Hall of Fame.

She had plans drawn up, seriously began lining up property,
and actively sought political support through contacts in Ralph
Klein's Conservative government. She even had her retired police
friend, Jim Fisher, agree to head security for her. "She was a lot of
fun to listen to and talk to," says Fisher. "She always had big
plans, and she went after them too, which I found really interesting. She tried for years to generate investment and she went to
great ends to try to produce a real good package that she could
present to investors."

And Julian Austin says, "Elly and I and Bill used to sit at the
Top Brass in Calgary and shoot the breeze for hours. She had this
big park she wanted to build. She had the plans for it and was
raising money, and she wanted to call one of the theatres the

Julian Austin Memorial Theatre. She had all that in place. I said, 'I'm very flattered, but I'm sure you could think of somebody more deserving than me.' She had a lot of the bucks lined up. She was well up in the millions, and she even had all the blueprints done up."

At one point, Ella had a full prospectus put together for the resort hotel, including a grand circular driveway at the entrance, a large reflective pool and waterfall, and two lion sculptures similar to those in front of the New York Public Library. Inside the hotel, a sweeping double staircase would lead up from the lobby. "I had one investor willing to put up $50 million," she said. "I've known him quite a few years. He's very rich and he's got a lot of land and he knew I was looking for a place to put up a resort. I got a phone call about a month ago and he wanted to have a major meeting. It was three and a half hours and I wasn't feeling well. He's putting all the money up and looking at a 50:50 partnership, but I don't know yet. He would build the resort and I would run it top to bottom. He doesn't know a thing about running a resort. I would appoint people to run different areas. Jim Fisher would look after all the security. I know five or six retired detectives who would work under him."

Elly's son John Melanson said his mother "had all these schemes going all the time. I always thought that that was her fantasy world, and I said we were all entitled to those dreams. But I know she used to go out and take rundown hotels and restaurants for a year and turn them into something very profitable, and then she would give it to whomever and take off. Once she accomplished what she wanted, she would leave."

Jim Fisher says he knows Elly "talked to the head people in Marriott hotels. She really went after it. But she never was able to hook up with the right people who could carry the ball, and yet she didn't want anybody else. She wanted to run this whole thing herself. For years, I just told Elly, you know, if you get the right people, basically take a finder's fee—take a percentage and let somebody else run it. I said it actually might get going, but she held herself back by always wanting to have independent control."

Karen Gardiner says her mother had "some great ideas and great dreams, but she never followed through with them." And Bill Lyons says Elly "had all these things she put together, but they never materialized. She had twelve companies incorporated and functional on paper, but not in reality. Rocky Mountain Productions was the only one *really* functioning."

Elly had the opportunity to start a new career when she received a letter from Calgary's Mount Royal College asking whether she was interested in a teaching position. "I was checked out by them and they said I was well experienced," she said. "They wanted me to teach event logistics, event management, event marketing, and event production. I thought it was very strange that they came to me, I must be doing something right, I'll send them a letter. But I couldn't do that—it's away at the other end of the city in the far southwest. It would take me an hour just to get there in the morning."

The last major project Elly spoke of was establishing her own country music station on satellite radio. "My lawyer's working on the licence for me, and it could be up and running in six months," she said. "I'll record artists, and their CDs will be on the satellite worldwide and they can sell them off that. I just came up with this idea a few days ago."

A seventy-three-year-old bundle of energy with big dyed blonde hair, in a sparkling blue sequined jacket, bouncing around Calgary with a heart working at 30 per cent of capacity, chain-smoking cigarettes and drinking beer, introducing country performers at the Legion Hall at night, maybe squeezing in a dance or two, and meeting high-rollers in fancy corporate offices during the day to discuss multimillion-dollar deals, all the while living in a modest rented house with daughter Cindy and Bill Lyons and old John and getting around in used cars or vans that Bill had to work at to keep on the road—that's the enduring image of Miss Elly in full flight.

16

Ashes in the Snow

Stephanie Stevenson, 33. Brockville, Ontario. Mother of two.
A maternity nurse who was separated from her husband,
Stephanie was shot to death two days before Christmas as she
was walking to her car in the driveway of her home. A rela-
tive said that Stephanie's ex-husband had "bothered her in the
past, again and again, and she couldn't do anything." Andrew
Stevenson was charged with first-degree murder. (December
2006)

ELLY'S FIRST HEART ATTACK IN 1993 LEFT HER IN A WHEELCHAIR for a year and a half. Three years later, she went in for an angioplasty, but doctors discovered in the operating room that her heart had formed its own bypass around the blockage. Then one day her heart started to race. Rushed to a hospital emergency room and quickly surrounded by several doctors and nurses, Elly realized, "This is very serious and I'm going to be behind the eight ball."

Bill Lyons was with her and says, "They decided to try a new drug that one of them said was going to help her, 'Or that's it.'" The drug was to be administered intravenously, but they weren't sure if it needed diluting. Elly's condition was serious, and they were apparently running out of time when the nurse suggested they should "read the book on this" before proceeding.

"I could feel myself sinking, and I guess my eyes were closed, because I couldn't see anything, but I could hear them," said Elly later. Bill says that at that point, Elly sat right up and said, "Read the fucking book," and then lay down and "was gone—right out of it."

They read the book, the drug worked, and after five days in critical care, Elly was released.

ON THE NIGHT OF DECEMBER 8, 2005, Elly sat up in bed. She was short of breath and extremely weak. With Cindy's help, Bill got her to the car and rushed her to emergency at Peter Lougheed hospital. She was slumped over and not breathing by the time they arrived.

"She was in cardiac arrest," says Bill. "It was code blue, and the medical team ran in and about ten minutes later they brought her back out. She was in emergency for thirteen hours while they monitored her. Then she was sent up to a ward."

"I was unconscious most of the night," said Elly. "I didn't regain consciousness until the next day. They just filled me with all kinds of medication and did whatever they had to do."

A week later, Elly was allowed out on a day pass and as a prank showed up at a bar where a friend was performing. "And I walked in and she's singing 'Suds in the Bucket,' and all of a sudden she spots me wearing my red winter coat and she says right over the mike, 'Holy shit, Miss Elly's here.'"

Elly was suddenly surrounded by friends and admirers. Elly's intravenous connector was still taped in place, "And suddenly they were all over me. They were kissing me on the head and on the cheek and grabbing my hand." She pleaded with them not to touch her. "I was surrounded and I had no defence."

It reminded her of the day she was acquitted of murder. She had felt ill back at her parents' place in Westville, but she sat in the rocking chair greeting a long line of well-wishers until she could take no more and fled to her bedroom.

"Get me out of here," she said to Bill. "I can't handle any more of this."

After threatening to walk out of the hospital, Elly was put on blood thinners and allowed to go home for Christmas on December 20. "She always lived for Christmas, and she wasn't going to miss it," says Bill. He put up a tree and brought out her ornaments, many of which were from the family home in Westville.

"I have a set of bells that were my grandmother's," said Ella. "They're red, and I hang them on the chandelier in the dining room and they play Christmas carols that keep changing all the time. And I put a manger scene on top of the television."

When it came to Christmas, Elly wasn't politically correct. "Now you're not supposed to say Merry Christmas. It's Happy Holidays. Well, bullshit. What I was brought up with, that's what I use." As a treat, she and Cindy had their hair done.

"Usually I cook Christmas dinner with turkey and plum pudding and sauce. And I make a fruitcake, and normally I would bake homemade banana cream pies, but I couldn't do it this year." So Elly made the dressing and Bill did the rest of the cooking under her direction.

Bill took her out to Sam Buca's for New Year's 2006. "So she saw the new year come in. We were there for about three hours, and then she was played right out."

The place was packed, and once again Elly was mobbed by musicians and friends and was introduced to the crowd as a special guest. "They were standing and applauding when I left with Bill," says Elly. "Maybe they figured it was a final goodbye."

For most of them, it *was* a final goodbye. By a week later, Elly had lost twenty-seven pounds. She was in increasing pain and her appetite was gone. She ate fruit in small amounts and began taking two pain pills four times a day, on top of the other nineteen she was taking for her heart and other ailments. She was scheduled to return to the hospital at the end of the month for further tests and treatment.

"The pills take the pain away," she said. "I don't know what's going on in my body, but I'll find out. And if it's something they can't fix, they can cut it out."

Bill believes that by the middle of the month, Elly knew she was dying. "She told me she was too sick to look after me. That was her way of saying she wasn't going to be here that long. She always had it in her mind that she was looking after me, so I let her think that. In her mind, she thought she was protecting me. She didn't want to hurt me. She threw this big shield around me, and it made her feel good. She talked more to Karen about the things in her life. I just stayed beside her as much as I could. I had to work, but we talked on the phone three or four times a day. We always did that. But toward the end, I called her ten times a day, because she was losing it. She couldn't remember because the blood was so thin the brain wasn't getting enough oxygen."

Friday, January 13, was a dark day. Elly had tests the day before, "And they told me straight out that I have cancer and a short time. I only heard half of it, because I was in shock. The doctor told me to make plans for my daughter and her future. This all came down like a ton of bricks. I won't take chemo or radiation. I'm not going to lose my hair. They are going to start a drug regime in two weeks to treat the pain. They said it was melanoma in the ribs and they can't do anything about it."

Bill says Elly was crying when she phoned him at work and said, "I've got cancer." He left work and went to the hospital to be with her. He said her lungs were clear, as she had always said. "But there was bone cancer on one of her ribs and on her spine at the juncture with the lungs. They found multiple melanoma in the blood first, and from that they could tell it was in the bone cells, and then they did a CAT scan."

Elly came home that day and was to return to the hospital on January 25 to set up a treatment plan for her pain. On Sunday, three days before her appointment, she was at the Bowness Hotel to watch her friend, blues musician Gary Martin, play. "We were there a couple of hours," says Bill. "She wanted to go down and see him, and she was lively and clapping. She was on the move, and that kept her going. But you could see she was really, really sick."

Elly underwent four hours of tests on the 25th, and when they returned home, Bill noticed she seemed somewhat disoriented. "Her hand coordination was off and I could hardly understand her speech," he says. "And then she said she wanted fish and chips and coleslaw for supper. She had the whole thing laid out. She thought she was back in her restaurant.

He went out, bought fish and chips, and was "in the middle of cooking when the hospital called and said, 'Get her here as quick as you can—her blood is so thin she's going to bleed to death.' I fed Cindy and John and rushed her to the hospital. They took her into emergency and gave her plasma and transferred her to the Foothills Hospital, which deals with respiratory stress. They put her on oxygen and life support for almost three days, then partial life support, and she rallied in the middle of that. You could talk to her, but she wasn't coherent. It was hard to understand her, although she did tell Karen one of the nurses was a bitch."

Karen flew into Calgary on Saturday the 28th and says that by the next day, "Mother was improving although she was off life support and there was fluid in her lungs. I talked to her and told her she was an amazing woman. Her will was so strong, and without it she would have died a long time ago. On Monday, she had a bad turn, but Tuesday morning she didn't seem too bad."

Bill says Elly "had a minor heart attack just after her rally, and then she was going into a massive heart attack, and they said, 'She's going to die, and you can let her go that way, but it will be very painful and you won't want to see it. Or you can give her morphine in a quiet room without the oxygen and she can die peacefully.' That's what we did, and she died two and a half hours later.

Elly's daughters Pearl and Kathy and her son Don were also at the hospital. "Pearl and Kathy didn't want to go into the room where she died," says Bill. "So there was Karen, Don, and myself with her, and the hospital chaplain stayed with us until she passed away."

Elly died on Wednesday, February 1, at 5:30 p.m. "Her heart just gave out," says Karen. "It was peaceful and I stayed with her, because I didn't want her to die alone."

Elly had made it clear that she wanted to be cremated and didn't want a burial. "Just take me out to Banff and put me up the mountain," she'd said. "And just throw the ashes up there. I'll never be alone. There are always animals up there."

When Cindy heard the word "cremation," she asked Karen what it meant. "Well, she wanted her body to be burned to ashes and then have us spread them over the mountain," said Karen.

"So I don't have to see her in a casket?" asked Cindy.

"No."

"Okay, I'll go to the mountain too."

And so, on a clear, cool Sunday in early February, a family party of ten, including Bill and seven of Elly's eight children—son James was ill—rode with her ashes on the Banff Gondola to the promenade-style boardwalk atop Sulphur Mountain. "It was 7,300 feet up," says Karen. "You could see the mountains cutting through the clouds. Mother's favourite flowers were red roses, so we cut the stems off them and said our goodbyes with the petals.

Cindy did one for each of the animals and one for herself. It was heart-warming. We stepped off the walkway and we all took turns spreading the ashes. I was surprised at how heavy the urn was."

LIKE ELLY, JANE HURSHMAN HAD instructed that her remains be cremated. But before that there was a private family viewing. "I picked her clothes out and I went in to make sure she looked nice before the family came," said her sister Mona. "I put a little bit of colour on her cheeks—but she still didn't look like herself. I didn't think my dad was going to make it through. He broke right down, and I don't think my mom could really let her feelings out because she was worried about my dad and afraid she would fall apart."

Jane's son Allan understood why it was so difficult for the family. "If she had died from a heart attack, or old age, you could deal with that—but this [suicide] was too hard to accept."

In her first "suicide" tape, Jane said, "I do not want to be buried in the ground. I want to be cremated, and I definitely do not want to be put in any coffin. I want Mom to take my ashes, and in the spring, when she plants her flowers in her garden, I want her to sprinkle my ashes there. Then I will be at peace at last."

On Friday, February 28, 1992, the weather was crisp in Mahone Bay, Nova Scotia. More than a hundred of Jane's friends and relatives gathered for her funeral service at St. John's Evangelical Lutheran Church. On a small table at the front of the church stood a framed picture of Jane and the urn containing her ashes. "Ten years ago, we cheered her strong spirit when she took action to free herself and her children from a madman who was destroying them," said Reverend Margie Whynot. "And when she began to speak out in public about her experiences, she opened the door for many other victims to do the same—to break the conspiracy of silence that surrounded their lives.

"By making Jane our larger-than-life hero, we didn't give her the time or the space to stop and forget the past for a while. We kept her immersed in the past, with all its pain and ugliness, and she tried not to let us down. By asking so much of her, we were able to avoid our own responsibility for speaking out to help make our society a better, safer place."

Whynot omitted the part of her written speech that said that, regardless of how Jane had died, Billy Stafford "has reached out of his grave and finally claimed his victim."[1]

Three days after Jane's funeral, there was a candlelight vigil— billed as a celebration of her life—at St. John's United Church in Halifax. The church was packed. A battered woman stood to say that, inspired by Jane, she had decided to come out of the shadows and begin speaking out against violence. She vowed to speak out from then on. Jane's sister Mona said that Jane was "truly a symbol of hope for the abused people in our society" and that her death was not a defeat for them, "but a rallying point. And we vow to continue this work to create the society that Jane so desperately wanted—where love, caring, and respect for one another surpasses the evils of anger, hatred, and violence. We have to carry her banner until all the pain stops."[2]

ELLY ARMOUR'S PUBLIC GOODBYE was downright raucous compared to Jane's sombre and sedate memorial service. "Miss Elly's love was country music," stated her obituary, and "promoting country artists was her calling in life."

The celebration of her life took place at Sam Buca's on Sunday, February 19. It had been previously scheduled, and Elly had planned to attend. It would have been her very own "farewell tour."

The capacity at Sam Buca's is 210, but on Miss Elly's special day, more than 600 friends and fans were in and out of the place between 2 p.m. and 10 p.m., when the doors closed. Calgary still allowed smoking in bars then, and the air was pretty much a blue haze throughout the day.

The music and tributes to Miss Elly never stopped, as each group or soloist or band performed two or three numbers in her honour. Both Ray Griff and Gary Martin spoke about Miss Elly and played. Bill Lyons read a poem and said that Elly had unconditional love for him, "as well as all her family of musicians and friends." Jan Patterson-Levi said, "She had her fingers in so many pies in the music industry, and many of you here today were helped by her." Julian Austin, who'd flown in to perform in the memorial tribute, said, "You could tell she affected us all. For some reason, she had a big heart for us musical misfits. The world is not as good a place when people like that leave. She was too young to leave. She had the heart of a sixteen-year-old."

And in the men's washroom, a long-haired, thin man in his twenties who looked like he was going through hard times listened as yet another of the musicians expressed affection for Miss Elly. "It must be something to be loved like that," said the young man to no one in particular.

FIGHTING BACK

17

Battle Lines

Julie Crocker, 33, Markham, Ontario and Paula Menendez,
34, Toronto, Ontario. A radio station sales manager, Crocker
had recently separated from her husband, Chris Little. She
was found stabbed to death in the bedroom of her home
where she lived with her two young daughters. Menendez, a
physiotherapist, was found strangled on the floor of Crocker's
garage. The two women didn't know each other, but Crocker
was dating Menendez's estranged husband. Police said the
deaths were meant to look like murder-suicide, but forensic
evidence told them otherwise. Little was arrested and charged
with two counts of first-degree murder. (February 2007)

THE WAR ON WOMEN HAS RUN LONGER THAN ALL OF THE conflicts of the last two centuries combined, including the Cold War. Only in the past twenty-five years has there been any significant movement to end the conflict.

The fuel that keeps this war going is untenable gender inequality, manifesting itself in the abortion of a healthy female fetus in

China, a female circumcision in Africa, an honour killing in Pakistan, or a husband beating his wife in Toronto or New York.

Those fighting to end gender inequality and its often lethal effects find themselves swimming in a sea of red herring—in the form of a conservative backlash determined to prove that women are just as violent as men, and that solutions to the problem of domestic violence must be *gender neutral.*

IN 1993 THE UNITED NATIONS defined violence against women as *any act of gender-based violence that results in, or is likely to result in, physical, psychological or sexual harm or suffering to women, including threats of such acts, coercion or arbitrary deprivation of liberty, whether occurring in public or private life.* This definition would include spousal battering, sexual assault, marital rape, female genital mutilation, forced prostitution, intimidation, sexual harassment, and sexual abuse of female children.

In 1997 the World Health Organization defined domestic violence as the *range of sexually, psychologically and physically coercive acts used against adult and adolescent women by current or former male intimate partners.*

Strong words from two prestigious bodies.

Former United Nations Secretary-General Kofi Annan described violence against women as "pervasive worldwide" and the "most atrocious manifestation of the systematic discrimination and inequality women continue to face, in law and in their everyday lives...It occurs in every region, country, and culture, regardless of income, class, race or ethnicity."[1]

The World Economic Forum, an independent non-profit foundation based in Geneva, attempted in 2005 to assess the current size of the gender gap by measuring the extent to which women in fifty-eight countries have achieved equality with men in five critical areas: economic participation, economic opportunity, political empowerment, educational attainment, and health and well-being.[2]

"Even in light of heightened international awareness of gender issues, it is a disturbing reality that no country has yet managed to eliminate the gender gap," the Forum concluded. The most successful were the Nordic countries, especially Sweden. Canada ranked seventh, the U.S. ranked seventeenth. The lowest ranked of the fifty-eight included Korea, Jordan, Pakistan, Turkey and Egypt.

The report said that "Even in highly developed countries, violence against women of all kinds is routine, and often condoned. Female sexual slavery and forced prostitution are still terrible 'facts of life' for poor, often very young, women. Genetic testing for defects of the unborn is used in some parts of the world to determine the sex of the fetus, so that females can be aborted, while in some countries, female infants are buried alive. Forced marriage and bride-burning are still prevalent in the Asian sub-continent ..."

The Council of Europe, a political organization representing forty-six countries, reported in 2006 that violence against women is still widespread in all European countries.[3] And, further, that boys who witness violence against their mothers are more likely to become violent against their partners in adult life, while girls who do are more than twice as likely to be victims of domestic violence, and four times as likely to encounter sexual violence in their adult lives.

Although many European countries treat domestic criminal acts less severely than they do crimes against strangers, some countries, including France and Luxembourg, punish violence *more* severely when it occurs within the family or against an intimate partner or spouse. The Polish Criminal Code states that batterers may be imprisoned for between three months and five years, increasing to ten years if particular cruelty was used, or up to twelve years if the victim attempted suicide because of the abuse.

Cyprus considers domestic crime as an aggravating factor leading to a more severe penalty than that for other forms of violence, and recognizes that physical or psychological violence committed in the presence of a child is likely to cause the child psychological injury and "is a serious offence in itself."

The UN's *State of the World Population Report 2000*, states that actual rates of women affected by men's violence "range from a low of 16 per cent of women in Cambodia to a high of 67 per cent in Papua New Guinea." For Canada the rate is 29 per cent, and for the United States, 22 per cent.

Those last two numbers are not surprising considering the participation rate of women in government in those countries. In the U.S., 16.3 per cent of the members of Congress are women, while at the state level, the number rises to 23.5 per cent.[4] In Canada's Parliament, women hold 20.8 per cent—64 of 380—of the seats. But in the provincial and territorial parliaments the average number drops to 18.4 per cent.[5]

Stephen Lewis believes numbers like these won't change significantly without the United Nations leading the way by creating the new directorate for women and by bringing true gender equality to its own house. It was no accident that the scathing brief attacking the world body over its inaction on the issue of gender equality came out of his office in July of 2006. Written by his colleague, Paula Donovan, it said the UN embraced the "systematic oppression of women" and "its culture, evident in employment, in decision-making, and in allocating resources, is harmful to women. It's time to remove the UN's aura of morality."

"When it comes to women, western governments cry poverty whenever large sums are discussed," says Lewis. "It's just unconscionable. How dare the leaders of the G8 crow about progress on aid and debt...while continuing to watch the economic, social, physical and psychological decimation of so many of the world's women? How in heaven's name can they be sanguine about the cat-astrophic loss of so much human potential?"[6]

Lewis proposes a "full-fledged agency with real operational capacity on the ground" that would work with governments to design and finance programs and give "community-based women's groups the support their voices and ideas have never had."

Paula Donovan told the *Toronto Star* that with this new agency "all of those programs and projects that women have designed, but could never get off the ground because of lack of staff and resources could be implemented. They haven't been sitting around waiting for outside help. They've been doing what they can to help themselves. These women know what needs to be done and they just need support to do it."[7]

GIVEN THE ASSAULT THEY face from the burgeoning "father's rights" movement, these women in Canada and the U.S. need all the support they can get.

Deborah Sinclair and Susan Harris of Education Wife Assault (EWA) in Toronto say the "foundational work" of the 1980s and early '90s "was stalled by diminishing funds and the rise of a right-wing agenda in many parts of the country.

"Along with the rise of the influence of the right, we also began to feel the weight of the backlash. This was evidenced as the lan-guage of women abuse fell into the morass of gender-neutral, victim-of-crime terminology."[8]

These days, according to Eileen Morrow, it's a sin to say "vio-lence against women." Only "family violence" will do. The coordinator for the Ontario Association of Interval and Transition Houses says that anyone who talks about violence against women is seen as "a *feminist radical*...now it's all gender neutral because they are trying to tell us that men and women are equally victimized.

And of course all of the [government] systems are terrified of not being *gender neutral*, so they say privately, 'Of course we know it's mostly women but we say *family violence* because we can't say *violence against women.*' Well, you're not going to solve the problem if you even refuse to say what it is."

And Monica Townson, in a report for the Canadian Centre for Policy Alternatives, said public discussion of solutions has also focused on "tightening up" on offenders as well as pouring money into programs for male batterers. "Male batterer programs are as yet unproven in their effectiveness and cannot, in any case, be seen as a priority over much-needed programs and services for women. Years of cuts to social programs, legal aid, direct anti-violence services and neighbourhood supports have left women in a hardened state of inequality, leaving us increasingly defenceless in the face of abuse."[9]

Batterer programs are, in fact, "only marginally effective at best in stopping abusers, and their effect is limited to low-risk abusers," according to domestic violence research analyst Andrew Klein, who, in his 2004 report to the U.S. Congress, said that's why the Justice Department won't fund them.[10]

Klein is adamant that we have been unsuccessful in reducing homicides of women by their male intimates "because we have failed to appreciate the true danger and intransigence of abusers." Consistently, that's what women's advocates have argued: stop asking the victim what's wrong with *her* or why she doesn't leave, instead ask him why *he's* beating her, and focus on ending the violence.

In other words, stop blaming the victim and quit coddling the batterer—that doesn't work.

Pamela Cross, former legal director of the Ontario Women's Justice Network, said it is an undeniable fact that "femicide and other forms of violence within families are systemic and gender-based... Ontario's Domestic Violence Death Review Committee noted in its 2004 report that 100 per cent of the victims in the cases it reviewed were women, concluding that domestic violence *is not* gender neutral. More than 60 women killed in Canada each year by their partners is not a fluke, is not a series of unconnected events, is not an isolated tragedy. It is a horrific and preventable death toll that should cause outrage in the citizens of this country."[11]

Cross and other vocal women's advocates have been vilified as "feminazis" and worse on the Internet sites of some fringe 'father's rights' organizations. These sites run headlines like "Who Are the Real Killers and Abusers in Canada? Women!" They back up the headlines by stating, accurately, that in Canada men are more than twice as likely to be murdered than are women. Based on that fact, they ask: "Where is the outcry? Where are the shelters and the grants for men?"

But the use of that statistic is misleading because their totals include *all* homicides, the vast majority of which are male-on-male, including street and gang killings, and have little to do with women or domestic violence. As study after study, including those from Statistics Canada, show, in cases of lethal and severe violence, the perpetrators by a wide margin are *men*.

Another statistic that these fringe groups are quick to exploit was included in a 2000 government report stating that 8 per cent of women and 7 per cent of men had been assaulted by their intimate partners at least once in the previous five years. Much attention was paid to the fact that the two numbers were almost identical, with several Internet sites crowing that this proved that women were just as violent as men.

But the violence studied in that report included pushing, shoving, scratching, slapping, or throwing things. And when another government study broke down the numbers, it revealed that women intimates are six times more likely to be sexually assaulted;

five times more likely to be choked; three times more likely to be physically injured; and five times more likely to require medical attention.

Women also die at a much higher rate. In the years 2004 and 2005 there were 157 women killed in Canada by their intimate partners (including boyfriends and ex-boyfriends), compared to thirty-two men killed by their intimates or ex-intimates.

And University of British Columbia psychologist Don Dutton concludes that those women who kill their male intimates usually do so in self-defence, "to put an end to their own terror," while "male-perpetrated homicide was estrangement-related: 'If I can't have you, nobody else will.'"[12]

What gets lost in this debate is the fact that the vast majority of divorcing parents in Canada do not engage in knock-down legal battles and usually settle custody issues outside the courtroom and in the best interest of their children. And the fact that, although fathers who do petition the courts end up with sole or joint custody more than 50 per cent of the time, there is a small percentage of non-abusive good fathers who have suffered obvious injustices over child support and custody matters. Unfortunately, some fringe groups try to use them as poster boys in an attempt to legitimize themselves.

As former *Toronto Star* columnist Michele Landsberg put it: "...that's part of what is so frustrating about the way the agenda has been commandeered by the fathers' rights activists. The tenor of their attack is so extreme, and their allegations so far-fetched, that the whole debate gets shoved to the far end of the scale. In tackling all of their misrepresentations, I couldn't afford to spend a word or a line of column space to acknowledge those loving and responsible fathers I believe to be in the majority."[13]

Janet Normalvanbreucher, a U.S. lawyer and former mental health professional, initially supported the idea of "father's rights" and still believes that children need positive male role models, "although not necessarily the biological father." But in her 1999 work, *Stalking Through the Courts,* she wrote that most father's rights groups are not part of the legitimate men's movement, but "arose as a backlash against women's demands to be free from domestic violence and unreasonable male domination in their daily lives."[14]

Through the Internet, Normalvanbreucher says, "misogynists and batterers find each other, fuel each others rage, obtain emotional support and information for their vendettas, [and] learn how to harass their victims without violating restraining orders by using the courts and state administrative agencies." They also disseminate *how to* information for dragging out legal proceedings, and other tactics "aimed at allowing the batterer to subpoena his victim into court, put her on the stand, and publicly demean her under the guise of 'cross-examination.'"

Normalvanbreucher said that "overwhelmingly" men join these groups after a former intimate or spouse, in an attempt to escape physical abuse, leaves them or files for divorce. She said they frequently garner public sympathy by making outrageous claims about bias against fathers in the courts. "Recent Congressional fact-finding has proved that not only are these claims false, but also that discrimination tends to be against *mothers,* not the fathers as claimed," she said. "Most of the men...have lost custody or visitation due to persistent physical abuse or extremely abusive behavior—not due to judicial bias."

The aggressive public posture of the father's rights movement, the spurious argument that women and men are equally violent, the demonizing of feminists and women's advocates, and the stalling of hard-fought gains made against intimate-partner violence in the past thirty years—all abet the continued battering and killing of women in their homes. In Canada, while overall homicide rates have been decreasing, the *domestic* killings of women have not, despite claims to the contrary.

Part of the problem is that, unlike similar agencies in the U.S., Statistics Canada does not include boyfriend/girlfriend or extramarital relationships in their intimate-partner assault and homicide totals. With those categories included, seventy women were killed by their intimates and ex-intimates in 2000. But in each of the five years after that, an average of seventy-five women were killed.

WHAT IS THE TRUE NATURE of violence against men in spousal relationships? In fact, many men killed by their intimates have a history of severe violence against their partners.

Martin Daly and Margo Wilson of the psychology department at McMaster University, said that, unlike men, "women kill male partners after years of suffering physical violence; after they have exhausted all available sources of assistance; when they feel trapped; and because they fear for their own lives."[15]

In an extensive study, Daly and Wilson found several differences between men who killed their spouses and women who killed their spouses. Men often hunt down and kill spouses who have left them; women hardly ever do. Men kill wives as part of planned murder-suicides; women almost never do. Men kill in response to revelations of wifely infidelity; women almost never do, even though their mates are more often adulterous. Men kill wives after subjecting them to lengthy periods of coercive abuse and assaults; women seldom do. And men perpetrate familicidal massacres, killing spouses and children together; women do not.

A 2006 Statistics Canada report says police determined that in 41 per cent of spousal killings of men, the male victim "was the first to use or threaten to use physical force or use physical force in the incident," while in the spousal killings of women only 5 per cent of victims initiated the violence.[16]

In a study for Health Canada's Family Violence Prevention Unit, Leslie Tutty at the University of Calgary examined the true extent of violence against men in intimate relationships. In her introduction, she said "even the most vocal proponents of the view that husband abuse is not a significant social issue in Canada do not deny that some men are abused by women partners. The existence of husband abuse is not an issue. Rather, the debate concerns how common it is and the degree of harm inflicted."

Tutty included data from a 1998 Canadian study of almost 22,000 incidents of spousal assault reported to police, in which 89 per cent of the incidents involved female victims, and 11 per cent involved male victims.

"The available evidence that woman abuse is a more serious and widespread social issue in Canada than husband abuse is difficult to refute," said Tutty. "Women who live with assaultive husbands suffer violence that is both serious and chronic, and frequently results in life-threatening injuries. Nevertheless, even the most vocal critics do not deny the existence of husband abuse or that some men are seriously injured by their women partners.

"At this point, however, there is no evidence that the number of Canadian husband abuse victims warrants the type of specialized services that have been developed for women abuse victims. Nor does the current research support changing the wording of family violence materials from being specific to women victims to being gender neutral."[17]

Numbers don't lie. And the only numbers that count in the domestic violence debate are the killings, the injuries, and the shelters. The vast majority of deaths and serious injury that occur in intimate-partner relationships are to women, not men. And the 400,000 or so women and children that fill North American shelters are neither imaginary nor phantom. They are real and they just keep coming. There appears to be no real need for shelters for male intimates abused by women. The evidence shows that most women who kill their spouses—like Jane Hurshman and Elly Armour—do so in self-defence or in defence of their children.

However, as Tutty reported, a miniuscule percentage of non-abused women do batter and sometimes kill their male intimates, and the justice system should, and usually does, deal with these women as it would any other criminal. Medical aid, counselling, and protection is available from existing social and law enforcement services to the battered men who need or want it.

MANY GOVERNMENTS AND their agencies, including justice and law enforcement, have been hoodwinked into playing the gender-neutral game. As a result, the very women's organizations which know best how to fix the problems have been marginalized, funding has been misdirected or wasted, and superfluous or meaningless studies have been commissioned. There's been a lot of talk but little action while the deaths and injuries continue to mount.

Within months of the minority Conservative government coming to power in Canada in January 2006, many workers in women's organizations were convinced their new prime minister, Stephen Harper, didn't like them. And they had a lot of reasons not to like him, perceiving his "family values" government to be hard-right, pro-gun, anti-abortion, more interested in pushing gender *neutrality* than seeking gender *equality* and an end to domestic violence.

They felt betrayed by Harper. During the election campaign, in a letter to the Canadian Feminist Alliance for International Action (CFAIA), he had said, "Yes, I'm ready to support women's human rights and I agree that Canada has more to do to meet its international obligations to women's equality. If elected, I will take concrete and immediate measures, as recommended by the United

Nations, to ensure that Canada fully upholds its commitments to women in Canada."[18]

But within a year, the new Conservative government eliminated "equality" from the mandate of Status of Women Canada (swc), and cut its operational budget by 43 per cent. Half its staff had to go, and twelve of sixteen regional offices had to close. It eliminated funding for women's groups that did research and advocacy, cut $3.7 billion from programs for Canadian children, and announced it would not implement the recommendations of the Federal Pay Equity Task Force to introduce a proactive pay equity law.

When Bev Oda, the minister responsible for Status of Women Canada, announced that a dozen of its sixteen offices would be closed, she said the offices didn't necessarily provide "the help directly to women. There was a lot of lobbying groups, there was a lot of advocacy.

"We don't need to separate the men from the women in this country... This government as a whole is responsible to develop policies and programs that address the needs of both men and women."[19]

Canadian Auto Workers national president Buzz Hargrove was quick to respond, saying "to proclaim that Canadian women are now equal and to eliminate women's equality as a goal from the mandate of the Status of Women is a clear signal to the women of our country that their equality does not matter to this government." Hargrove said the government "still does not get the link between violence faced by women and their economic, social and political inequality."[20]

Another issue that pitted women's organizations—and many other Canadians, including the three federal opposition parties—against the minority government was its plan to scrap registration provisions in the Firearms Act for "long guns," including rifles and shotguns. The Conservatives held back on this plan because it lacked the votes to change the law. Instead it granted *amnesty* to those who have yet to register their long guns—a move that is gradually eroding the effectiveness of the registry, making it less useful to the police and more dangerous for battered women.

The Canadian Firearms Registry is important to the police. Since it was launched on December 1, 1998, law enforcement officers have queried the registry online over six million times. In the last quarter of 2006 alone, police averaged 5,800 registry searches every day.

From the launch to the end of 2006, fully 19,600 firearms licences were refused or revoked "for public safety reasons," including a history of domestic or other violence, mental illness, unsafe firearm use and storage, drug offences, or providing false information.[21]

Gun advocates complain that the government should be going after illegal handguns and criminals instead of "law-abiding" gun owners. But the reality is that *legally acquired* rifles and shotguns are the weapons of choice in domestic homicides. On average, 80 per cent of husbands who shoot their wives use a legally owned rifle or shotgun.[22]

The Canadian Medical Association (CMA) reports that the estimated cost of gun injuries and deaths in Canada is $6 billion per year, and that gunshot wounds are the third-leading cause of death among Canadians aged fifteen to twenty-four. The CMA says that compulsory registration is key to reducing deaths and injuries "resulting from the misuse of privately owned guns" and that it "provides police with the information needed to enforce firearm prohibition orders and to recognize risks in volatile situations such as domestic violence."[23]

In the U.S., the *American Journal of Public Health* reports that a firearm in a house increases the risk of intimate-partner homicide five-fold. The findings also suggest that abusers who possess guns tend to inflict the most severe abuse. "An abuser's threats with a weapon or threats to kill his victim also were associated with substantially higher risks for her murder."[24]

Given the ongoing firefights between women and the Harper government over everything from the gun registry to day care and pay equity, there was bound to be political fallout. In July 2007, a *Globe and Mail/CTV News* poll showed the Conservatives were backed by only 26 per cent of Canadian women.[25]

BATTERED WOMAN LIVE in a world of shelters, police and courtrooms.

The police have come a long way in understanding domestic violence, but it wasn't always that way and there is still a long way to go.

Roy McMurtry, who retired as Chief Justice of Ontario in May 2007 and who served as that province's attorney general for ten years, remembers the days "when women would phone the police and, more often than not, the attitude of many working police officers was, 'Well, you get over there and they will both be attacking you.' And certainly during my years as attorney general one of my priorities was to have this whole issue taken more seriously. When there was an allegation, the police were to investigate, and they weren't simply to tell the women to go down to city hall to see a justice of the peace and swear out a warrant."

McMurtry attended a family and domestic violence conference in France, "I think in the 70s. And I was giving a paper from the law enforcement side. But a great majority of delegates were from the social service industry and they didn't think this was an issue for the criminal courts, unless it was a very serious assault. They thought these issues should be dealt with by social workers, and there was this long-held view that once you involved the police and the courts, you were going to create a permanent division in-so-far as the family is concerned. And, of course, the clergy was in the background saying, 'Stay there for the good of the family.' For many generations this conduct was merely swept under the rug."

Nowadays most police departments thoroughly screen new recruits to ensure they are not themselves potential batterers, and train them to ensure that new officers understand the nuances and dynamics of family violence.

One of the problems facing police recruiters is that young officers often dread domestic violence calls. It's not glamorous work.

"They need a big paradigm shift in recruitment to make people realize what police work really is," says Jan Reimer's Alberta Council of Women's Shelters. "Everyone wants to be like the cops they see on TV, chasing robbers and going undercover to do the big drug busts and all this exciting work...and instead they're coming into a home and there is a kid crying in the corner and a woman with a black eye. That's not what they thought they signed up for, but that's a lot of what police work is."

Pamela Cross says that for years battered women and their advocates have argued that the criminal law provides little protection from persistently abusive partners and former partners.

"Despite Ontario's mandatory charging policy, police response is inconsistent. In some parts of the province, it appears police are reluctant to lay charges where the assault is, in their minds, minor. And, increasingly, women face the risk of being charged themselves, as dual charging becomes more common." (Dual charging involves charging an abused woman who calls police for help, along with charging her spouse, if she had tried to fight back to defend herself. It's more of the fallout from gender neutrality.) Because of this, Cross says, many women won't call police at all when they are in danger.

That battered women don't trust, or are afraid of, the system is reinforced by Statistics Canada, which said that more than 70 per cent of abused victims fail to report violent attacks against them to police. Police implementation of mandatory charging policies across the country in the 1980s was supposed to remove the onus from the victim and encourage them to come forward. "Despite the implementation of such policies...reporting spousal abuse to police has remained stable: 28 per cent of spousal violence victims reported to police in 2004, compared to 27 per cent in 1999."[26]

Kim Pate, Executive Director of the Canadian Association of Elizabeth Fry Societies, says it's a question of political will, "and there isn't the will on the part of police to respond every time they are called, despite what they say. Crowns must recognize this as a gendered reality."

Pate said it's true that women are sometimes reluctant to call the police because they fear being charged for trying to defend themselves against a battering spouse.

"In what context would a woman reporting violence see any benefit to making it all up?" asks Pate. "There may be the very, very rare cases, but if you took this seriously it would be far easier to weed those out instead of presuming that every woman who calls saying she's being beaten is making it up."

Charging women along with, or instead of, the abuser is a bastardization of the "pro-charging" policy introduced specifically as a weapon against violence against women. It's another example of gender-neutral fallout from the backlash against feminists.

To counter this, some jurisdictions in the U.S. have adopted "primary aggressor" models, which require police to identify the primary assaulter, based on the history of violence between the parties and the probability that one person may have been acting in self-defence.[27]

Pate says punishing women for resisting abuse is a "gender-neutral, zero-tolerance" policy that has "helped make women the fastest growing prison population in Canada and around the world. Prior to incarceration, 71 per cent of federally sentenced women had experienced physical abuse and 56 per cent had experienced sexual abuse."

Pamela Cross says problems in the justice system go well beyond policing and charging of abused women. She said that a "lack of consistency and accountability persist throughout the criminal process. Charges are reduced or dropped in exchange for peace bonds. Sentencing is consistently lighter in cases of intimate assault, compared to assault in the general population. Most commonly, male partners are placed on probation for a first offence. That probation order almost always contains a no-contact provision, but enforcement of these provisions is spotty.

"Because bail is seldom denied to men on their first charge, and because many succeed in receiving bail when they are charged a second, third, and fourth time, the women who are their victims are forced to confine their lives to very small safe zones. These women establish safety plans, never go anywhere alone, change their daily routine, install security systems in their homes, leave their jobs and, in some cases, their communities and their identities, just to try to stay alive. They imprison themselves because we will not imprison their assaulters."[28]

Although the province of Alberta has had historically high rates of domestic violence and intimate-partner homicides, it is a leader in trying to combat them. Alberta's *Protection Against Family Violence Act* allows access to a judge or justice of the peace twenty-four hours a day to obtain an emergency protection order, with an automatic review by a Queen's Bench judge within seven days. Free legal assistance is available for the review process from Legal Aid.

Starting first in Calgary in 2000, and then Edmonton, Alberta has set up special domestic violence courts in several cities. And the RCMP's "K" Division in Alberta has set up a special office to deal with domestic violence and has teamed with several partners, including Jan Reimer's Alberta Council of Women's Shelters, to ensure its officers are "trained, skilled and collaborative...from both prevention and enforcement perspectives."[29]

Ontario was the first province to set up special domestic violence courts and there are now more than forty-five around the province. When they follow the procedures laid down on paper they work well but, as Cross and Pate have said, they are often inconsistent.

Cross cites a 2004 Statistics Canada report that, "probation was the penalty in 72 per cent of spousal violence cases, making it the most common sanction. But in cases where the offender was not a spouse, probation was used less frequently—in only 53 per cent of cases. This study establishes clearly that intimate violence against women continues to be taken less seriously than other crimes of violence in Canada."

The Woman Abuse Council of Toronto has monitored the city's special domestic courts since they were established more than a decade ago, and its latest report states that "in almost every area tracked, we found that the criminal justice response in 2006 was less vigorous than three years ago." It found a smaller percentage of serious charges laid; more charges withdrawn; less jail time ordered; less time in pre trial custody (especially for offenders who failed to comply with existing court orders); shorter probationary periods; and higher percentages of absolute discharges.[30] The Council says that these courts are "sliding backwards" in conveying the message that abuse is not acceptable.

Reacting to complaints that some judges and justices of the peace are insensitive to or uneducated about the dynamics of domestic violence and manipulation of the justice system by batterers, Roy McMurtry says "if these issues are not treated seriously in the courts then the public has to know about that. I've always felt very strongly about the accountability of our fundamental institutions, and certainly the courts are a fundamental institution. And I'd be the first one to say that if the justice system isn't treating it seriously enough then people should be free to criticize the system, as some are now doing."

The people who know the most about domestic violence, including the judicial aspect, are the survivors, and of course their advocates, many of whom have worked with survivors for thirty years. But this pool of priceless knowledge is largely ignored.

"The government comes in, and they come up with some hairbrained idea and then they'll latch on to somebody that agrees with them and off they go," says Eileen Morrow of the Ontario Association of Interval and Transition Houses. "And they put millions of dollars into some project that won't work and if you criticize them, they just don't talk to you anymore. If you think *we're* angry you should talk to some survivors. They are *really* angry."

She says the women's movement "has been under a lot of backlash for at least ten years now" and that in some ways government treats advocates and shelter workers the way abusers treat battered women: "if you speak out, if you don't obey, if you don't shut up, or soften everything, then the guys come out and there's a big backlash and pretty soon everybody is talking about how you're a bunch of radical feminists, and not just feminists but *lesbians,* and then it becomes all this sexist thing—it's just awful."

And like a battered spouse, women advocates and shelter workers "get worn down after a while and they just want to protect themselves, so they start using gender-neutral language and they go and sit in all these coordinating committees that accomplish little or nothing.

"We're virtually at the point where independent women's organizations are being told that if you don't work together with the police and the Crowns and all these people you won't get your funding for your counselling or your shelter programs. Here in Ontario we now are in a mandatory relationship with the child welfare system, which quite frankly is terrible. They don't know a hell of a lot about violence against women, and so women are getting charged with 'failing to protect' and they're always training—we're spending all this money on training, but they don't do anything."

Morrow says that in the domestic violence courts there is a good policy "on paper" that states there is supposed to be a "special" Crown that follows a case all they way through "but it turns out that half the time it's not the *special* Crown, just *some* Crown. Essentially what it boils down to is: They're not doing what they're supposed to be doing—so *do* it."

ROY MCMURTRY BELIEVES there must be a multi-pronged approach to combating domestic abuse, including a look at the movie and television industries "where the most horrific examples of violence are almost glorified as entertainment. It's something that has been worrying me for years. And yet, any time we talk about it, of course there are screams of 'censorship' or 'Big Brother' and the people who produce this stuff say, 'Well, it's just entertainment and nobody takes it very seriously.' If you see a fine film or read a good book you're supposed to be influenced by that, but if it's negative or very violent they try to tell you it isn't going to influence you. It's absurd. Look at the violent video games and the bullying that goes on with kids. It's a huge, huge problem that has to be addressed at a young age."

McMurtry says domestic violence has to become as socially unacceptable as drinking and driving became under his watch as Ontario's attorney general. "When I took the job in 1975 there was a high tolerance for alcohol abuse on the highway," he says. "It was still regarded as good old Charlie having too many and then going off and driving his car—it was almost a source of humour, rather than the source of carnage which it was. Then Ride programs were developed but it was also education amongst young people and they started to get smarter and the whole business of the designated driver developed.

"I believe very strongly that by education we reduced alcohol abuse on the highway to a considerable extent—although we still have a problem—and people have to be educated at a young age to eschew violence. Domestic violence has to be condemned continually and the public has to be reminded continually that it's a serious problem, and not one just affecting a few people that we don't want to know about."

In their own way, Jane Hurshman and Elly Armour tried to be educators when they went public with their stories. They wanted to help other abused women and their children, wanted their message to get to other women, and to men of goodwill and good conscience.

Most men do not beat up women, nor do they condone it when others do. But some people think men have to do more than wear a white ribbon once a year, have to begin speaking out. Jan Reimer thinks it is crucial that male role models in sports, business, politics, policing, the judiciary, and education begin speaking against domestic violence to boys and young men. Her shelter organization sponsors special breakfast meetings. The first was in Edmonton in November 2006, the second in Calgary in March 2007. In total more than five hundred men and women participated and heard former hockey players Lanny McDonald and Kelly Buchberger declare that domestic violence is a *men's* issue as well as a women's issue.

The keynote speaker at both events was Jackson Katz, a U.S. author and filmmaker and a leading anti-sexist male activist. "We need a whole lot more men involved...It takes guts for men to start speaking out and challenging other men's sexism and challenging other men's attitudes and entitlements to women's bodies and other forms of male power and privilege," he said. "It takes guts and strength and self-confidence and a lot of men."[31]

In London, Ontario, when Mayor Anne Marie DeCicco-Best launched her Task Force to End Women Abuse, Chief of Police Murray Faulkner said, "The vast majority of us, who are not involved in these violent acts, need to stand up to these other guys and say, 'Listen, this isn't what a man's about. Don't remain silent. That's the worst thing to do.'"

Don't remain silent. That was the message Jane Hurshman always left with her audiences of battered women. If more men run with that, Jan Reimer believes, things might actually change. Pamela Cross used a military analogy in her July 2007 *Toronto Star* article: "It is no exaggeration to say that women who suffer abuse and violence at the hands of the men who claim to love them live in a war zone where every day survived becomes a battle victory.

"It is time that the same media and political attention given to other victims of war be given to women killed by their partners. Perhaps then, we would see that these women—who spend every day of their lives trying to outwit the enemy, stay one step ahead of him, protect the children, stay alive for one more day—are heroes as much as any soldier serving in a war."

One of the powerful weapons aimed against women in this war bears the name gender neutrality. The phrase sounds innocuous, and in a perfect world it would be. That it sounds so reasonable is what makes it so dangerous.

But there can never be gender neutrality without gender equality. The two will never co-exist until all of the patriarchal red herring swimming around this issue are swept up in the nets of truth and reality, and discarded to rot in the sun.

18

Recommendations

MOST LONG-TIME ACTIVISTS, SHELTER WORKERS, AND SURVIVORS, and some enlightened prosecutors, judges, and police officers, know what has to be done to reduce the number of women being abused and killed by criminal domestic violence. They appear to be blocked, however, by legislative and systemic apathy, combined with the failure consistently to follow proven measures already on the books.

Activists are convinced that if these existing policies and protocols were diligently executed and enforced, most murders of women could be prevented.

The principles and recommendations in this chapter are based on numerous studies and interviews with front-line workers, abuse survivors, lawyers, judges, prosecutors, police officers, psychologists, and many other experts who deal with domestic violence. What's most appalling about the recommendations is that versions of many of them have been made over and over again, by inquest juries, by innumerable studies, and by dedicated women's organizations across North America.

Principles

- Domestic violence laws must be gender specific, *not* gender neutral, because by a wide margin women are the ones who end up in the hospital or the grave.
- Domestic violence is such a breach of trust it should be considered as serious a crime as attacking or murdering a police or corrections officer.
- The penalty for murder of an intimate partner must be severe—twenty-five years without parole. Otherwise, what's to deter a batterer who sees news stories about men who kill their spouses being charged with manslaughter or second-degree murder and sentenced to five, ten, or fifteen years, of which they will likely serve only a third?
- Whenever possible, the abuser should be removed from the home—to jail or a halfway house—instead of forcing women and children to hide out in shelters.
- An abuser confined to a halfway house would be required to wear an electronic ankle bracelet and undergo counseling until the courts were through with him.
- A battered spouse, meanwhile, would be offered counseling and would be supplied with a form of electronic "panic button" that directly alerts police if she suddenly comes under threat. (They are being used more and more in England, Israel, and several U.S. states. In 2005 the Ontario government announced plans to put them in shelters, but they've been used successfully in individual homes. Calgary police have even experimented with a panic button on a bracelet that alerts 911 without having to dial.)
- A batterer breaking the terms of bail or court orders against him would be arrested on a new (and serious)

breach of trust charge. Break bail, you go to jail—no second chances. Second chances have proved deadly for too many women and their children.

Government

LEGISLATION

- Create a category of crime called *femicide* with penalties the same as those for first-degree murder (twenty-five years without parole).
- Whenever there is a history of abuse and a woman is killed by her male intimate the charge should be *femicide,* and the *provocation* defence ("she left me and I just lost it") should not be allowed.
- Establish halfway houses for batterers so that women and children aren't the ones forced to leave the home.
- Implement legislation (with adequate funding) for universal daycare and provide women with opportunities to earn income and escape a battering spouse.
- Provide sustained funding for shelters and second-stage (medium-term) housing, with counselling services and income support so that women who flee are not forced to return to a batterer for economic reasons.
- Restore full funding for Status of Women Canada and other women's advocacy groups.
- In cases of domestic violence, transfer jurisdiction for restraining and protection orders from civil courts to criminal courts, with mandatory incarceration when orders are breached.
- When restraining or protection orders are in place, make it an offence for a private investigator or other third party,

aware of such orders, to find, or seek to find—on behalf
of an abuser—an estranged intimate partner who is in hiding or a shelter.

- Implement full registration and licensing of all firearms.
- Ensure adequate long-term funding of the front-line services needed by aboriginal women to escape violence.
- Undertake comprehensive national research on the magnitude of domestic violence in aboriginal communities.
- Ensure the full participation of aboriginal women in the
planning and implementation of the policies that directly
affect their welfare.

EDUCATION

- Include mandatory courses for those studying to be teach-
ers to train them to recognize students who are from
abusive homes, and alert appropriate authorities who can
provide counselling and intervention (including police)
when necessary.
- Develop courses to teach students from a young age that
physical and emotional abuse in the home is unacceptable,
illegal, and a gross breach of trust.
- Engage older students in meaningful discussions on the
dynamics of abuse and engage willing survivors of severe
abuse to provide first-hand accounts of their experience
(similar to school presentations on the tragic consequences
of drunk driving).

MEDICAL PROFESSION

- Require private practice and hospital doctors and nurses to
keep up to date on available community resources for
domestic violence victims so they can pass on this information to patients requiring help.

Justice

COURTS

- Require prosecutors, judges, and justices of the peace to have an understanding of domestic abuse and, in particular, the elevated danger women and children face when they attempt to leave, or have left, a batterer.
- Eliminate time delays between bail hearings and trials in domestic abuse cases, to reduce the risk to battering victims.
- Coordinate criminal and family law systems in domestic violence cases to ensure that no-contact protection orders, criminal or civil, take precedence over family law orders until safety measures are in place to protect women and children threatened by violence.
- Order electronic monitoring (ankle bracelets) with global positioning technology for those charged with domestic violence offences who are on parole, out on bail, or in a halfway house.
- Because the risk of harm increases dramatically for a woman seeking a peace bond, deal with such applications immediately, or issue an emergency temporary order until a court date is set.
- Amend the "best interests of the child" test in the *Children's Law Reform Act* to direct courts to consider the impact of domestic violence on children when custody and access are being determined.
- Order mandatory risk assessments in all bail hearings relating to domestic violence cases.
- Require that those charged with domestic violence offences who breach their bail conditions be immediately incarcerated.

- Upon conviction for a domestic violence offence, the Crown should seek an order requiring the offender to attend a batterer intervention program such as Partner Assault Response (PAR) as probation requirement.
- When an accused batterer is to be released on bail, police, prosecutors, or corrections officials must, without fail, notify (warn) victims ahead of time.

LEGAL PROFESSION

- Ensure that every law school has mandatory courses so all potential lawyers will understand the issues and dynamics relating to family violence.
- Engage domestic violence "experts" from the police, prosecution, defence, and the judiciary as guest lecturers in law schools, and, when possible, violence survivors who can give first-hand accounts of what they and their children have been through.
- Lawyers involved in family law practice should engage in continuing education on the dynamics of domestic violence to keep fully aware of the lethal risks associated with separation, divorce, and custody and access.
- Never pressure women into joint custody arrangements or mediation when violence is involved in a relationship.

POLICE

- In all domestic violence calls, have a "without delay" response.
- Recruit more aboriginal officers.
- Work with aboriginal communities to develop protocols ensuring appropriate and effective response to reports of missing aboriginal women and children.

- Identify, monitor, and manage high-risk cases and vigorously enforce bail conditions arising from a violent offence or threat of violence.
- Institute a dedicated police unit that has links to community-based experts to deal specifically with high-risk domestic violence cases, to ensure an appropriate response.
- Train 911 operators and dispatch personnel in the issues surrounding domestic violence, and provide them with prioritized questions to help them assess immediate risk to callers and to first responders.
- Enter restraining orders into the Canadian Police Information Centre (CPIC) system immediately so that if there is a breach, there can be a quick police response under the Family Law Act.
- Establish a protocol between police and prosecutors to ensure that persons proposed as surety be properly investigated and fully informed about their responsibilities and potential penalty should they breach their duty.

Business, Industry, and Unions

- Establish a zero-tolerance policy regarding sexual harassment and inappropriate abusive or degrading behaviour, and make sure every employee, manager, or executive is aware of it.
- Provide training on the issue of domestic violence to executives, managers, and company or union officers.
- Provide confidential reporting and counselling services to employees or union members who may be victims of domestic abuse or workplace harassment.

Churches and Clergy

- Meet with police, battered women's advocates and/or social workers to understand the dynamics and consequences of domestic violence.
- Assist victims of domestic violence and do not hesitate to call in police or government social services if there is ongoing abuse within a family.
- Speak out publicly and often against domestic violence, and do not put "survival of the family" or "staying together for the sake of the children" ahead of a spouse's safety.
- Where appropriate, inform immigrant congregations that some of the practices involving the treatment of women and girls in their original countries may be inappropriate and/or illegal in Canada or the U.S.

Civic Organizations and Service Clubs

- Have executives and event planners meet with knowledgeable police officers, prosecutors, social workers, or survivors who work with domestic violence victims to gain a thorough understanding of the issue.
- Invite police, prosecutors, front-line social workers and/or survivors of domestic abuse to speak at meetings or conventions.
- Plan annual, major fund-raising efforts to raise community awareness of the problem and to provide financial aid to emergency shelters or second-stage housing for battered women and their children.

- Engage male volunteers in shelter- or house-building projects sponsored by their organizations.
- Have a core of knowledgeable male spokespersons ready to respond to false or misleading claims in the media from fringe groups who diminish or discredit those legitimately seeking to redress issues of gender equality and violence against women.
- Engage in visible and persistent lobbying efforts with governments at all levels for legislation promoting gender equality and an end to criminal violence in the home.

Endnotes

Except where noted, websites were accessed between March and July 2007.

Foreword

1 The panel included senior international officials and politicians such as Prime Minister Shaukat Aziz of Pakistan; Prime Minister Jens Stoltenberg of Norway; Louis Michel, European Commissioner for Development and Humanitarian Aid; Robert Greenhill, president of the Canadian International Development Agency (CIDA); Keizo Takemi, Japan's Senior Vice Minister of Health, Labour and Welfare; Josette Sheeran, U.S. Undersecretary of State for Economics, Business and Agricultural Affairs; and former Chilean president Ricardo Lagos.

2 Then a member of Britain's Parliament and Chancellor of the Exchequer. In June 2007, Brown succeeded Tony Blair as prime minister.

3 World Health Organization and International Labour Organization.

About This Book

1 Hurshman is Jane's family name. She was Jane Whynot after her first marriage but went by the name of Jane Stafford when she lived common-law with Billy Stafford. She legally reverted from Whynot to Hurshman after her trial [and became Jane Corkum when she remarried].

2 Brian Vallée, *Life and Death With Billy*, Toronto: Seal Books, 1998, 79–80.

[3] From 1984 to 1988.

[4] From June 2001 until the end of 2006.

[5] Speech at Harvard Law School, February 26, 2006.

[6] Speech at Harvard Law School, February 26, 2006.

Chapter 1: Domestic Terrorists

[1] Federal Bureau of Investigation (U.S.), Uniform Crime Reports, *Law Enforcement Officers Killed and Assaulted, 2005.*

[2] The numbers for 2000 to 2005, inclusive, are from the FBI report cited in note 1. Numbers for 2006 were conservatively estimated because the report wasn't ready at the time of writing this book. But preliminary figures from both the FBI and Statistics Canada for 2006 indicate that the final figures will likely be higher than the estimates here because of an upswing in overall homicide rates.

[3] Rita F. Fahy and Paul R. LeBlanc, National Fire Protection Association, Fire Analysis and Research Division, *Firefighter Fatalities in the United States – 2005.*

[4] Howard Witt, *Chicago Tribune*, April 18, 2005.

[5] Department of Homeland Security, U.S. Fire Administration.

[6] U.S. Department of Defense, Defense Manpower Data Center.

[7] Such as the cost of jailing perpetrators.

[8] U.S. Department of Health and Human Services, Centers for Disease Control and Prevention, *Costs of Intimate Partner Violence Against Women in the United States*, March 2003.

[9] World Health Organization, 2004.

[10] Ontario Women's Directorate, Prevention of Violence Against Women: It's Everyone's Responsibility, 1997.

[11] Total includes actual numbers from thirty-two states that provide user statistics and estimates from the remaining eighteen states, based on comparison with states with a similar population and demographics.

[12] Statistics Canada, the Juristat, results from the biennial Transition Home Survey, "Canada's Shelters for Abused Women, 2003/04."

Chapter 2: Shelters and Fear

[1] Leslie Tutty, *Effective Practices in Sheltering Women: Leaving Violence in Intimate Relationships, Phase II Report,* 2006, 1. Available at www.ywca.ca/public_eng/advocacy/Shelter/YWCA_ShelterReport_EN. pdf. Accessed June 4, 2007.

2 National Coalition Against Domestic Violence (U.S.).

3 U.S. Department of Justice, Bureau of Justice Statistics, *Homicide Trends in the United States,* which covers 1976 to 2004. Available at www.ojp.gov/bjs/pub/pdf/htius.pdf. Accessed June 4, 2007.

4 Alan Elsner, Reuters, January 4, 2001.

5 Andrew Robert Klein, in a report to the U.S. House of Representatives House Ways and Means Committee, February 10, 2005.

6 Leslie Tutty, *Effective Practices in Sheltering Women,* 1.

7 Leslie Tutty, *Effective Practices in Sheltering Women,* xii, 43.

8 *The Globe and Mail,* June 2, 2006.

9 Leslie Tutty, *Effective Practices in Sheltering Women,* 6.

10 Statistics Canada, 1996.

11 Andrew Robert Klein, report to the House of Representatives.

12 Aysan Sev'er, "Recent or imminent separation and intimate violence against women: A conceptual overview and some Canadian examples," *Violence Against Women: An International and Interdisciplinary Journal* 3(6) (1997): 566–589.

13 Carolyn Goard, director of integrated services, Calgary YWCA, in a panel discussion on violence against women, April 19, 2006.

14 Walter S. DeKeseredy, McKenzie Rogness, and Martin D. Schwartz, "Separation/Divorce Sexual Assault. The Current State of Social Scientific Knowledge," *Aggression and Violent Behavior* 9 (2004): 676.

15 Leslie Tutty, *Effective Practices in Sheltering Women,* 5.

16 Domestic Abuse Women's Network (DAWN), www.dawnonline. org/aboutdv.htm. Accessed June 1, 2007.

17 *R. v. LaVallée* (1990) SCR 852, delivered by Madam Justice Bertha Wilson.

18 Brian Vallée, *Life With Billy,* New York: Simon & Schuster, 1989, 6.

19 Andrew Robert Klein, report to the House of Representatives.

20 www.dawnonline.org. Accessed June 1, 2007.

21 Brian Vallée, *Life and Death With Billy,* 165.

22 *R. v. LaVallée.*

23 Brian Vallée, *Life and Death With Billy,* 80

24 Natalya Brown, *The Globe and Mail,* November 29, 2005.

25 Brian Vallée, *Life and Death With Billy,* 4.

26 Carolyn Goard, panel discussion on violence against women.

27 Brian Vallée, *Life and Death With Billy,* 91–92.

28 Angela Browne, *When Battered Women Kill,* New York: The Free Press, 1987.

Chapter 3: Ella

1 Brian Vallée, *Life With Billy*, 20–21.
2 Ibid., 22.
3 Ibid., 24–25.
4 Ibid., 28–29.
5 *Pictou: Nova Scotia's Northern Ocean Port*, 1916. Available at www.parl.ns.ca/pictou/index.htm. Accessed June 5, 2007.
6 The Burns Encyclopedia, www.robertburns.org/encyclopedia. Accessed June 4, 2007.
7 Obituary, *The Evening News* (New Glasgow), November 14, 1956.
8 www.empireco.ca/our_company/Profile.asp. Accessed June 4, 2007.
9 Obituary, *Halifax Herald*, February 27, 1942.
10 Public Archives of Nova Scotia, *Place-Names and Places of Nova Scotia*, 1967. Available at www.gov.ns.ca/nsarm/cap/places. Accessed June 4, 2007.

Chapter 4: Vernon

1 An experienced miner who keeps the roof, sides, and floor of a passage in good repair.
2 A mine car into which coal dug from the face is loaded to be sent to the surface.
3 A blacksmith's heavy, sledge-type hammer.
4 U.S. Department of Justice, Bureau of Justice Statistics, *Family Violence Statistics: Including Statistics on Strangers and Acquaintances,* June 2005. Available at www.ojp.usdoj.gov/bjs/abstract/fvs.htm. Accessed June 4, 2007.
5 James Ptacek, *Battered Women in the Courtroom: The Power of Judicial Responses,* Boston: Northeastern University Press, 1999.
6 Donald G. Dutton, *The Batterer: A Psychological Profile*, New York: Basic Books, 1995. Edward W. Gondolf, "Discussion of Violence in Psychiatric Evaluations," *Journal of Interpersonal Violence* (1992).
7 Brian Vallée, Life with Billy, p. 14.
8 Bill Ibelle, "Debate Rages on Batterers' Treatment," *South Coast Today,* May 26, 1995.
9 Gus B. Kaufman, Jr., *Individual Therapy for Batterers?* Men Stopping Violence, 2001. Available at www.menstoppingviolence.org/LearnMore/articles/IndividualTherapyForBatterers.pdf. Accessed June 4, 2007.

10 Bill Ibelle, "Debate Rages on Batterers' Treatment."

Chapter 5: Tarnished Knights

1 Women's Rural Advocacy Programs (Minnesota), *Let's WRAP!*, Summer and Fall 1996.
2 Kristi Sayles, "My Knight in Shining Armor That Wasn't," *The Plain Truth*, November/December 2000. Available at www.ptm.org/ooPT/NovDec/Knight.htm. Accessed June 4, 2007.
3 Jennifer Landhuis, "Domestic Violence Discussion," at www.exploring-womanhood.com/interviews/domestic-violence-1.htm. Accessed June 4, 2007.
4 David Mandel, *Issues in Family Violence Newsletter*, 2(3), Fall 1999. Available at www.endingviolence.com/newsletters/fall1999entitle.php. Accessed June 4, 2007.
5 Kathleen Waits, "Battered Women and Their Children: Lessons from One Woman's Story," *Houston Law Review* 35(1) (1998): 29–108.
6 Ibid.
7 Brian Vallée, *Life With Billy*, 56.
8 Ibid., 59.
9 Kathleen Waits, "Battered Women and Their Children."
10 Brian Vallée, *Life With Billy*, xii.
11 Domestic Abuse Helpline, www.domesticabusehelpline.org.
12 University of Wisconsin–Stout, Dating and Domestic Violence, www.uwstout.edu/cvpp/domestic_violence.html#warningsigns. Accessed June 4, 2007.
13 www.centennialcollege.ca/extra/wsa/signs_AP.htm.
14 Brian Vallée, *Life With Billy*, 41.

Chapter 6: You Make Your Bed

1 University of Wisconsin–Stout, Dating and Domestic Violence, www.uwstout.edu/cvpp/domestic_violence.html#warningsigns. Accessed June 4, 2006.
2 Murry J. Cohen and Caroline Kweller, "Domestic Violence and Animal Abuse: The Deadly Connection," Support Network for Battered Women, Santa Clara County, California. Available at www.snbw.org/articles/animalabuse.htm. Accessed June 4, 2007.
3 Her expertise is in animal-assisted counselling and therapy.

4 Sue C. McIntosh, "The Links Between Animal Abuse and Family Violence, as Reported by Women Entering Shelters in Calgary Communities, 2004." Available at http://canadianveterinarians.net/pdfs/McIntoshCalgarystudy.pdf. Accessed June 4, 2007.

5 Ibid.

6 Statistics Canada, Family Violence in Canada: A Statistical Profile, 1999.

7 University of Michigan Health System, "Abuse During Pregnancy," at www.med.umich.edu/1libr/wha/wha_batpreg_bha.htm. Accessed June 4, 2007.

8 Public Health Agency of Canada, Canadian Perinatal Surveillance System Fact Sheet, "Physical Abuse During Pregnancy," 2004. Available at www.phac-aspc.gc.ca/rhs-ssg/factshts/abuseprg_e.html. Accessed June 4, 2007.

9 Ibid.

10 Brian Vallée, *Life and Death With Billy*, 57.

11 Ibid., 57.

12 Ibid., 57–58.

13 Ella became very emotional while recounting this incident.

14 Brian Vallée, *Life and Death With Billy*, 71, 73.

15 Ibid., 80.

Chapter 7: The Deer Hunter

1 Abuse Counseling and Treatment (ACT), www.actabuse.com./cycleviolence.html. Accessed June 4, 2007.

2 Brian Vallée, *Life With Billy*, 62.

3 Kathleen Waits, "Battered Women and Their Children: Lessons from One Woman's Story," *Houston Law Review* 35(1) (1998): 29–108.

4 R. Lundy Bancroft, "Understanding the Batterer in Custody and Visitation Disputes," 1998. Unpublished article, precursor to Chapter 5, *The Batterer as Parent*, Thousand Oaks, CA: Sage Publications, 2002.

5 Nova Scotia Department of Natural Resources.

Chapter 8: Expectant Inmate

1 *Toronto Telegram*, November 8, 1951, p. 1

2 Ibid.

3 Brian Vallée, *Life With Billy*, 131.

4 Ibid., 117.

5 "R. v. Farmer: *Nova Scotia's Last Hanging for Murder, 1937*," at www.courts.ns.ca/history/milestones.htm. Accessed June 4, 2007. Farmer—poor, black, a father of eight—claimed he shot his half-brother, Zachariah, in self-defence in a dispute over a keg of home-brewed beer. There was evidence the victim was sitting in a chair when he was shot, casting doubt on Farmer's claim that his own life had been in danger, and the jury convicted him of murder. Before Farmer, the last person to die on the gallows in Nova Scotia, one other black and four whites had been hanged in the province in the 1930s.

6 Richardson held the position of magistrate for the Town of Stellarton until 1953, when he was appointed a provincial magistrate. He retired in 1969 and died at home in Stellarton in 1971 at the age of 69.

7 Brian Vallée, *Life With Billy*, 131.

8 Brian Vallée, *Life and Death With Billy*, 217. How went on to become Nova Scotia's Chief Provincial Court Judge until he retired in 1988.

9 http://en.wikipedia.org/wiki/County at _seat. Accessed June 4, 2007.

10 Nova Scotia Department of Justice, *Correctional Services Employment Systems Review*, 2002–2003, September 22, 2004.

11 Fred Honsberger, "Nova Scotia Custody Configuration Project," 1997.

12 Ibid.

Chapter 9: Cellmates

1 *Traditional Lifetime Stories: A Collection of Black Memories*, Vol. 2. Dartmouth, NS: Black Cultural Centre for Nova Scotia, 1990, 57. Available at www.ourroots.ca/e/toc.aspx?id=8800. Accessed June 4, 2007.

2 Ibid.

3 Cora Mae Jackson was eighty-eight when the Black Cultural Centre for Nova Scotia published its second volume of *Traditional Lifetime Stories: A Collection of Black Memories in 1990*. It included a short biography of Cora, stating that she was a member of Second Baptist Church and its choir, an honourary member of the Women's Missionary Society and the Ladies Auxiliary, and, "She has also been on the social committee for twenty years. At the time of her interview, Mrs. Jackson was healthy and strong. She is another one who has overcome."

Chapter 10: Relative Justice

1 The Courts of Nova Scotia, www.courts.ns.ca.Accessed June 4, 2007. The building was burned to the ground by an arsonist in 1985.

2 Richard Clark, "Timeline of Capital Punishment in Britain," at www.richard.clark32.btinternet.co.uk/timeline.html. Accessed June 4, 2007.

3 Ibid. Clark writes that in the first half of the nineteenth century, in rural county towns, murderers were usually executed on a market day, often a Saturday, to draw the biggest crowd and "very little was done to in any way to lessen the suffering" of women being executed, and in some cases "it was increased by the judge." In 1825, the famous prison reformer, Elizabeth Fry, recorded one of her visits to Newgate prison, where she went to comfort a young woman called Eliza Fricker, aged about thirty, who had been condemned for burglary. Fry protested the severity of her sentence and was attacked for being a sentimentalist by the Lord Chancellor, Lord Eldon, who stated, "If hanging was abolished for theft, the property of Englishmen would be left wholly without protection." Clark says Eliza was duly hanged outside Newgate on Wednesday, the 5th of March 1817, together with six men.

4 Phyllis Goldfarb, "Review of *The Penalty is Death: U.S. Newspaper Coverage of Women's Executions,* by Marlin Shipman," Boston College Law School Faculty Papers, Paper 19. Available at http://lsr.nellco.org/bc/bclsfp/papers/19. Accessed June 4, 2007.

5 Marlin Shipman, *The Penalty is Death: U.S. Newspaper Coverage of Women's Executions,* Columbia: University of Missouri Press, 2002.

6 Victor L. Streib, *Death Penalty for Female Offenders, January 1, 1973, through March 31, 2007,* Issue 58. Available at www.deathpenalty-info.org/FemDeathMar2007.pdf. Accessed June 4, 2007.

7 Goldfarb, "Review of *The Penalty is Death.*"

8 Maurine Watkins and Thomas H. Pauly, *Chicago: With the* Chicago Tribune *Articles That Inspired It,* Carbondale: Southern Illinois University Press, 1997.

9 *The Evening News* (New Glasgow), May 30, 1952, p. 13

10 Shipman, *The Penalty is Death.*

11 William A. Schabas, "Review of *Uncertain Justice: Canadian Women and Capital Punishment, 1754–1953,* by F. Murray Greenwood and

Beverley Boissery." Available at https://www.ccjaacjp.ca/en/cjcr/
cjcr14.html. Accessed June 4, 2007.

12 Brian Vallée, *Life With Billy*, 135–136.

13 Ibid., 157.

14 Ibid., 135.

15 Ibid., 177.

16 Ibid., 178.

17 Ibid., 182.

18 Ibid., 183.

19 Ibid., 183–184.

Chapter 11: Troubled Odyssey

1 Vernon's family eventually marked the grave with a flat, ground-level
headstone.

2 Brian Vallée, *Life and Death With Billy*, 248.

3 Ibid.

4 Ibid., 259.

5 Ibid., 262.

6 Ibid.

7 Ibid., 264.

8 According to Bill Gidley, executive director, RCMP Veterans' Association.

9 In 1955, King was transferred from Nova Scotia to RCMP headquarters
in Ottawa. He was promoted to sergeant major in 1962 and transferred
back to H Division headquarters in Halifax, where he remained until
his retirement in June of 1964. He died in Chatham, New Brunswick,
in December 1981.

Chapter 12: And Then There Was One

1 Brian Vallée, *Life With Billy*, 45.

2 Dr. Neilson was interviewed by the author in May 2007.

3 Brian Vallée, *Life and Death With Billy*, 215.

4 Margaret J Hughes and Loring Jones, *Women, Domestic Violence, and
Posttraumatic Stress Disorder (PTSD)*, January 2000. Available at
www.csus.edu/calst/government_affairs/reports/ffp32.pdf. Accessed June
4, 2007.

5 Ibid.

6 Dr. Cathy Humphreys, "Mental Health and Domestic Violence: A

Research Overview." Paper presented at The Impact of Domestic Violence on Women's Mental Health and Well-Being: Key Messages from Research and Practice, a conference sponsored by Making Research Count at Coventry, England, 2003. Available at http://www2.warwick.ac.uk/fac/soc/shss/mrc/violence/cathy. Accessed June 4, 2007.

7 She listed other symptoms, but those included here are significant to Jane's and Ella's experience.

8 Ibid.

9 Hughes and Jones, *Women, Domestic Violence, and Posttraumatic Stress Disorder.*

10 Humphreys, *Mental Health and Domestic Violence.*

11 Brian Vallée, *Life With Billy,* 163.

12 Ibid., 165.

13 Ibid., 167.

14 Brian Vallée, *Life and Death With Billy,* 249.

15 Hughes and Jones, *Women, Domestic Violence, and Posttraumatic Stress Disorder.*

16 C.J. Newton, "Domestic Violence: An Overview," TherapistFinder.net, *Mental Health Journal,* February 2001. Available at www.aaets.org/article145.htm. Accessed June 4, 2007.

17 With massive newspaper and television coverage, followed by three books. Buxbaum's wife reportedly begged him seconds before the shooting, "No, honey, please, not this way." But he watched impassively as the killer he hired pulled the trigger. Another accomplice said later that Buxbaum "didn't blink an eye." Key to his conviction was the testimony of forensic accountants that in the eighteen months before the murder, nearly $2 million had gradually disappeared from his bank accounts (to feed his nefarious habits) and he had taken out a $1-million life insurance policy on his wife.

Chapter 13: Elly's Place

1 Brian Vallée, *Life and Death With Billy,* 220–21.

2 Ibid., 342

3 Doreen Pitkeathly, "At the Clubs," *Hamilton Spectator,* March 20, 1980.

4 David Wesley, *Hamilton Spectator,* June 14, 1980.

5 *Hamilton Spectator,* November 8, 1980.

6   Judy Nyman, *Hamilton Spectator*, February 9, 1981.
7   *Hamilton Spectator*, February 19, 1981.

Chapter 14: Cowtown

1   Reeves died of emphysema at his home in Texas on New Year's Day 2007.
2   "David" is a pseudonym.
3   To protect his relationship with his children, he doesn't want the details to be divulged.

Chapter 15: All That Glitters

1   Unable to overcome her addiction to alcohol, she died of liver and kidney failure in Calgary in February 2002 at age sixty-six.
2   He remarried in 1996 and died of cancer at his home near Fenelon Falls, Ontario, ten years later at the age of seventy-two.
3   *Calgary Herald*, June 26, 2007.
4   Lyrics by Paul Brandt.
5   David Olive, *Toronto Star*, December 11, 2006 p. D1.
6   Anne Kingston, *Maclean's*, March 27, 2006, p. 16
7   Ibid.
8   Ibid., p. 20.
9   Alberta Council of Women's Shelters (ACWS), "Fiscal 2006–2007 Statistics." Available at www.acws.ca/questions/stats.php. Accessed June 4, 2007.
10   Alberta Crime Reduction and Safe Communities Task Force interim report, *Building Safe Communities and Reducing Crime: Summary of What Was Heard*, June 19, 2007. Available at http://justice.gov.ab.ca/downloads/documentloader.aspx?id=47761. Accessed June 4, 2007.
11   Panel discussion on domestic violence against women, Calgary YWCA, April 19, 2006.
12   In 2006, Reimer received a Governor General's Award in Commemoration of the Persons Case, for working tirelessly "to promote safe communities and ensure the well-being of society's most vulnerable members—seniors, youth and women in abusive relationships." The government of Canada established the Governor General's Awards in Commemoration of the Persons Case in 1979 to celebrate the 50th anniversary of the case's decision and to annually salute the

contributions of contemporary women to the advancement of gender equality. The landmark 1929 Persons Case involved five Canadian women—Emily Murphy, Henrietta Muir Edwards, Louise McKinney, Irene Parlby, and Nellie McClung—who became known as the "Alberta Five" or the "Famous Five." They fought and won the right for women to be recognized as persons and, therefore, eligible to sit in the Senate.

13 Alberta Council of Women's Shelters, "Fiscal 2006–2007 Statistics."

14 *Calgary Sun*, September 25, 2005.

15 *Calgary Sun*, September 26, 2005.

16 CBC *News*, December 21, 2005.

17 To protect the identity of shelter workers, the judge at the inquiry allowed them to give only their first names.

18 *National Post*, May 7, 2005.

19 CBC *News*, October 6, 2005.

20 CBC *News*, February 22, 2006.

21 Lori Haskell, *Bridging Responses: A Front-Line Worker's Guide to Supporting Women Who Have Post-Traumatic Stress*, Toronto: Centre for Addiction and Mental Health, Toronto, 2001. Available at www.camh.net/Publications/Resources_for_Professionals/Bridging_responses/bridging_responses.pdf. Accessed June 4, 2007.

22 In one of dozens of interviews with the author.

23 Brian Vallée, *Life and Death With Billy*, 218.

Chapter 16: Ashes in the Snow

1 Brian Vallée, *Life and Death With Billy*, 355.

2 Ibid., 357–58

Chapter 17: Battle Lines

1 Kofi Annan, United Nations Development Fund for Women (UNIFEM), November, 25, 2005.

2 Women's Empowerment: Measuring the Global Gender Gap, 2005 World Economic Forum.

3 Dr. Carol Hagemann-White, *Combating Violence Against Women, Stocktaking study on the measures and actions taken in Council of Europe member States*, Directorate General of Human Rights, Council of Europe, 2006.

4   Center for American Women and Politics, Eagleton Institute of Politics, Rutgers University, 2007.

5   Nova Scotia Advisory Council on the Status of Women, Women's Political Representation in Canada, January 24, 2006.

6   Speech to Panel on UN Reform, Geneva, July 2, 2006.

7   Olivia Ward, *Toronto Star*, July 1, 2006.

8   Deborah Sinclair and Susan Harris, *Twenty-Five Years Later: Still Holding the Hope*, Education Wife Assault EWA, Toronto, 2004.

9   Monica Townson, *A Report Card on Women and Poverty*. Canadian Centre for Policy Alternatives, 2000.

10 Andrew Klein, Advocates for Human Potential Inc. Statement to House Committee on Ways and Means, 2004.

11 Pamela Cross, *Violent Partners Create War Zone for Women*, Toronto Star *(theStar.com)*, July 6,2007.

12 Chris Wood, *Maclean's*, August 7, 2000.

13 *Toronto Star*, May 2, 1998.

14 Janet Normalvanbreucher, *Stalking Through the Courts*, 1999, http://www.thelizlibrary.org/liz/FRtactic.html.

15 Wilson, M.I. & Daly, M. "Who kills whom in spouse killings? On the exceptional sex ratio of spousal homicides in the United States." *Criminology*. 30:189–215.

16 Holly Johnson, *Measuring Violence Against Women: Statistical Trends 2006*, Statistics Canada.

17 Leslie Tutty, *Husband Abuse: An Overview of Research and Perspectives*, for the Family Violence Prevention Unit, Health Canada, 1999.

18 http://www.fafia-afai.org/images/Conservative_response_Jan1 82006.pdf.

19 CBC *News*, November 30, 2006.

20 CAW press release, December 5, 2006.

21 Canadian Firearms Centre, March 2007.

22 Kwing Hung, *Firearms Statistics*, March 2006.

23 "Reasonable control: gun registration in Canada." CMAJ, February 18, 2003; 168 (4).

24 "Risk Factors for Femicide in Abusive Relationships: Results from a Multisite Case Control Study," *American Journal of Public Health*, July 2003, Vol. 93, No. 7.

[25] *Globe and Mail*, July 19, 2007.
[26] Statistics Canada, *Family Violence in Canada: A Statistical Profile – 2006.*
[27] Holly Johnson, Statistics Canada, *Measuring Violence Against Women: Statistical Trends 2006.*
[28] Pamela Cross, *To Bail or Not to Bail*, Ontario Women's Justice Network, August 8, 2002 .
[29] K Division RCMP, Alberta.
[30] Woman Abuse Council of Toronto, Women's Court Watch Project.
[31] Shannon Woodward, *Calgary Herald*, Saturday, March 17, 2007.

Index